KIERKEGAARD

C. Stephen Evans provides a clear, readable introduction to Søren Kierkegaard (1813–55) as a philosopher and thinker. His book is organized around Kierkegaard's concept of the three "stages" or "spheres" of human existence, which provide both a developmental account of the human self and an understanding of three rival views of human life and its meaning. Evans also discusses such important Kierkegaardian concepts as "indirect communication," "truth as subjectivity," and the Incarnation understood as "the Absolute Paradox." Although his discussion emphasizes the importance of Christianity for understanding Kierkegaard, it shows him to be a writer of great interest to a secular as well as a religious audience. Evans' book brings Kierkegaard into conversation with western philosophers past and present, presenting him as one who gives powerful answers to the questions which philosophers ask.

C. STEPHEN EVANS is University Professor of Philosophy and Humanities at Baylor University. His most recent published works include *Kierkegaard: Fear and Trembling* (2006), co-edited with Sylvia Walsh, and *Kierkegaard's Ethic of Love: Divine Commands and Moral Obligations* (2004).

KIERKEGAARD

An Introduction

C. STEPHEN EVANS

CAMBRIDGE
UNIVERSITY PRESS

CAMBRIDGE
UNIVERSITY PRESS

University Printing House, Cambridge CB2 8BS, United Kingdom

Cambridge University Press is part of the University of Cambridge.

It furthers the University's mission by disseminating knowledge in the pursuit of
education, learning and research at the highest international levels of excellence.

www.cambridge.org
Information on this title: www.cambridge.org/9780521700412

© C. Stephen Evans 2009

First published 2009
Reprinted 2010

A catalogue record for this publication is available from the British Library

Library of Congress Cataloguing in Publication data
Evans, C. Stephen.
Kierkegaard : an introduction / C. Stephen Evans.
p.   cm.
Includes bibliographical references and index.
ISBN 978-0-521-87703-9 (hardback)
1. Kierkegaard, Søren, 1813–1855.   I. Title.
B4377.E92 2009
198'.9–dc22
2008053488

ISBN 978-0-521-87703-9 Hardback
ISBN 978-0-521-70041-2 Paperback

To Jan Evans
Fellow Kierkegaard Scholar and So Much More

Contents

Preface

It is customary for scholars who write about Kierkegaard to apologize for doing so. Kierkegaard made constant fun of the "professor" and predicted, with some bitterness, that after his death, his literary corpus would be picked over by the scholars for their own purposes. And so it has been.

Nevertheless, I offer no apologies for this effort to introduce Kierkegaard as a philosopher to those who are interested in reading him. Those of us who love Kierkegaard and who regularly teach Kierkegaard know how stimulating and provocative an encounter with his works can be. Nevertheless, for the contemporary student, and even for the professor, there are cultural and philosophical differences between Kierkegaard's world and our own that make it difficult to understand his writings. The current work is by no means an attempt to "summarize" Kierkegaard's thought as a substitute for reading him. It is rather an attempt to remove some of the barriers to a genuine reading of Kierkegaard.

Obviously, there are many ways one might organize an introduction to Kierkegaard's thought. One would be to discuss and explain some of Kierkegaard's major works, such as *Fear and Trembling, Concluding Unscientific Postscript,* and *The Sickness Unto Death.* I have chosen not to follow this route, for several reasons. One is that I feared it would encourage a kind of "Cliff's Notes" approach involving summaries of these works. A second is that the important works are many, and their complexity is such that any adequate account of them would make this a lengthy book. Hence, I have chosen instead to introduce Kierkegaard thematically, focusing on important concepts in his works.

The major organizing structure is provided by the Kierkegaardian notion of the three "stages of existence" or "spheres of existence," a key set of concepts in Kierkegaard's writings. When understood as "stages" these provide an account of a path to authentic selfhood; understood as "spheres" these concepts provide a description of three rival views of human existence and its meaning. It is thus well-suited to serve as a basis for understanding Kierkegaard's thought. After two introductory chapters discussing Kierkegaard's life and works, including his distinctive views on communication, the book therefore takes its readers through the aesthetic, ethical, and religious spheres of existence, culminating with an analysis of Kierkegaard's understanding of Christian thought and its relevance to the contemporary world. Since many courses on Kierkegaard use this same trio of concepts as an organizing tool, my hope is that the book will be useful as a supplementary text for students who are reading the primary sources.

In going through the three stages of existence, the book takes Kierkegaard seriously as a philosopher, giving full treatments of what I take to be his epistemological, ethical, and metaphysical views. On my reading, Kierkegaard poses a sharp challenge to the dominant tradition of modern philosophy. However, in several important respects he also does not fit well into the categories of "existentialist" or "postmodernist" which some have attempted to apply to him. In looking at Kierkegaard as a philosopher, I have also tried to do justice to Kierkegaard's uniqueness as a thinker, the ways in which his work does not fit the standard philosophical mold.

Naturally, I do discuss specific works of Kierkegaard at specific places in the book. Therefore, those who are looking particularly for introductions to specific works may profit from looking closely at those sections. Chapter 2, for example, discusses *The Point of View for My Work as an Author* and several sections of *Concluding Unscientific Postscript* that deal with "indirect communication." Chapter 3 has an extensive discussion of the view of the self found in *The Sickness Unto Death*, and returns to *Concluding Unscientific Postscript* to treat the themes of "truth as subjectivity" and the critique of the Hegelian idea that reality can be thought of as a "system." Chapter 4 focuses mainly on *Either/Or*, volume I, while Chapter 5 looks at the portrait of the ethical life given in *Either/Or*, volume II, as well as the picture given in *Fear and Trembling*, where the ethical life is contrasted with the life of faith. Chapter 6 returns to *Concluding Unscientific Postscript* for yet another account of the ethical life, one that sees the ethical as the starting point for a religious life shaped by resignation, suffering, and guilt. Chapter 7 examines a number of philosophical issues raised by Kierkegaard's understanding of Christian faith, especially the relation of faith to reason, the Incarnation understood as the "Absolute Paradox," and the relation between faith in Christ and historical evidence. To accomplish these tasks, this chapter discusses mainly *Philosophical Fragments*, but also *The Book on Adler* to shed light on Kierkegaard's understanding of Christianity as a revealed religion. Finally, Chapter 8 returns to *The Sickness Unto Death* for a concrete picture of human existence as it relates to faith, but it also includes a discussion of *Works of Love*, where Kierkegaard as a Christian thinker presents his mature understanding of ethics as summarized in the great commandments to love God and the neighbor.

Kierkegaard's literary output was vast, even though he died at age 42. I am only too conscious that there are many themes in Kierkegaard as well as whole works that this book barely touches on or omits entirely. Some readers will certainly object that I have focused mainly on the pseudonymous writings and have not given adequate attention to the *Upbuilding Discourses*. The reason for this slant is simply that I wanted to treat Kierkegaard primarily as a philosopher, albeit a Christian thinker, and therefore I decided to focus mainly on the works that are taught in philosophy departments and that treat issues recognizable as philosophical. In any case, since my goal was not to summarize Kierkegaard's thought, but to motivate readers to encounter him for themselves, I chose to keep this work relatively short and accessible. For the same reason, references to the secondary literature are relatively few, although I have included a very personal guide to further reading about Kierkegaard in place of a traditional bibliography or list of works cited.

I have supplied almost all the translations for quotations from Kierkegaard's published works, working from the first Danish edition of the *Samlede Værker* (Copenhagen: Gyldendals, 1901–1907). However, for the convenience of English-speaking readers I have cited the pagination for the Princeton University Press *Kierkegaard's Writings* editions, edited by Howard V. Hong. This English edition contains the pagination of the Danish edition I have used in the margins for any reader who wishes to consult the Danish.

In conclusion, I wish to thank the hundreds of students who have studied Kierkegaard with me since 1972, for all you have taught me. In many ways this is a book that you helped me write, and I have written it for you. Special thanks must go to Merold Westphal, who has taught me so much about Kierkegaard over the years, and was kind enough to read this work for Cambridge University Press, and give me a large number of helpful comments and suggestions. I must also thank my friend and colleague Robert Roberts for detailed comments on several chapters. I also thank the other members of the Baylor Philosophy Department, the members of the Philosophy Department of the University of St. Andrews, and the participants in the Theology Research Seminar at the University of St. Andrews, for helpful discussion of chapters read to these groups. The final work on this book was done while I was in residence at the University of St. Andrews, and the staff and community of St. Mary's College there provided a wonderful place to work. My doctoral student Mike Cantrell, who was back in Waco, Texas, and had access to my library, provided me with some crucial research help during this period. Another doctoral student, Andrew Nam, is owed my gratitude for doing the index.

Chronology

1813	Søren Kierkegaard is born in Copenhagen
1830	Enters the University of Copenhagen as a theology student
1838	Publishes his first book, *From the Papers of One Still Living*, a critique of Hans Christian Andersen as a novelist
1840	Becomes engaged to Regine Olsen but breaks the engagement the next year
1841	Successfully defends his doctoral thesis, *The Concept of Irony with Constant Reference to Socrates*, and goes to Berlin to hear Schelling lecture, returning the following year
1843	Publishes the pseudonymous *Either/Or* in two volumes, the first book in what he will later call his "authorship," and also begins to publish a series of *Upbuilding Discourses* under his own name. *Either/Or* is followed by *Repetition* and *Fear and Trembling*
1844	Publishes *Philosophical Fragments*, *The Concept of Anxiety*, and *Prefaces*
1845	Publishes *Stages on Life's Way* pseudonymously and *Three Discourses on Imagined Occasions* under his own name
1846	Publishes *Concluding Unscientific Postscript*, with the thought that he would complete his authorship and take a pastorate, and also *Two Ages: A Literary Review*. He also becomes embroiled in a controversy with a satirical magazine, *The Corsair*, and decides that he must remain at his literary "post" rather than become a pastor. He also works on *The Book on Adler*, a work that reflects on the case of a Danish pastor deposed for claiming to have received a revelation from God, but Kierkegaard never publishes his work, though sections are later incorporated into *Two Ethical-Religious Essays*

1847   Publishes *Upbuilding Discourses in Various Spirits* and *Works of Love*

1848   Publishes *Christian Discourses* and *The Crisis and a Crisis in the Life of an Actress*. He completes *The Point of View for My Work as an Author*, but the work is only published posthumously

1849   Publishes *The Sickness Unto Death, Two Ethical-Religious Essays*, and two books of religious discourses: *The Lily in the Field and the Bird of the Air* and *Three Discourses at the Communion on Fridays*

1850   Publishes *Practice in Christianity* and *An Upbuilding Discourse*

1851   Publishes *Two Discourses at the Communion on Fridays, On My Work as an Author*, and *For Self-Examination. Judge for Yourself!* is written but not published until after his death

1854   Begins a public, polemical attack on the Danish Lutheran Church as a state church, first waged in *The Fatherland*, and later, in a periodical Kierkegaard himself published, *The Moment*

1855   Publishes *What Christ Judges of Official Christianity* and *The Changelessness of God*. In the midst of his controversial attack on the Church, collapses on the street and dies in a hospital a few weeks later on November 11

Sigla used for Kierkegaard's published writings

BA   *The Book on Adler*, ed. and trans. Howard V. and Edna H. Hong (Princeton, New Jersey: Princeton University Press, 1998)

CA   *The Concept of Anxiety*, ed. and trans. Reidar Thomte in collaboration with Albert B. Anderson (Princeton, New Jersey: Princeton University Press, 1980)

CD   *Christian Discourses* and *The Crisis and a Crisis in the Life of an Actress* (Princeton, New Jersey: Princeton University Press, 1995)

CUP   *Concluding Unscientific Postscript to* Philosophical Fragments, vols. I and II, ed. and trans. Howard V. Hong and Edna H. Hong (Princeton, New Jersey: Princeton University Press, 1992) [Vol. I contains complete text of work, and hence all quotations are from it; II contains index, scholarly notes, and related materials.]

EO I and II   *Either/Or, Vols. I and II*, ed. and trans. Howard V. Hong and Edna H. Hong (Princeton, New Jersey: Princeton University Press, 1987)

EUD   *Eighteen Upbuilding Discourses*, ed. and trans. Howard V. Hong and Edna H. Hong (Princeton, New Jersey: Princeton University Press, 1992)

FT   *Fear and Trembling/Repetition*, ed. and trans. Howard V. Hong and Edna H. Hong (Princeton: Princeton University Press, 1983)

JY   *For Self-Examination* and *Judge for Yourself*, ed. and trans. Howard V. Hong and Edna H. Hong (Princeton, New Jersey: Princeton University Press, 1990)

PF   *Philosophical Fragments*, ed. and trans. Howard V. Hong
        and Edna H. Hong (Princeton, New Jersey: Princeton
        University Press, 1985)
PV   *The Point of View* (includes *On My Work as an Author* as
        well as *The Point of View for My Work as an Author*), ed.
        and trans. Howard V. Hong and Edna H. Hong
        (Princeton, New Jersey: Princeton University Press, 1998)
SUD   *The Sickness Unto Death*, ed. and trans. Howard V. Hong
        and Edna H. Hong (Princeton, New Jersey: Princeton
        University Press, 1980)
TA   *Two Ages: The Age of Revolution and the Present Age: A
        Literary Review*, ed. and trans. Howard V. Hong and
        Edna H. Hong (Princeton, New Jersey: Princeton
        University Press, 1978)
UDVS   *Upbuilding Discourses in Various Spirits*, trans. Howard
        V. Hong and Edna H. Hong (Princeton, New Jersey:
        Princeton University Press, 1993)
WL   *Works of Love*, ed. and trans. Howard V. Hong and Edna
        H. Hong (Princeton, New Jersey: Princeton University
        Press, 1995)

CHAPTER I

Introduction: Kierkegaard's life and works

Søren Kierkegaard is acknowledged to be one of the most influential thinkers of the nineteenth century. Born on May 5, 1813, in Copenhagen, where he spent almost all of his life, Kierkegaard was not widely known outside Scandinavia in his lifetime, and was not hugely popular even in Denmark. Most of his books were published in editions of 500 copies that never sold out prior to his death in 1855, at age 42. However, around the beginning of the twentieth century he exploded upon the European intellectual scene like a long-delayed time bomb, and his influence since then has been incalculable.[1] Although Kierkegaard was not widely read in the English-speaking world until the mid-twentieth century, his works are today translated into all major world languages and his impact is strongly felt in Asia and Latin America as well as in Europe and North America.

IS KIERKEGAARD A PHILOSOPHER?

Kierkegaard's influence is broad not only geographically but also intellectually. One could go so far as to call him "a man for all disciplines," given his importance for theology, psychology, communications theory, literary theory, and even political and social theory, not to mention philosophy. Kierkegaard himself clearly wanted to be remembered primarily as a religious thinker. Indeed, he famously goes so far as to say that he was really a missionary, called not to introduce Christianity into a pagan country, but rather to "reintroduce Christianity into

---

[1] For an interesting account of the early reception of Kierkegaard, and particularly how Kierkegaard became known outside of Denmark, see Habib Malik, *Receiving Søren Kierkegaard: The Early Impact and Transmission of His Thought* (Washington, D.C.: Catholic University of America Press, 1997).

Christendom."[2] Some have actually questioned whether Kierkegaard is really a philosopher at all, given his diverse interests and fundamentally religious purposes.

Is Kierkegaard a philosopher? It would be awkward to write an introduction to his philosophy if he were not, of course. Yet this question must be faced, because Kierkegaard was clearly doing something different than most professional philosophers today. One must certainly concede that Kierkegaard was not a philosopher in the usual academic sense. Although he wrote a philosophical doctoral dissertation (*The Concept of Irony with Continual Reference to Socrates*), he never held an academic position and never published the kinds of works philosophy professors are expected to write. Kierkegaard's works are dazzling in their variety and hard to categorize. Many are edifying or "upbuilding" works that are intended to help the reader become a better person. A large number are "literary" in character, attributed to pseudonymous "characters" whose voices are in some cases clearly different from Kierkegaard's own and who interact with each other as well as their creator. Moreover, little of the work seems to have a straightforward philosophical purpose. Kierkegaard does not write treatises whose primary aim is to expound and defend epistemological or metaphysical theses.

However, those facts are surely not sufficient to deny Kierkegaard the title of "philosopher," for similar things could be said about Nietzsche, and hardly anyone questions Nietzsche's position as one of the seminal philosophers of the last 150 years. Though Kierkegaard's primary intentions may be edifying or religious or literary, he certainly deals with many recognizable and important philosophical issues in the course of doing what he does, and he discusses and interacts with many of the great philosophers of the western tradition, including (from ancient philosophy) Socrates, Plato, and Aristotle and (from the modern period) Hegel, Kant, and Spinoza. I suspect that uneasiness about Kierkegaard's status as a philosopher stems primarily from his self-professed religious aims rather than his unconventional way of doing philosophy.

This suspicion about whether work with religious aims can be properly philosophical is a distinctively modern and western one. Such a worry would be virtually unintelligible in traditional Indian and Chinese philosophy, just as it would have been for Plotinus, and for all of the western

---

[2] Kierkegaard considered using a variant of this phrase as a title for a whole section of his later works. See *Kierkegaard's Journals and Papers*, Vol. VI, trans. and ed. by Howard V. Hong and Edna H. Hong (Bloomington, Indiana: Indiana University Press, 1978), Entry 6271, pp. 70–71.

medieval philosophers, Christian, Jewish, or Islamic. It stems, I think, primarily from a post-Enlightenment conception of scholarly work as inspired by a passion for objectivity, grounded in a disinterested search for truth that requires the scholar to bracket out personal and human concerns in the interest of finding such truth, regardless of the consequences.

I think the best response to this worry that can be made on behalf of Kierkegaard is to note that the question "What is philosophy?" is itself philosophical and always has been one about which philosophers have disagreed. Philosophy is not a "natural kind." It is, at least to some degree, simply that activity carried on by those thinkers we call philosophers. The view that philosophy demands a kind of objectivity in which the philosopher must strive to think, in Spinoza's words, "under the aspect of eternity" (*sub specie æternitatis*), is one to which Kierkegaard is deeply opposed, and his opposition is at least partly philosophical in character. When Hegel affirms that "philosophy must beware of the wish to be edifying,"[3] he is affirming a view of philosophy that Kierkegaard thinks is mistaken, not merely because Kierkegaard finds the perspective religiously objectionable, but because Kierkegaard believes that such a view is rooted in a misunderstanding of the human condition. Kierkegaard's counter-claim that "only the truth that edifies is truth for you" may be misguided or mistaken, but it is grounded in a philosophical vision of human beings as finite, historically-situated beings whose primary task is to become whole persons.[4] It cannot be ruled out at the beginning as unphilosophical without begging some significant philosophical questions. If anything would be contrary to the spirit of western philosophy, it would be to hold that fundamental questions, including

---

[3] See G. W. F. Hegel, *Phenomenology of Spirit*, trans. by A. V. Miller (Oxford: Oxford University Press, 1979), p. 6.

[4] Strictly speaking, the words "only the truth that edifies is truth for you" do not come from Kierkegaard, but from one of his literary characters, in this case the "country priest" whose sermon concludes the second volume of *Either/Or*, trans. and ed. by Howard V. Hong and Edna H. Hong (Princeton, New Jersey: Princeton University Press, 1987), p. 354. Despite the pseudonymity of the country priest, I think most readers would agree that the claim is one that aptly characterizes all of Kierkegaard's work. For the convenience of the English-speaking reader, references for quotations from Kierkegaard will be taken from English language translations, using the *Kierkegaard's Writings* edition from Princeton University Press unless otherwise noted. However, the translations will be my own, and often will be different from Hong, as in the current case. The translations are based on Kierkegaard's *Samlede Værker* (Copenhagen: Gyldendals, 1901–1906). Since the Princeton edition contains the pagination for this edition in the margins, it will be easy for English readers to find the corresponding Danish passages if they wish to examine the original texts. Subsequent references to Kierkegaard's writings will be made parenthetically in the text, and a list of the abbreviations used is found at the beginning of the book.

questions about the nature of philosophy itself, cannot be asked or that rival answers to those questions should not be seriously considered.

In many ways, taking Kierkegaard seriously as a philosopher is to return to the kind of conception of philosophy that inspired the Greeks, for whom philosophy was intensely concerned with questions about the good life. Such a conception of philosophy does seem strange or even quaint in the contemporary world, where philosophy has become a kind of specialized, technical profession, one which does not clearly tend to make its practitioners practically wiser or better people. However, a challenge to this contemporary conception of philosophy seems well within the domain of the philosophical tradition. I conclude that Kierkegaard's edifying concerns, both ethical and religious, do not preclude entering into a serious philosophical conversation with him, including a conversation about the relation between philosophical reflection and edification.

A BRIEF SKETCH OF KIERKEGAARD'S LIFE

I begin with a brief and highly selective recounting of Søren Kierkegaard's life. Any account of Søren's life must begin with Kierkegaard's father, Michael Pedersen Kierkegaard, whose influence on Søren was profound and permanent. Michael Kierkegaard came from a poor family on the western side of Jutland, but at age 11 he was invited to Copenhagen to be apprenticed to an uncle who was a merchant. Michael parlayed his business smarts and hard work into a flourishing business of his own. He became his uncle's heir, made some shrewd investments in a time when Denmark was suffering financial collapse as a result of picking the wrong side in the Napoleonic Wars, and eventually became one of the wealthiest men in Copenhagen.

Despite his financial success, Michael Kierkegaard by all accounts suffered from what was then called "melancholy," and would today doubtless be termed depression. His first wife died childless after two years of marriage, and just over a year later Michael married his servant, Anne Sørensdatter Lund, already four months pregnant with their first child. Søren would be the seventh and last of their children, born when the mother was 45 and Michael 56. Michael was a devout and pious man, but his melancholy mingled with a strong dose of guilt to produce a strict and severe form of Christianity for his children. Staunch and loyal members of the State Lutheran Church, the Kierkegaard family also attended the Moravian meeting that met on Sunday evenings, giving young Søren a strong dose of what might loosely be termed "evangelical pietism" to leaven Lutheran orthodoxy.

What caused the old man's strong sense of guilt? Speculation has centered on two things: sexual sin and an episode in Jutland when the young Michael had cursed God because of his poor, miserable life, though it was shortly to be almost miraculously transformed. Whatever the cause, we know that somehow the older man's feelings of guilt were transferred to his sons. In Danish, the term for "original sin" is *Arvesynd*,[5] literally "inherited sin," and it appears that Søren believed quite literally that his father's sins had been transmitted to him as well.

This "inherited sin" was fraught with significance for Kierkegaard's life. Søren struggled all his life with the melancholy and sense of guilt that he shared with his father. Perhaps even more important, the relation to the father played a key role in what may have been the most determinative episode in Kierkegaard's life: his broken engagement to Regine Olsen.

In 1840 Kierkegaard had become engaged to Regine, but almost immediately he realized he had made a terrible mistake. After an agonizing period in which he foolishly (from my perspective) played the scoundrel in a vain attempt to free Regine (and her family) from any attachment to him, he finally broke the engagement the following year, and fled to Berlin for a period of intense writing. His reasons for breaking the engagement may not have been completely clear even to himself, and we shall probably never know them with certainty. However, the following facts seem reasonably firm: (1) Kierkegaard came to believe that he had some personal impediment or flaw that made it impossible for him to marry. (2) Whatever this problem was, he could not explain it to Regine without divulging his (now deceased) father's deepest secrets, something Søren could not do. (3) Kierkegaard gave the whole situation a religious interpretation; he believed he was called by God to be an "exception" who must sacrifice Regine and the joys of married life. (Though it is also true that at times Kierkegaard had doubts about this, and thought that if he had truly had faith, he would have remained with Regine.)

Despite the broken engagement, Kierkegaard loved Regine deeply. He continued to think about her and write about her in his journal until the end of his life. There is ample evidence that Kierkegaard's writings, especially the earlier books, are partly intended as ways of communicating with Regine. In any case, the broken engagement allowed Kierkegaard

---

[5] I shall in this book follow Kierkegaard's nineteenth-century Danish spelling, in which all nouns were capitalized.

truly to become an author, and between 1843 and 1846, he produced an astounding array of works, a number of which will be discussed in subsequent chapters. Many of these early works are pseudonymous and literary in character. Some, such as *Either/Or* and *Repetition*, have some of the character of a novel. However, it is important to note that from the beginning of his authorship, Kierkegaard also produced a series of religious works that he termed *Edifying Discourses* ("Upbuilding Discourses" in the Hongs' literal translation of the Danish "Opbyggelige.")

Even a brief sketch of Kierkegaard's life must mention two other episodes: the *Corsair* controversy and the "attack on Christendom" at the end of his life. In 1846 Kierkegaard intended to conclude what he called his "authorship" and accept a post as a Danish pastor, preferably in a rural parish. However, during that year he became embroiled in a quarrel with a Danish literary magazine, *The Corsair*. *The Corsair* was a satirical magazine, poking fun at Denmark's intellectual elite. Much of the writing for the magazine was anonymous, and this anonymity allowed for scurrilous and irresponsible attacks. (One might think of the kind of meanness anonymous postings on internet blogs allow today.)

The Corsair had up until this point exempted Kierkegaard from its biting ridicule. However, after a nasty review of Kierkegaard's *Stages on Life's Way* by a man named P. L. Møller, one of the people who regularly wrote for *The Corsair*, Kierkegaard responded, in the name of his pseudonym Frater Taciturnus, and in the response complained that it was unjust for him to be the only important Danish author who had not been "abused" in *The Corsair*. Also, in a passing remark, he revealed Møller's association with the magazine. *The Corsair* responded by making Kierkegaard the object of its ridicule in a long-lasting, sustained attack that went beyond the boundary of criticism or even ridicule of Kierkegaard's ideas, making fun of his physical appearance, the uneven length of his trousers, his supposed arrogance, and many other things, both in texts and in cartoons.

This may seem an inconsequential series of events, but it was fraught with consequences for everyone involved. Meir Goldschmidt, the editor of *The Corsair*, was later to write in his memoirs that the events were "a drama and a catastrophe for three people, of whom I am the only survivor."[6] Goldschmidt obviously came to regret the episode and eventually gave up the lucrative magazine as an act of repentance. Møller,

---

[6] Quoted in Joakim Garff, *Søren Kierkegaard: A Biography*, trans. Bruce H. Kirmmse (Princeton: Princeton University Press, 2005), p. 376.

who had hoped to become a professor at the University of Copenhagen, was ruined by the controversy, left for France, and soon died there, befriended only by two women he had seduced. Kierkegaard's own life was completely transformed. Prior to these events his main recreation had been walking the streets of Copenhagen, where he spent literally hours in conversation each day with people from all walks of life. After *The Corsair* made him an object of public ridicule, the character of his interchanges with ordinary people changed dramatically, as it became literally impossible for him to walk around Copenhagen without crowds of curious and sometimes jeering onlookers. Kierkegaard describes the pain he thereby suffered as the equivalent of being "trampled to death by geese."[7]

Biographers have offered vastly differing assessments of Kierkegaard's behavior in these events. In his journals, Kierkegaard portrays his action as selfless and even courageous, voluntarily taking a stand against a disreputable and demoralizing organ, and suffering the consequences for that stand, and Walter Lowrie is sympathetic to these claims.[8] Some other writers, however, have tended to see Kierkegaard's actions as unjustly ruining Møller's life and as motivated by spite against Møller, whose review of *Stages on Life's Way* had contained a wounding personal attack on Kierkegaard himself. Joakim Garff, for example, calls Kierkegaard's treatment of Møller an "assassination," and views Kierkegaard's own account of his motivation as self-deceived rationalization.[9]

My own view is that Kierkegaard's motives in this matter were probably mixed, as is so often the case with most of us. He surely did see *The Corsair*, as well as Møller, whose sexual promiscuity as well as looseness with the truth were abundantly evident, as malicious and malevolent, and therefore had good reason to see himself as standing for the right. So I see no reason not to take Kierkegaard at his word when he claims that his action was one that was "prayerfully" undertaken. But it is not impossible that personal resentment of Møller, who had attacked Kierkegaard cruelly, also played some role in his response. It is hardly surprising that in retrospect Kierkegaard preferred to focus on his virtuous motives and ignore, as we humans generally do, any motives that were less than noble.

---

[7] See *Søren Kierkegaard's Journals and Papers*, 7 vols., ed. and trans. Howard V. Hong and Edna H. Hong (Bloomington, Indiana: Indiana University Press, 1967–1978), Vol. V, entry 5998, p. 376.

[8] See Walter Lowrie, *A Short Life of Kierkegaard* (Princeton, New Jersey: Princeton University Press, 1942), pp. 176–187.

[9] See Garff, pp. 393–394.

Though Kierkegaard's motives may have been more complex than he was willing to admit, I cannot agree with Garff and others that Kierkegaard's actions towards Møller amounted to an "assassination." Kierkegaard was drawing public attention to a fact already widely known, and forcing Møller to take responsibility for his anonymous literary activity. Møller had long had an association with *The Corsair*, and this was hardly a secret around Copenhagen; in fact, even Garff admits that Møller had revealed this publicly in T. H. Erslew's *Encyclopedia of Authors*.[10] It is true that Møller lost hope for a university appointment after the clash with Kierkegaard, and even that his life began to unravel after this episode, but there is every reason to believe that the causes of this were the deep flaws in Møller's own character and had little to do with Kierkegaard. Robert Perkins has given a definitive argument that Møller was unqualified for the university post he aspired to, and had no realistic chance of ever getting it, so the claim that Kierkegaard "assassinated" Møller simply seems factually wrong.[11]

Regardless of how one evaluates Kierkegaard's conduct here, there is no question that the affair fundamentally changed his life. He gave up the idea of becoming a country pastor, and instead decided that he must "remain at his post," i.e., continue his activity as a writer in Copenhagen. The persecution and resulting isolation he suffered gave him a profound sensitivity to the evils that can stem from an anonymous "public," egged on by the press and what we would today term the instruments of "mass media." He came to believe that true Christianity necessarily was linked to outward suffering, since Christian faith requires a break with the values that established societies always embody. Since the true follower of Christ must be willing to suffer opposition and persecution from society, and even expect such persecution, genuine Christianity must be distinguished from "Christendom," a term Kierkegaard uses to denote the kind of "establishment Christianity" that equates being a Christian with being a

---

[10] Garff, p. 394. Howard Hong was the first to show that Møller's self-revelation in Erslew preceded Kierkegaard's connection of Møller with *The Corsair*. See Hong's discussion of the whole affair in the "Historical Introduction" to *The Corsair Affair*, ed. and trans. by Howard V. Hong and Edna H. Hong (Princeton, New Jersey: Princeton University Press, 1982), p. xxvii and also n. 279. Erslew's *Forfatter-Lexicon* has a title page dated 1847, but Hong discovered the book was printed in fascicles beginning in 1843, and that the fascicle containing the information about Møller had appeared in 1845. See also Robert L. Perkins' discussion of this issue, and his note about the Hong research, in his "Introduction" to *International Kierkegaard Commentary: The Corsair Affair*, ed. Robert L. Perkins (Macon, Georgia: Mercer University Press, 1990), pp. xiii–xxv, particularly n. 3, p. xviii.

[11] See Perkins' brilliant account of the whole affair in the "Introduction" cited in the previous note.

respectable member of a given society. All of these themes become prominent in the works Kierkegaard wrote from this period on, most of which were non-pseudonymous, such as *Christian Discourses* and *Works of Love*.

Kierkegaard became increasingly convinced that establishment Christianity in Denmark, as embodied by the official Lutheran church, made authentic Christian life difficult and even impossible. A genuine Christian is someone who has found forgiveness for sin through faith in Christ. Kierkegaard does not doubt this bulwark of Christian (and Lutheran) orthodoxy. However, the person who has genuine faith necessarily expresses this faith by being a follower, an imitator, of Jesus; it is not merely an abstract, propositional belief.

Christendom tones down the radical character of God's demands on a person's life. Christ's life was a decisive challenge to the established order of his day, and he paid the price for this challenge with his life. On Kierkegaard's view, the Christian who becomes a follower of Christ can expect to suffer opposition and persecution from the established order as well. Christendom claims that this is no longer the case since western society has itself become Christian. Kierkegaard rejects this assumption that society has become truly Christian. He believes that the Church in this life must always be a Church militant, struggling to define itself over against the world. It cannot expect to become a Church triumphant that has made society essentially good.

This opposition to Christendom can already be detected in some of Kierkegaard's early pseudonymous writings, but it becomes an increasingly dominant theme in the writings composed after the *Corsair* affair, and is expressed strongly in many entries in his Journal from 1846 onwards. Kierkegaard made no open break with the church as long as Jakob Peter Mynster, Bishop of Zealand, was alive, partly out of reverence for Mynster as his father's pastor and partly because Kierkegaard hoped that in some way Mynster would address the situation of Christendom, perhaps making a "public confession" that contemporary Christianity fell far short of the New Testament standard. Things came to a head in 1854, when Mynster passed away, and was eulogized by his soon-to-be successor, Hans Lassen Martensen, as a "link in this holy chain of witnesses to the truth," a chain "stretching across the ages, from the days of the Apostles up to our own times..."[12]

---

[12] Quoted in Garff, p. 729.

Kierkegaard's own later writings had employed the concept of a "witness to the truth" (*Sandhedsvidne*) as the definitive embodiment of Christian faith.[13] A witness to the truth is someone willing to suffer persecution to the point of death for the sake of the truth proclaimed, and this usage is supported by the New Testament concept of the martyr. Etymologically, the New Testament Greek word for a martyr, transliterated *martus*, has, as its basic meaning, one "who affirms or attests (often in legal matters)," and hence is close to the English term "witness."[14] This sense is extended in the New Testament to "one who witnesses at cost of life, martyr."[15] One can see this sense clearly at work in Acts 22:20, where Paul says, "And when the blood of Stephen your witness [*martus*] was shed, I also was standing by and approving."[16]

Martensen's eulogy outraged Kierkegaard for several reasons. Martensen had taken a concept that Kierkegaard himself had used to distinguish genuine Christianity from its Christendom counterfeit and used it to praise the foremost representative of that establishment Christianity. Mynster had lived a long and comfortable life at the pinnacle of Danish society. Thus, in Kierkegaard's eyes, Martensen's praise of Mynster equates such a life with the life of the martyrs who had provided the foundation for the Church. The eulogy provoked a public response from Kierkegaard in a newspaper: "Was Bishop Mynster a 'Witness to the Truth', one of 'the genuine witnesses to the truth' – is this *true*?" This polemical blast was followed by a series of newspaper articles, and eventually by a magazine, *The Moment*, that Kierkegaard began in order to carry on his polemical battle with the established Church. In all of this Kierkegaard campaigns for the view that "the Christianity of the New Testament no longer exists," and that the cause of Christianity would be best served if this were honestly admitted.

Kierkegaard published nine issues of *The Moment*, and had the tenth and final issue ready for publication when he collapsed on the street, and was eventually taken to the hospital with paralysis. He died a few weeks later on November 11, 1855, refusing to take communion from a priest who was a "state functionary," but nevertheless affirming "Yes, of course,"

---

[13] See, for example, the following passage : "Christianity . . . was served by *witnesses to the truth*, who instead of having profit and every profit from this doctrine, sacrificed and sacrificed everything for this doctrine, . . . lived and died for this doctrine." (JY, 129).

[14] See Walter Bauer, Frederick William Danker, William A. Arndt, and F. Wilbur Gingrich, *A Greek–English Lexicon of the New Testament and Other Early Christian Literature*. Third Edition (Chicago: University of Chicago Press, 2000), pp. 619–620.

[15] Ibid.

[16] My thanks to New Testament scholar Mikeal Parsons for help with this point.

to his life-long friend, Emil Boesen (a pastor in the state church), who asked him whether he continued to "believe in Christ and take refuge in Him in God's name."[17] The attack on Christendom was still rooted in faith in Christ.

Kierkegaard's attack on Christendom should not be viewed merely as a rejection of an established, state Church. It should be seen rather as a rejection of any attempt to identify Christianity with a particular human culture or society. The attack was thus felt not just by the leaders of the state Church, such as Mynster and Martensen, but also by Nikolai Grundtvig, the inspiration for the leading reform movement within the Danish Church, a movement that included Kierkegaard's brother Peter Christian among its adherents. (Kierkegaard's relationship with his brother was, unfortunately, not good, and his brother's association with Grundtvig made the situation even worse.) Grundtvig also had his difficulties with the established Church, but Grundtvig, whose brand of Christianity involved a strong admixture of Danish nationalism and enthusiasm for everything Scandinavian, could neither see the depths of the problem of Christendom nor recommend a proper cure. From Kierkegaard's perspective, Grundtvig's brand of cultural Christianity was simply another form of Christendom.

Kierkegaard's critique of Christendom is doubtless of more importance for understanding his work as a theologian than as a philosopher, but it is such a strong element in his later writings that it cannot be ignored even by his philosophical interpreters. Contemporary debates about the place of religion in public life show the importance of the issues he is grappling with, and I am inclined to think that Christendom is today most alive and well in parts of the U.S., which, despite the lack of an established church, has communities that continue to identify Christian faith with the prevailing culture.

MAKING SENSE OF KIERKEGAARD'S WORKS: IS KIERKEGAARD "POSTMODERN"?

Kierkegaard claims, in *On My Work as an Author*, that his "authorship, viewed as a *totality*, is religious from first to last" (PV, 6; italics original).[18]

---

[17] Virtually all of Kierkegaard's biographers depend on Boesen's recollections of conversations with the dying Kierkegaard. See Garff, p. 787.

[18] The suspicious attitude Garff takes towards Kierkegaard's Journals is partially grounded in some of the work of Henning Fenger, *Kierkegaard: The Myths and Their Origins* (New Haven, Connecticut: Yale University Press, 1980).

This is repeated and echoed in the posthumously published *The Point of View for My Work as an Author*: "the whole of my authorship relates itself to Christianity"(PV, 23). I believe that these claims are essentially correct, and that Kierkegaard was right to say that this is something "anyone who can see, if he wants to see, must also be able to see" (PV, 6). Most writers about Kierkegaard in English have accepted this point of view, at least until the last twenty-five years or so.

Recently, however, Kierkegaard's self-assessment has been severely challenged. Joakim Garff, in his massive biography, claims that Kierkegaard's self-understanding, as expressed both in his writings and in his Journals, was essentially a literary expression of how Kierkegaard wanted to be understood by history rather than an accurate account of his true intentions. Garff himself therefore takes a critical stance towards Kierkegaard's own accounts of his life and writings, so as to avoid "the danger of being an unintentional collaborator in writing the *myth* of Kierkegaard," a myth that "lurks everywhere in the materials."[19]

Implicit in Garff's work is a claim that was earlier made explicitly by Louis Mackey. Mackey did not merely question whether Kierkegaard's own account of the "point of view" for interpreting his authorship was correct, but argued that no such point of view, whether Kierkegaard's or anyone else's, could be correct.[20] Mackey affirms that there is no underlying unity to Kierkegaard's authorship, only "points of view." Even the "Søren Kierkegaard" who affixed his name to the non-pseudonymous books is ultimately just another pseudonym, a character Kierkegaard invented.[21] Taking note of the literary character of so much of Kierkegaard's authorship, with pseudonyms layered within pseudonyms, Mackey cautions us that "[w]hen a man fabricates as many masks to hide behind as Kierkegaard does, one cannot trust his (purportedly) direct asseverations. And when he signs his own name, it no longer has the effects of the signature."[22] In the end Kierkegaard as an integral human being vanishes from our eyes: "Søren was never the same person. At most a free variable (an *x*), he is at last an absolute absence. A constant evanescence."[23]

---

[19] Garff, p. xxi.
[20] See Louis Mackey, *Points of View: Readings of Kierkegaard* (Tallahassee, Florida: Florida State University Press, 1986).
[21] See Mackey, pp. 187–190. As Mackey notes, the suggestion that "Søren Kierkegaard" should be viewed as just another pseudonym was first made by Søren's brother, Peter, and certainly reflects the sad estrangement of the two brothers.
[22] Mackey, p. 188.   [23] Mackey, p. 187.

What is the effect of taking Kierkegaard as an "evanescence"? It gives us a Kierkegaard who is essentially "postmodern," who does not write to edify or make us aware of any religious truth, but who helps us to see the way human language inevitably fails to convey what is intended. This postmodern Kierkegaard is ironical and "deconstructive" through and through. Roger Poole, who was a professor of literature and a strong advocate of what may be termed the literary approach to Kierkegaard interpretation, tells us that Kierkegaard as a philosopher is really a kind of anti-philosopher: "Kierkegaard writes text after text whose aim is not to state a truth, not to clarify an issue, not to propose a definite doctrine, not to offer some meaning that could be directly appropriated."[24] According to Poole, Kierkegaard writes this way because he sees something that Derrida and Lacan were later to articulate. To be true or false, propositions must refer, but if language can never refer in this way, then it is impossible to convey truth straightforwardly. Kierkegaard's "texts demonstrate to a nicety the Lacanian perception that all we are ever offered in a text is an endless succession of signifiers."[25] Since Kierkegaard (actually one of his pseudonyms) is notorious for the claim that "truth is subjectivity," it might appear that it is a mistake to treat him as a philosopher who is in dialogue with other great western philosophers, ancient and modern, who tried to convey such truths.

Ultimately, this kind of radical postmodern view cannot be consistently maintained. The person who tells us that language cannot successfully refer has himself referred to something; he or she has made a claim *about* human language. Similarly, the individual who tells us that we cannot make true statements has made a statement that purports to be true. I see no reason to saddle Kierkegaard with such self-stultifying claims. Kierkegaard is certainly a philosopher who has a clear grasp of the limits of human language and human knowledge, but he is equally far removed from a philosophy that denies the value of rigorous thought and careful distinctions. The radical postmodern Kierkegaard is a Kierkegaard who is an object of aesthetic appreciation. Such an approach to Kierkegaard allows a person to enjoy the style and literary techniques of Kierkegaard without fear of being challenged by Kierkegaard as one human person speaking to another about issues of ultimate importance. Paradoxically, such an aesthetic Kierkegaard is much less interesting, even aesthetically, than a

---

[24] Roger Poole, *Kierkegaard: The Indirect Communication* (Charlottesville, Virginia: University of Virginia Press, 1993), p. 6.
[25] Poole, p. 9.

Kierkegaard who has something to say to me, someone whose voice can challenge my beliefs and assumptions, and even the way I live my life. A conversation with a human being is much more interesting than a "conversation" with an "evanescence."

What about the claim that Kierkegaard's own understanding of his work is a retrospective falsification? We must begin by separating out the question of whether the perspective is a retrospective one from the question of whether it is false. There is little doubt that Kierkegaard's understanding of his work evolved as the work progressed, and thus that the perspective he took at the time he wrote *The Point of View* differs from the views he may have held at the time of writing some of the earlier works. In fact, Kierkegaard affirms this himself in *The Point of View*, claiming that it would be "unfairness to God" if Kierkegaard were to affirm that he had understood his authorship in the beginning in the way that he now does (PV, 76–77). Rather, he says that his understanding of what he was about developed as he wrote, as God providentially educated him: "It is Governance that has educated me, and the education is reflected in the process that led to the production" (PV, 77). Non-believers will of course not be inclined to accept Kierkegaard's claim that the unity of the authorship is to be ascribed to the role God played in the whole enterprise. However, even a religious skeptic can take seriously Kierkegaard's claim that his understanding of the authorship evolved. And such a skeptic may be interested in the personal view of the authorship that Kierkegaard developed, and even take Kierkegaard's claims as sincere and illuminating.

As an author of a number of books myself, including several dealing with Kierkegaard, I have some sense of what such an affirmation on the part of an author might mean. In the process of writing, I have frequently found myself in the position of making discoveries about my own writing, moments where in effect I realized, "That is what I have been trying to say all along." The experience is one in which a person has a clear view of what he or she is doing only in retrospect. And yet in some sense and in some cases there is a recognition that this "retrospective" understanding is an articulation of what one was trying to do all along, perhaps confusedly and unclearly. This is true at every level of writing. Every writer has had the experience in which one finally gets the sentence or paragraph *right*, is able to say what one has been trying to say all along.

What is true for the sentence or paragraph can be even more true of a book or series of books. I recently edited a selection of my own articles on

Kierkegaard, written over a twenty-year period.[26] In reading over the essays I was struck by the unity and coherence of them, and it became clear to me that throughout my whole career I had been laboring to develop and articulate a particular view of Kierkegaard. Yet I by no means could have articulated what I was attempting to do at the beginning of this period. The fact that Kierkegaard sees his own authorship in a similar way as a coherent attempt to realize a particular project is therefore no reason to think his perspective is false, even if the realization on Kierkegaard's part is one that came into being along with the work itself. Everything depends on whether the coherence Kierkegaard saw in his authorship is really there. If it is, it is of course natural for a religious individual such as Kierkegaard to attribute this coherence to providence (rather than fortune), but readers do not have to accept Kierkegaard's religious explanation of his writing to find his interpretation of what his authorship is about credible.

However, even if one agrees that this kind of retrospective view of an authorship can be truthful and insightful, are there special reasons to be dubious about the particular account Kierkegaard gives? Kierkegaard recognizes that some will be inclined to be suspicious, and in fact he does not rely in *The Point of View* "on a simple declaration by the author himself." Rather, he tries to take "a completely objective attitude" towards his own works: "If I cannot, as a third party, as a reader, make good from the writings the claim that things are as I say, that it cannot be otherwise, it would never occur to me to want to win what I then perceive as lost" (PV, 33). In other words, we do not simply have a claim from Kierkegaard, made retrospectively, that the authorship has a religious purpose. Even if all we had was the claim, it would still be important to have an understanding of how an author himself views his works and have his testimony to that effect. However, we do not have to take Kierkegaard's word for what he was about. He challenges us to look at his authorship in light of his claims, to see if the books make sense as a coherent whole when viewed as Kierkegaard himself views them.

In a sense the current book is an attempt to develop the argument that Kierkegaard here describes: to give a reading of Kierkegaard's authorship as a whole in light of his declared intentions. Perhaps it will be clear only at the end whether I have succeeded or failed, but I shall try to show that what Kierkegaard says is true or at the very least highly plausible. The

---

[26] *Kierkegaard on Faith and the Self: Collected Essays* (Waco, Texas: Baylor University Press, 2006).

books do appear to hang together in just the way Kierkegaard says, and when read in light of what we might call his overall project, the works are illuminated both individually and in their complex inter-relationships.

This of course does not mean the books cannot be read in other ways, or that none of those other ways are interesting and helpful. In *The Point of View* Kierkegaard himself refers to the fact that he has had many readers who have read him only for aesthetic enjoyment or appreciation, which shows that he understands that there are ways of reading his works other than the one he suggests. Depending on what the reader wishes to gain, such ways of reading may be profitable. Perhaps it makes no sense to say that a person who reads the corpus differently and for different purposes is "wrong." However, if we want to learn what Kierkegaard hoped we would learn from his texts, it is only fair to take his intentions as our starting point, both as known from his own testimony and, even more significantly, as these can be seen in the writings themselves.

IS KIERKEGAARD OF INTEREST ONLY TO RELIGIOUS PEOPLE?

If Kierkegaard is fundamentally a religious writer who wants to "reintroduce Christianity into Christendom" does this make him philosophically less interesting? It may seem so to some, particularly those who are strongly opposed to religious perspectives, or perhaps especially to those who are, or at least claim to be, indifferent to such perspectives. I shall argue, however, that this is not the case. The peculiar way Kierkegaard sees the predicament of Christianity in the modern world makes aspects of his thought interesting to those who have little or no interest in his own religious faith.

I begin by simply noting the fact that historically Kierkegaard has been deeply interesting to non-Christians. In the twentieth century he powerfully influenced writers such as Heidegger, Sartre, and Camus. Even more surprising, perhaps, is the way Kierkegaard has been eagerly read and appreciated in non-Christian cultures such as Japan.[27] That Kierkegaard's philosophical thought has been found interesting and powerful to non-Christians is no accident, I will argue. To see why, we must look at Kierkegaard's analysis of what we might call the crisis of the decline of Christian faith.

---

[27] For the fascinating history of Kierkegaard's reception in Japan, which considerably antedates his recognition in the English-speaking world, see an article on the internet by Kinya Masugata, found at www.kierkegaard.jp/2005/masugata2.html.

Most scholars will recognize that such a decline is a real historical phenomenon. For whatever reason, by Kierkegaard's day, the majority of intellectuals in Europe were no longer serious, believing Christians, as probably had been the case two to three hundred years earlier. The roots of the decline go back at least to the period of the Enlightenment and probably before that, and the decline has continued to the present day. One of the remarkable differences between Europe and the United States is the much higher percentage of active believers in the U.S.

The reasons for the decline are no doubt various, complex, and disputed. However, one particular account is, I think, popular enough to be called "the received view." The basic story of the received view is that religious faith in general and Christian faith in particular have declined for reasons that are primarily intellectual. There are many versions of the received view, depending on which intellectual factors are chosen for emphasis. Philosophers may focus on the attacks on natural theology given by David Hume and Immanuel Kant, or Hume's critique of miracles. Others may look at the development of skepticism about the historical parts of the Bible as the result of "higher" critical scholarship about the Bible in Germany. Others may trace the decline to the development of modern science and the alleged way in which a scientific worldview undermines a religious perspective. (Of course the development of Darwinism could also be cited, but this occurred after Kierkegaard's death.) Whatever the supposed reasons, the basic idea is that while religious faith, including Christian faith, was at one time reasonable, it is no longer so, because the evidence on which it rests is no longer credible.

I shall try to give a detailed account in later chapters of Kierkegaard's account of religious knowledge and how it is attained. For now, I must simply register his disagreement with this "received view." Kierkegaard's account of religious faith is not one that sees faith as primarily the result of evidence or reflection on evidence. Evidence is not the ground of faith, and the lack of evidence cannot be the reason for the loss of faith. From Kierkegaard's perspective, faith has not declined because humans have become smarter or have developed a better understanding of natural science. Rather, faith has declined in contemporary western culture because contemporary westerners have become emotionally and imaginatively impoverished. We have ceased to care in the right ways about the right things.

The crux of the issue can be seen in *Concluding Unscientific Postscript*, a book to which Kierkegaard added his own name as "editor" on the title page, and which he essentially endorsed, despite its pseudonymity, in *The Point of View* as "the turning point in the whole authorship" (PV, 55). *Postscript*, according to Kierkegaard, both "appropriated all the pseudonymous aesthetic writing as a description of one way along which one may go to becoming a Christian," and itself described the second way: "*back* from the system, the speculative, etc. to becoming a Christian" (PV, 55). So we may safely assume that the analysis of the problem of Christianity given in *Postscript* by the pseudonymous Johannes Climacus is one that Kierkegaard himself endorses.

The diagnosis Climacus presents of the ailment of the modern world is stark and simple: "My principal thought was that, those of our time, because of so much knowledge, have forgotten what it is *to exist*, and the meaning of *inwardness*" (CUP, 249; italics original). The problem is not merely that people have lost a sense of what it might mean to exist religiously but "had forgotten what it means to exist humanly" (CUP, 249). For Kierkegaard, as for Climacus, Christianity is not primarily a set of doctrines (though it requires some particular beliefs), but a way of life, a particular way of answering the questions that human existence poses. However, if we do not understand those questions, or have ceased to ask them or even care about them, we will find it impossible to understand Christian faith if that faith is essentially an answer to those questions.

We can now see why Kierkegaard's mission to "reintroduce Christianity into Christendom" led him to another mission that can hardly be described as sectarian – that of describing the basic structure of human existence as it is lived. It is of course for this reason that Kierkegaard is justly famous as the "father of existentialism," however much he would have disliked and rejected many of the views of the twentieth-century existentialist "children" who paid him homage. Kierkegaard is a genuine philosopher, and a philosopher of the first rank, because he has given a penetrating description and analysis of what human life is actually like, and how it is lived. It is hardly surprising that his writings are deeply interesting to other humans as humans, regardless of whether they have any interest in his own project of articulating Christian faith in the modern world.

What exactly does Kierkegaard have to tell us about human existence? Does he have anything to tell us that we do not already know? Oddly, in one sense the answer to that second question is no. Kierkegaard himself, in commenting on his pseudonymous authorship, disclaims any grand new theories: the pseudonymous authors' significance "unconditionally does not lie in making any new proposal, some unheard-of discovery, or in founding a new party and wanting to go further" (CUP, 629).[28] Instead, the goal of the pseudonyms is said to be "to read through once again the original text of individual human existence-relationships, the old familiar text handed down from the fathers, as a solo, if possible in a more inward manner" (CUP, 629–630). In one sense the Kierkegaardian texts in question then tell us nothing we do not already know, or at least nothing that "the fathers" did not know.

Kierkegaard was not the first or last philosopher to think of philosophy as an activity in which we come to understand what in one sense we already know. After all, Plato himself taught that learning is just "recollection," a claim that Kierkegaard reflected deeply upon, and attached great significance to. Plato thought that there are different ways of "knowing" or "understanding" something. As another of Kierkegaard's pseudonyms, Anti-Climacus, tells us in *The Sickness Unto Death*, even Plato's teacher Socrates recognized that "to understand and to understand are two different things" (SUD, 90). It is one thing to have a detached, propositional understanding of a truth; quite another to understand what that truth might mean for human existence, or to bring into clear conscious awareness an insight that is already present in a vague and perhaps even unnoticed way.

In *Concluding Unscientific Postscript* Johannes Climacus gives several examples of what it might mean to truly understand things which in one sense everyone already knows (CUP, 165–183). We humans all know that all of us will die; we may know statistics about the average life expectancy and the major causes of death. However, it is one thing to know this and another to have asked what the fact of death implies for the meaning of life and how it should be lived. All humans know what it means to be grateful; everyone has experienced some good. Religious people may respond to this by saying that one should be thankful to God. However, for what should humans be thankful? What is actually good for us humans? Is human life itself good, so that all humans should be grateful? These are merely examples, Climacus says, of what it means to "think subjectively" about human existence.

The results of Kierkegaard's attempt to "read through the original text of individual human existence-relationships" will be spelled out in detail in subsequent chapters. At this point, however, something must be said about the notion of "inwardness" or "subjectivity" (terms that

---

[28] This quotation comes from "A First and Last Explanation," which is attached to the pseudonymous *Concluding Unscientific Postscript*, but signed by Kierkegaard himself.

Kierkegaard uses interchangeably). As seen above, for Kierkegaard to talk about human existence is to talk about inwardness. What then is inwardness?

A good starting point is to notice what we might call the unfinished, open-ended character of human existence. Kierkegaard, like Nietzsche a half-century later, sees the human self not simply as a finished product, a kind of entity, but as a developing process. A self is not simply something I am but something I must become. To be sure, there is also a sense in which the self must have a kind of substantial reality, for there must be something that is undergoing the process of becoming. But the substantial reality of the self includes potentialities, and thus selfhood is a process in which a person must try to "become what one already is" (CUP, 130).

This unfinished self gives shape to itself through its choices; every decision I make is also a decision about what kind of person I want to be. Kierkegaard's analysis of existence thus turns on his analysis of human choice, and it is here where inwardness is vital. Kierkegaard is no friend of thoughtlessness or enemy of reflection. He understands, with a tradition of philosophers that goes back at least to Aristotle, that part of what makes human choice distinctive is our ability to conceive the possibilities from which we must choose and reflect on the desirability and achievability of those possibilities.[29] Far from decrying this kind of reflection, part of Kierkegaard's goal is to "make people aware" of the choices that confront them, helping them to choose consciously rather than mindlessly.[30]

However, though not an opponent of reflection, Kierkegaard also holds firmly to the view that reflection by itself cannot determine a choice. Johannes Climacus makes the case for this view clearly in *Concluding Unscientific Postscript*, arguing that rational deliberation has within it no principle of closure, no way of bringing the process of deliberation to an end.[31] When I think about a decision I can and should

---

[29] For a detailed analysis of Kierkegaard's understanding of choice, including both his agreements and disagreements with the Aristotelian tradition, see my essay, "Where There's a Will There's a Way: Kierkegaard's Theory of Action," reprinted in *Kierkegaard on Faith and the Self: Collected Essays* (Waco, Texas: Baylor University Press, 2006), pp. 311–326.

[30] See PV, p. 50, where Kierkegaard says that he cannot determine a reader's choice, but can compel a reader to "become aware."

[31] See CUP, 335–338, where Climacus criticizes and satirizes the Hegelian notion that reflection somehow continues "so long until" it "cancels itself."

reflect on the reasons for one action over against another, but reason itself provides no natural end to this process. I can always think longer, look for more reasons, reflect more on the reasons I have, or reconsider the weight I have placed on my reasons. Of course humans do not deliberate forever prior to action, but why not? According to Climacus, it is because there is something more to the human self than reason. We bring the process of deliberation to a close because we want something or care enough about something to cease thinking and act. Though Kierkegaard affirms human freedom and responsibility, he consistently rejects the notion of a *liberum arbitrium* (a disinterested or indifferent will) as a myth.[32] We can make choices only because we have desires, hopes, fears, wishes, hates, and myriads of other "interested" attitudes towards the possibilities that confront us. It is these "carings" that move us to act and give our lives the "push" that is needed to move beyond reflection. The transition from possibility to actuality is a movement, a movement that Climacus metaphorically terms "a leap," a leap that is made possible by "interestedness" (CUP, 340).

This means that an understanding of human existence must include an understanding of what today would be termed our emotional lives. The motto on the title page of *Either/Or* could well be the motto for the whole of Kierkegaard's pseudonymous authorship, and a good deal of his edifying writings besides: "Is reason then alone baptized, are the passions pagans?" However, there are emotions and there are emotions. Kierkegaard knows that much of the time what moves a person to act are momentary feelings. Perhaps many such feelings are emotions that we have little control over. That is certainly sometimes the case. I have little control over the fear I feel if I am in a strange, dark room and hear a sudden, unexpected noise. A person who is completely dominated by such involuntary urges is close to what philosopher Harry Frankfurt has called a "wanton," a person who is barely recognizable as a person.[33] Such a person lurches through life, with wild reverses in direction possible if these immediate impulses change.

However, Kierkegaard does not share the view of many of our contemporaries that all of our emotions are like this, things we have no control over. He believes it is possible for a human life to acquire

---

[32] See *Kierkegaard's Journals and Papers*, Vol. II, entry 1268.
[33] See Harry Frankfurt, "Freedom of the Will and the Concept of a Person," in *Free Will*, ed. Robert Kane (Oxford: Blackwell, 2002), pp. 127–144, esp. pp. 133–134. This article first appeared in *The Journal of Philosophy*, LXVIII (January 14, 1971), pp. 5–20.

continuity, to manifest what Nietzsche would later call "a long obedience in the same direction" and thereby acquire what ethicists call character.[34] For this to occur, the individual must have or develop what Kierkegaard calls a passion, which might be defined as a sustained, enduring emotion, an emotion that gives shape and direction to a person's life.[35] The difference between a momentary feeling and a passion is the difference between a feeling of infatuation and a couple that is deeply in love for a lifetime.

Passions in this sense do not simply happen to a person. To be sure, there is an element of passivity in a passion, since by definition a passion must be something that moves us, and in the normal case this means that in some way a passion involves a response to something. Still, genuine passions can be cultivated, and indeed must be worked at if they are to endure. In the normative sense in which existence is equivalent to becoming a true self, "existing, . . . cannot be done without passion" (CUP, 311). Existence is indeed "motion," but there must be "a continuity that holds the motion together," and this is provided by passion (CUP, 312).

Some passions for Kierkegaard can endure because they do not merely reflect some temporal whim, but are grounded in what he and his pseudonyms call "the eternal." Though there are "earthly passions" that may be relatively long-lasting, authentic passions must be passions for goals that are in some sense eternal. He uses the term "eternal" in different and complicated ways, but one is simply to designate ideals, timeless possibilities that can in some way move us, become part of us.

Subjectivity or inwardness are simply Kierkegaardian terms for this affective dimension of human life that must take center stage if we are to understand human existence. In the next two chapters, I will explore Kierkegaard's view of subjectivity, first by discussing his view of whether and how one can communicate about subjectivity. I will look at Kierkegaard's claims about "indirect communication," giving close

---

[34] Nietzsche actually speaks of "*obedience* over a long period of time and in a *single* direction." See Friedrich Nietzsche, *Beyond Good and Evil*, in *Basic Writings of Nietzsche*, trans. and ed. Walter Kaufmann (New York: The Modern Library, 2000), p. 291. Interestingly, the religious writer Eugene Peterson has appropriated Nietzsche's phrase for his own un-Nietzschean purposes. See Eugene Peterson, *Perseverance: A Long Obedience in the Same Direction* (Downers Grove, Illinois: InterVarsity Press, 1996).

[35] Alternatively, if one wishes to reserve the term "emotion" for occurrent feelings, one could define a passion as a long-term disposition to have emotions of a specific kind.

attention to the way he attempted to practice this art through his use of pseudonyms and the irony and humor that are pervasive features of his work. Then, in Chapter 3, I will look concretely at Kierkegaard's view of human existence by beginning a discussion of Kierkegaard's view of the "stages" or "spheres" of human existence.

CHAPTER 2

Pseudonymity and indirect communication

Kierkegaard described what he called his "authorship" as beginning with the publication of *Either/Or* in 1843, although prior to this he had published a little-read and hard to understand critique of Hans Christian Andersen called *From the Papers of One Still Living*, as well as a very interesting doctoral dissertation, *On the Concept of Irony With Continual Reference to Socrates*. Most commentators have followed Kierkegaard on this point and have viewed *Either/Or* as his first real book. However, if one looks at the title page of the original Danish edition of *Either/Or*, Kierkegaard's name is nowhere to be found. Instead, the name of Victor Eremita (Victor the Hermit) appears as editor, with the two volumes of the work purportedly containing the writings of two other individuals, termed by Victor "A" and "B", though Victor reveals that B is actually a judge named William. The whole apparatus is made still more complicated by the fact that A's papers include a "Diary of a Seducer," supposedly written by another man named Johannes, though Victor argues there is good reason to believe that the true author of the Diary is A himself (EO I, 8–9). Volume II, which contains two long letters William has written to A, concludes with a sermon sent to William by yet another character, a country priest.

Either/Or was the first in a large number of such pseudonymous books. *Repetition*, by Constantine Constantius, and *Fear and Trembling*, by Johannes de silentio, also appeared in 1843. In 1844, Kierkegaard published the following: *Philosophical Fragments*, attributed to Johannes Climacus, *The Concept of Anxiety*, authored by Vigilius Haufniensis, and *Prefaces*, by Nicolaus Notabene. In 1845 *Stages on Life's Way* appeared, "compiled and published" by Hilarius Bookbinder, though the book, like *Either/Or*, contains a host of characters, some of whom had first appeared in *Either/Or*. Finally, in 1846 what some have called Kierkegaard's "First Authorship" concludes, appropriately enough, with *Concluding Unscientific Postscript to Philosophical Fragments*, also attributed to Johannes

Climacus. Kierkegaard's later writings also contain some important pseudonymous works, most notably *The Sickness Unto Death* and *Practice in Christianity*, attributed to Anti-Climacus.

Kierkegaard's authorship is not all pseudonymous. As I noted in Chapter 1, from the very beginning he also published edifying or "upbuilding" works, explicitly religious in character, under his own name, a fact that he appeals to as evidence that his religious concerns were present from the start. However, the pseudonymous section of the authorship, particularly in Kierkegaard's early writings, looms very large, both in sheer number of pages and in influence. Hence any attempt to understand Kierkegaard's writings must begin by asking why Kierkegaard chose to write under pseudonyms and what purposes his pseudonyms serve.

We can begin by ruling out the hypothesis that Kierkegaard chose to write this way to protect his anonymity. Very soon after *Either/Or* appeared, most people in Copenhagen who were "in the know" at least suspected that Kierkegaard was the author. Copenhagen in this era was not a very large city, and the number of people who could possibly be the author of such a book was small. Certainly, there was a general assumption that all the pseudonymous books were by the same individual, and after the publication of *Philosophical Fragments* in 1844, it was pretty clear to everyone that this individual was Kierkegaard, since he placed his own name on the title page of this work as "Editor." If anyone still had doubts about this, Kierkegaard allayed them in 1846 by publishing "A First and Last Explanation" at the end of *Concluding Unscientific Postscript*, in which he formally acknowledged that he was the author of all the works, while requesting that his readers understand that the pseudonymous "authors" have their own perspectives, much as characters in a novel have views that may differ quite a lot from the author of the novel.

But if anonymity was not the aim of Kierkegaard's use of pseudonyms, why did he write in this way? In all likelihood, there were many reasons. Perhaps Kierkegaard simply was exercising what we might call his literary exuberance. Kierkegaard was inexhaustibly creative, and clearly enjoyed the "mystification" and puzzles his artistic creativity posed for his readers. In one place he describes his early literary work as a "poetic element" that "had to be emptied out" (PV, 85). The suggestion is that although Kierkegaard's ultimate purposes were religious, he understood his own need to write creatively and satisfied that need through his early pseudonymous works, creating his "novel-like" characters as authors.

This cannot be the whole story, however. Suppose, for example, that Kierkegaard had actually written novels instead of just writing in this novel-like manner. We could certainly see this as a way of exercising his creativity, just as we would in the case of other writers of novels. However, writers of novels typically have motivations of a different kind as well. They write to inspire, to challenge, to make moral or political points, to make money, to become famous, and for hundreds of other reasons. Which of these additional motivations might be present for Kierkegaard?

We can rule out a desire for financial gain. Kierkegaard's Denmark was a small country with a very few cultured readers, so there was little prospect of making much money through writing sophisticated books. Some have suggested that Kierkegaard wanted fame and recognition, and this possibility is more plausible. He had a sense of his own talents and gifts, and it is understandable that he was, like most young people, eager to see those talents recognized.

However, there must still be more to the story than this. This would be true even if Kierkegaard was an ambitious person who wanted to be known for his literary accomplishments. For no one simply wants recognition; people want to be recognized *for* something, something significant and valuable. So what exactly did Kierkegaard hope to accomplish as a writer, and how did his use of pseudonyms help him accomplish this?

As I have already said, Kierkegaard testifies that his primary goals were religious. At least by the time he wrote *The Point of View for My Work as an Author*, he was clear that his major purpose was to "reintroduce Christianity into Christendom," to breathe life into the nominal Christian faith that dominated his society. Perhaps at the beginning he was less clear about this calling, but it seems plausible that from the beginning he was indeed on some kind of religious mission. The fact that his earliest writings include the series of *Upbuilding Discourses* is strong evidence for this, as is the fact that many of the early pseudonymous books themselves clearly center around religious issues. *The Concept of Anxiety*, for example, focuses on what one might call the psychology of original sin, while *Fear and Trembling* is a series of reflections, inspired by the Biblical story of Abraham's willingness to sacrifice his son Isaac upon God's command, on what it means to be a person of faith.

There are a number of ways of understanding how Kierkegaard's pseudonymous authorship might serve this religious calling, but the concept that is the key to linking them is that of "indirect communication." Both Kierkegaard and many of his pseudonyms claim that at least some communication that is ethical and/or religious or serves ethical-religious ends must have the character of being "indirect." An understanding of what indirect communication is and why it is important for religious communication will go a long way towards helping us understand Kierkegaard's use of pseudonyms.

CAN WE RELY ON *CONCLUDING UNSCIENTIFIC POSTSCRIPT*'S ACCOUNT OF INDIRECT COMMUNICATION?

Probably the fullest account of indirect communication (and its contrasting counterpart, direct communication) is found in *Concluding Unscientific Postscript*. One might worry that it is illegitimate to draw on this source to explain Kierkegaard's motivation for using indirect communication as the reason for pseudonymity, since *Postscript* is itself one of the pseudonymous books. However, I believe this worry is misplaced, for several reasons.

First, at the very least, *Concluding Unscientific Postscript*, though attributed to Johannes Climacus, is the work of Kierkegaard. Climacus is his poetic creation, and thus in some sense the work of Climacus is "Kierkegaardian" even if Climacus had advanced views that differ from those of Kierkegaard personally. We would still be interested in what Climacus has to say about communication as one of Kierkegaard's characters, and it would be reasonable to assume that the large amount of space Climacus devotes to discussing this topic reflects some concern of Kierkegaard himself. Moreover, it would be an error to infer that Kierkegaard's views must always be different from those of his pseudonyms, since he might well agree with some of what they say even if they were actually different individuals rather than being his own creations.

However, Johannes Climacus is in many ways special among the pseudonyms, and has a close relation to Kierkegaard. First, the two books attributed to Climacus both have "S. Kierkegaard" on the title page as editor, something not done for the other pseudonyms. Kierkegaard himself affirms in *The Point of View* that putting his name on the title page as editor was "a hint, at least for someone who concerns himself with such things and has a sense for them" (PV, 31–32). He means, I think, that the writings of Climacus, especially *Concluding Unscientific Postscript*, have a much closer relation to himself and his own purposes than the other early pseudonyms.[1] The privileged position of Climacus is also evidenced by the fact that, in *Postscript*, he gives a kind of analysis of all the earlier pseudonyms, one that explains how they relate to each other and how they all serve the purpose of helping individuals gain an understanding of what it means to be a Christian. Nor is this analysis merely that of Climacus. Kierkegaard appropriates the analysis himself in *The Point of View*, endorsing the claim that *Postscript* is "the turning point in the whole authorship" because "[i]t poses *the problem*: becoming a Christian" (PV, 55). The book can serve as the turning point because it describes what could be called the two paths to authentic Christianity: "After first having appropriated the whole of the pseudonymous aesthetic writings as a description of one way down which one may go to becoming a Christian – *back* from the aesthetic to becoming a Christian, the book describes the second way – *back* from the system, the speculative, etc. to becoming a Christian" (PV, 55).

However, besides all this evidence that the views of Climacus in *Postscript* are close to Kierkegaard's own, there is strong independent evidence that Kierkegaard holds similar views about communication. Although *Postscript* contains the most detailed and elaborate account of direct and indirect communication in the published writings, Kierkegaard frequently discusses these notions in other works under his own name, and what he says in these contexts, often in passing while addressing other issues, agrees pretty closely with what is found in *Postscript*.[2] The most extended of these discussions is in *The Point of View*, which I will discuss below. There are also many discussions of communication in Kierkegaard's *Journals and Papers*, including extensive notes for a lecture course Kierkegaard proposed to give on the subject, and once again, there is broad agreement with what is said in *Concluding Unscientific Postscript*. Kierkegaard's account of indirect communication is complex, to the point that we may doubt that all the things he says about it are completely consistent. But at least some of the inconsistencies and problems are present in the account Climacus gives in *Postscript*. I shall

---

[1] Philological work has established that in the case of *Philosophical Fragments*, Kierkegaard wrote the book intending to publish it under his own name. The pseudonym was a late invention. For a detailed account, see Johnny Kondrup, "On the Genesis of Philosophical Fragments," in *Kierkegaard Studies Yearbook 2004*, ed. Niels Jørgen Cappelørn, Hermann Deuser, and Jon Stewart (Berlin and New York: Walter de Gruyter, 2004), pp. 1–17.

[2] For a list of significant passages in Kierkegaard's works, both published and unpublished, that deal with indirect communication, see p. 597 in *Kierkegaard's Journals and Papers*, Vol. II. Also see the entries from the Journals on the theme in the same volume, pp. 383–388.

begin therefore by looking at what is said about indirect communication in that work.

INDIRECT COMMUNICATION AND "DOUBLE REFLECTION"

Many of Kierkegaard's key ideas are inextricably intertwined in such a way that it is impossible to explain one of them in isolation. This makes things hard for the commentator, since it appears that everything must be explained at once, which is obviously impossible. The best remedy, when expounding a concept such as indirect communication, is simply to give preliminary sketches of key related ideas that will be given a fuller discussion later. (It is for this reason that this work will also unavoidably contain some repetition of themes.) In *Concluding Unscientific Postscript*, indirect communication is linked to a number of key concepts. These include the basic notion of existence itself, the notion of the "stages" or "spheres" of existence, the basic contrast between objectivity and subjectivity that pervades the book, and the Socratic ideal of the teacher as a midwife, which I will refer to as "the maieutic ideal."

This idea of "the maieutic" may be unfamiliar to some readers, but it plays a key role in Kierkegaard's self-understanding. Briefly, the term stems from Socrates' understanding of himself as a teacher who had no knowledge to pass directly on to others. Rather, Socrates, as Plato portrays him in his dialogues, teaches by helping others to "recollect" the truth that is already present within them. Thus, Socrates does not give birth to new ideas himself, but assists his hearers, in the manner of a midwife, to "give birth" to their own ideas. This is famously illustrated in Plato's *Meno*, where Socrates, simply by asking questions, helps an uneducated slave boy to come up with a geometrical truth. Kierkegaard in many ways aspires to be a modern-day Socrates, and the maieutic ideal embodies his affirmation of the idea that individuals must discover the truth for themselves.

Johannes Climacus, the pseudonymous author of *Postscript*, distinguishes between objective and subjective communication by linking them to other contrasting concepts, such as the distinction between objective and subjective thinking, and the distinction between objective and subjective understanding. Objective understanding is understanding that can be directly or immediately passed on to another person. Climacus characterizes this kind of understanding as an understanding of "results"; perhaps historical and mathematical knowledge are proper domains for this kind of understanding, where communication is appropriately direct.[3] Subjective understanding, by contrast, is not communication of "results" but of "a way," and this kind of understanding cannot be directly or immediately passed on to another person, but requires an indirect or "artful" form of communication (CUP, 72–80).

The idea that lies behind this seems to be something like this. An historian may, by dint of arduous research, discover some fact. Suppose, for example, that an American historian learns that Thomas Jefferson fathered an illegitimate child. Learning such a fact may have cost the historian a tremendous amount of effort ("the way"), but once the discovery has been made, this new knowledge ("the result") can be transferred to someone else with little effort on the part of the beneficiary. All that is really necessary is trust in the work of the historian and the ability to grasp the meanings of the relevant concepts that the historian uses to articulate this fact. Even direct communication requires a kind of reflective understanding on the part of the recipient, but this understanding can be an abstract understanding of the relevant concepts.

Subjective understanding, by contrast, is an understanding that bears on a person's own existence, how life should be lived. Climacus does think that it is possible to think about such things and to communicate one's thought to others. However, in this case, for genuine communication to occur and genuine understanding to be achieved, the recipient of the communication must be able to do more than grasp what the communicator says in an abstract way. The recipient must in some way think through the meaning of what is said concretely in relation to his or her own life. Here the effort that the communicator has exerted to gain this understanding cannot be directly or immediately passed on as a "result," but something like the "way" the communicator has followed to gain the understanding must be reduplicated by the recipient.

Climacus describes this as the requirement of "double reflection" (CUP, 73). Genuine subjective understanding requires that a person first grasp the relevant concepts (first reflection), but then go on and think through what it would mean to apply those concepts to the person's own life (second reflection).

Consider the concept of gratitude, one that Climacus himself uses as an illustration of what it means to "think subjectively" (CUP, 177–179).

---

[3] I say "perhaps" because Climacus sometimes seems to deny that there is any such thing as historical knowledge, because it is only "an approximation." See CUP, 81 and 316, for example. However, in CUP, 193, Climacus does mention mathematical and historical knowledge "of various kinds" as the outcome of "objective reflection."

Pastors tell us, says Climacus, that we should be thankful to God for the good he gives us, even that we should always be thankful (CUP, 178). It is one thing to understand these words in the sense that one could give a roughly synonymous equivalent or perhaps even translate them into a foreign language. It is quite another thing to understand what it means to live a life of gratitude. If I wish to live in this way, do I thank God only for those things I recognize to be good? But perhaps God understands that some things will ultimately be for my good that I do not recognize to be good. Suppose I believe that I ought to be thankful in all circumstances. Does this mean I must literally be thankful for everything that happens to me, or merely that I should be able to be grateful for the goods I have enjoyed no matter what happens to me?

These are difficult questions, and yet without answering them it is not clear that we really understand what it means to live in a grateful manner. Another way of putting this, one that Climacus himself is fond of, is to note that without such a subjective understanding, any agreement between speaker and hearer may be purely verbal. Both may agree that "we ought always to be thankful to God" and yet have vastly different, even contradictory, ideas about what this means. Climacus thus claims that "objective" communication, communication that does not require this "second reflection," can amount to "patter" and lead only to "rote understanding." Kierkegaard's critique of "Christendom" partly stems from this point, because Kierkegaard believed that much of what the Danish people of his day "knew" and "understood" as baptized, confirmed Christians was a purely verbal kind of knowledge. People knew what one is supposed to *say* about how life should be lived as a Christian, but showed little understanding of what this might mean for them concretely.

Climacus thinks that communication that essentially bears on human existence must be indirect because the "second reflection" that must be done requires a kind of active involvement and appropriation by the person receiving the communication, and this means that direct communication is of no value. However, one might wonder whether it is really true that direct communication cannot be helpful to others about such matters. Cannot one individual who knows another person well tell that person some helpful, concrete things about what it might mean for that other person to live gratefully? This certainly seems possible, and I think we must understand what Climacus says in a way that is consistent with this truth. To see how this is so we must explore the basic Kierkegaardian understanding of human existence in more depth. This will help us distinguish two different ways Kierkegaard talks about indirect communication that are not always kept separate: indirect communication as an art or strategy by which one *attempts* to help another, and indirect communication as the *successful* impartation of existential wisdom to another.

KIERKEGAARD'S UNDERSTANDING OF HUMAN EXISTENCE: PASSION AND CHOICE

It is widely recognized that Kierkegaard saw human persons as having a distinctive kind of being or reality, and that he took advantage of the fact that the Danish language has more than one word for "existence" or "being" to highlight the distinctive form of human being. (Once again much of the relevant Kierkegaardian literature on this point is found in Climacus' *Concluding Unscientific Postscript.* In what follows I draw on this Climacus literature but assume it is broadly representative of Kierkegaard's own views.) Human beings do not merely have a kind of abstract reality (*Realitet*), of the kind shared by formal entities such as numbers and propositions, and they do not merely exist in the sense of occupying a particular place in time (Danish *være til*), as plants and rocks do. Rather human beings *exist* (*existere*) in the sense that they form themselves through a process in which their own choices play an important role. It is of course this stress on the distinctive character of human existence that has led many to award Kierkegaard the honorary title (one he likely would have declined) "father of existentialism."

In *Philosophical Fragments* Johannes Climacus expresses this idea by saying that human existence contains a kind of doubling; it is a "coming into existence within its own coming into existence" (PF, 76). Human beings exist as part of nature in the way that other physical objects do; in that sense they have "come into existence." However, their being as part of the natural order of things includes possibilities, and their own existence as persons is a process in which some of these possibilities come into existence. Other parts of the natural order of course have possibilities as well; we can speak truthfully of the possibility that a plant will germinate early or a rock will fall off a ledge in a rainstorm. However, human beings do not merely have possibilities, but in some sense are constituted by their awareness of these possibilities. Possibility is constitutive of the being of persons in a way that is not the case for non-persons.

How do we actualize possibilities? How is existence possible? Thought or reflection obviously plays a crucial role. It is through reflection that we become aware of "the eternal," possibilities which, like all possibilities, are timeless realities, but which humans become aware of as ideals to strive to realize. However, thought by itself is never equivalent to existence: "It is one thing to think and another to exist in the thought. Existing is in relation to thinking just as little something that follows of itself as it is something thoughtless" (CUP, 254–255). One cannot exist without thinking, but thinking alone is not existing.

Why is this the case? In Chapter 1 I discussed Kierkegaard's reasons for claiming this, but I must here reiterate and expand on the points made there.[4] Climacus argues that for humans thought by itself cannot reach closure but action requires closure. Action definitely conforms to the Aristotelian principle of non-contradiction, which says that if some proposition p is true, then "not p" must be false.[5] "A person can *be both* good and evil, ... but one cannot *become* good and evil *at the same time*" (CUP, 420; italics original). Hegel had criticized this Aristotelian logical principle, and his own logic attempted to show how apparently contradictory propositions can both be partially true. Whether Hegel is right or not about speculative logic, Climacus argues that this Hegelian logic cannot be valid for the realm of action, for to perform some action A is definitely to reject not A.

But why can't thought bring about this closure that allows a human person to determine the will to action? We certainly can reflect on the reasons to perform or not to perform a particular action. However, this reflection by itself cannot lead to action. For any particular action we are considering, how do we know we have reflected long enough and hard enough? Are there other reasons we should consider? Should we reconsider the evaluations and weightings we have given to the reasons we have considered? Climacus thinks that in principle a person could go on reflecting upon an action forever. (My wife thinks that I come close to this in restaurants, where I am often paralyzed by the possibilities offered by the menu and have trouble making a decision.) Of course we don't deliberate endlessly; in most cases we are able to say, "I have thought

---

[4] See Chapter 1, pp. 20–21.

[5] See the discussion of the principle of contradiction in CUP 304–308, where Climacus argues that the Hegelian attack on the Aristotelian principle of non-contradiction may be valid for abstract thinking but is not valid for existence.

about this long enough; it is time to act." (Eventually I am able to tell the exasperated waiter what I want!) But what enables us to do this? Is it the thought that one alternative possibility looks like the best option? It is hard to see how that thought by itself could rule out further thinking, for we could certainly think more about whether this thought is itself correct. We bring the process of thinking to a close when something other than thought makes its presence felt, something that lies more in the region of what psychologists call our affective lives than our intellectual lives. We saw in Chapter 1 that Kierkegaard calls this dimension of our lives "passion."

Life is finite, and the time we spend thinking inevitably postpones action. We are able to stop thinking and act because we have passions: wants, desires, fears, hopes, wishes, loves, and a thousand other emotional attitudes. Even the thought that "A is the best action for me to perform, the most reasonable in light of all I know" will not necessarily move me to perform A unless I *care* about doing what is best, *want* to do what is reasonable. Kierkegaard has a variety of terms for this passionate dimension of the human self that makes it possible to act, sometimes referring to it as inwardness or subjectivity. We can now understand why Climacus says that "it is impossible to exist without passion" (CUP, 311).

However, there are passions and there are passions. Most human choices are formed by what Kierkegaard calls "aesthetic" or "immediate" passions, momentary inclinations that may be grounded in our biological urges or need to fit in with what others are doing. These kinds of passions are in one sense natural and many of them are involuntary; we just find ourselves wanting an ice cream, or fearing the person we see walking towards us on the dark street. Such passions hardly deserve the name, and in fact, Kierkegaard often reserves the term "passion" for something quite different, those enduring, sustained kinds of carings that give direction and continuity to a person's life.[6] (He is not, however, completely consistent about this usage.)

A classic example of an immediate passion would be "love at first sight." One person sees another person and immediately feels a desire to be with that other person and have a relationship. But such immediate "falling in love" experiences may not last. They certainly must be

---

[6] For an excellent attempt to order Kierkegaard's account of passions and emotions see Robert Roberts, "Existence, Emotion and Character: Classical Themes in Kierkegaard," in *Cambridge Companion to Kierkegaard*, ed. Alastair Hannay and Gordon Marino (Cambridge: Cambridge University Press, 1998), pp. 177–206.

distinguished from the deep, enduring love two people have nourished for each other over a lifetime. Love in this second sense is Kierkegaard's favorite example of an enduring passion. These kinds of passions are ones that can be formed, developed over time, and thus a person may have some responsibility for them. Since they give direction to a life, a self that is shaped by such passions is one that will have some unity at a given point of time, as well as some continuity over time.

To use contemporary language, Kierkegaard thinks that a person must have emotional intelligence in order to be wise, to know how to live rightly. It is not enough to know propositional truths. One must "perceive" the possibilities that confront one rightly, recognizing which are to be feared, which are to be desired, which are to be hoped for, and the passions are simply the means whereby we recognize in a "thick" way the character of these possibilities.

We are now in a position to see both why it is possible for one person to try to help another with respect to learning something about what it means to exist, and also the limitations of such help. On the one hand, the fact that passions can be developed and nourished makes it possible for one person to try to help another learn something about existence. However, there is clearly a sense in which each person must develop for himself or herself the passions that form the self. For it is the very nature of a passionate caring that it must be owned by the one who cares. Perhaps I can help another person learn to love what I love, but my love cannot simply be transferred to the other person. That other person must develop a passion that is truly personal. In that sense what I communicate to the other is necessarily indirect.

Perhaps something like this is true even for cases of communication about what Kierkegaard would call objective matters. Someone who wants to explain some difficult point about a computer program cannot simply "transfer" his or her knowledge to me without effort on my part. However, even if the contrast between objective and subjective communication is not as absolute as Kierkegaard thinks, there does seem to be a sense in which communication about subjective matters requires a deeper kind of involvement on the part of the recipient of the communication.

INDIRECT COMMUNICATION AS AN ART

Kierkegaard is convinced that this kind of practical wisdom or existential understanding has diminished in the modern world. Part of the reason for this is that we are under the illusion that truth about existence or life can be boiled down to a set of propositions and learned as one would learn supposedly "objective" subjects such as mathematics and history. There is at least some evidence that he is right in thinking that this error is widespread in our world. For example, take our response to unethical business practices, such as the ones that brought down the Enron Corporation. After this occurred, there was a flurry of proposals for adding courses in ethics to the curriculum of business schools, but it is far from clear that studying ethical theory makes people ethically better. Adding the courses may actually make the situation worse, by giving the illusion that knowledge about ethical theory constitutes ethical character or can substitute for such character.

Kierkegaard thinks that his own, predominantly Christian culture is one in which this kind of "objective knowledge" is much prized, but genuine subjective understanding is regarded as something easy, perhaps something to be left for the common people incapable of higher learning. Becoming an honest person who lives with gratitude and hope is supposed to be easy; giving a theoretical analysis of honesty, gratitude, and hope is supposed to be difficult. Climacus, who surely speaks for Kierkegaard here, says that it is his task to "introduce difficulties," to show how hard the simple existential tasks really are (CUP, 165–181, 186–187). In one sense people already know what he has to say to them; his job is to help them reflect on and understand what they already know. In the first chapter, I quoted from Kierkegaard's own view of the pseudonymous works, and it is worth hearing the words again:

> Their significance . . . unconditionally does not lie in making any new proposal, or some unheard-of discovery, or in founding a new party and wanting to go further, but precisely the opposite, . . . to read through the original text of individual human existence-relationships again, the old familiar text handed down from the fathers, as a solo, if possible in a more inward manner. (CUP, 629–630)

We can easily see why Kierkegaard worries a lot about how he communicates to his readers. The problem is that people already know a lot of moral and religious truths, but have not really thought them through in relation to their own lives. In such a situation, communication of such truths can easily amount to "patter" and learning of them can certainly be a matter of "rote understanding." Kierkegaard himself wants to avoid compounding this problem by simply adding to the avalanche of information available to people. He therefore sets himself the task of communicating indirectly, of assisting others to engage in the "double-reflection" that is essential for genuine subjective understanding. He wants to encourage not merely intellectual understanding, but the "second reflection" that requires understanding of what these concepts would mean for a person's own life.

In a culture that already suffers from an overload of objective knowledge and communication about such knowledge, Kierkegaard does not want to aggravate the problem by contributing yet another "theory" that could be learned by rote. Rather, he wants to communicate to his readers in a *form* that shows his awareness of the necessity for "double reflection" on the part of his readers, and that he hopes will encourage them to engage in this kind of subjective thinking.

The use of pseudonyms is certainly part of this "artful" communication, a strategy designed to encourage readers to think for themselves. Through the pseudonyms, Kierkegaard presents his readers with various views as to how human life should be lived, various answers to the question "How should a person exist?" The pseudonyms do not simply write about these various answers to this question; they embody those answers. They do not merely tell us about their views of life, but show us what it is like to live in a certain way. We might compare Kierkegaard here to a novelist such as Dostoevsky. In *The Brothers Karamazov* Dostoevsky does not simply tell us about an atheistic challenge to belief in God based on the problem of suffering; he embodies this challenge in the person of Ivan Karamazov. In a similar manner, Kierkegaard does not simply tell us about a view of existence that sees the purpose of life as the attainment of moments of aesthetic satisfaction; he shows us what such a view of life is like by creating the character of Johannes, the author of "The Diary of a Seducer" in *Either/Or I*.

The advantages of this novelistic strategy are clear. For one, Kierkegaard can give an honest portrayal of the strengths of a particular view of life, help us see what is attractive about it, even if it is a view that he himself sees as pernicious, just as Dostoevsky gives us an honest portrayal of the power of atheism in the person of Ivan Karamazov, even though it is at odds with his own Christian faith. Second, this novelistic strategy seems well-tailored to encourage the kind of existential or subjective reflection Kierkegaard wants his readers to engage in. It is natural for a person who encounters such a character to ask questions such as these: "Do I want to be like this person?" "Am I like this person?" "What do I find attractive and/or repulsive about this person?" The reader is thus encouraged to make an application to his or her own life from the start.

Kierkegaard himself believed that the possible ways of living a human life, though in one sense infinitely various, can be usefully categorized using a relatively small number of concepts. He termed the various ways of existing the "stages" or "spheres" of human existence, and I will discuss them in more detail in succeeding chapters. In a way then, he has a kind of descriptive "theory" about the existential choices that face human persons, and he is clear about this:

Even though I achieve nothing else, I nevertheless hope to leave very accurate and experientially based observations concerning the conditions of existence...

Using my diagram, a young person should be able to see very accurately beforehand, just as on a price-list, if you venture this far out, the conditions are thus and so, this is to win, and that to lose; and if you venture out this far these are the conditions, etc.[7]

However, although Kierkegaard has a theory of sorts, even one that could be presented in a "diagram," we can now see why he does not simply present his ideas in the *form* of a psychological theory. Such an "objective" way of presenting these views is likely to foster the problem of "parroting" and "rote-communication" that he sees as endemic in the modern world.

At the heart of the Kierkegaardian account of the "stages on life's way" lies his conviction that existential growth requires the development of the appropriate passions, and cannot be achieved simply through knowing propositions. If it is true, for example, that a particular form of the aesthetic life is a form of "perdition," it would not do Kierkegaard's readers much good simply to be told this. Somehow, they must come to "see" it for themselves, develop an emotional sense of repugnance for or even horror of such a life-possibility. Kierkegaard believed that this was best done by creating his pseudonymous "characters." These pseudonyms, he tells us, exhibit a "heedlessness with regard to good and evil, in broken-heartedness and hilarity, in despair and arrogance, in suffering and jubilation, and so on, only ideally limited by psychological consistency, which no factually real person within the moral limitations of actuality dares permit himself or can want to permit himself" (CUP, 625).[8]

We can therefore understand Kierkegaard's use of pseudonyms as part of a strategy to engage in "artful" communication that is intended to

---

[7] *Kierkegaard's Journals and Papers*, Vol. I, 1046.

[8] This quote is again from "A First and Last Explanation," in *Concluding Unscientific Postscript*, and thus reflects Kierkegaard's own voice rather than the pseudonym.

foster subjective understanding. However, it would be a mistake simply to identify indirect communication with pseudonymity. Kierkegaard uses a number of other strategies that encourage the same kind of existential understanding on the part of readers. For example, he often includes stories and parables in his works, both pseudonymous and those under his own name.[9] Several other techniques deserve special comment.

One is the use of irony and humor. It is not for nothing that Kierkegaard received the Master of Arts degree (the equivalent of a Ph.D. in today's university) for a dissertation on *The Concept of Irony with Continual Reference to Socrates*, so that he sometimes refers to himself, somewhat amusingly, as the "Master of Irony." Kierkegaard perceived his own situation in Denmark as strongly analogous to that of Socrates in ancient Greece. Although Socrates claimed not to possess any wisdom himself, he reluctantly accepted the judgment of Apollo's oracle that he was the wisest man in Greece. The reason, as Socrates explained at his trial, is that although neither Socrates nor his contemporaries possessed wisdom, Socrates was wiser than the others by virtue of recognizing his own lack of wisdom.[10]

Socrates famously attempted to help his contemporaries move towards his own negative wisdom by ironically engaging them in questioning. Encountering a politician or teacher with a reputation for wisdom, Socrates ironically accepts their confident self-estimates at face value, and asks them to help him gain the understanding of piety, or beauty, or knowledge that they supposedly already possess. Of course, through Socratic questioning he usually shows pretty quickly the gap between the claims and the actual insights of his discussion partners.

Kierkegaard saw the pretensions of bourgeois society in Christendom as equally shallow, and he seeks to follow the Socratic example of engaging his contemporaries through irony. In fact, he here gives another justification for his use of indirect communication. His society, he tells us, is in the grip of a "delusion," in which they have come to believe the "illusion" that Christendom actually is genuine Christianity (PV, 48). A delusion, however, cannot be dispelled directly. According to Kierkegaard, it requires that the communicator "does not begin *straightforwardly* with what one wishes to communicate but begins by taking the other's

---

[9] Some of these have been collected and published separately as *The Parables of Kierkegaard*, ed. Thomas Oden (Princeton, New Jersey: Princeton University Press, 1978).
[10] See Plato's *Apology* in *The Last Days of Socrates*, trans. Hugh Tredennick (Harmondsworth, Middlesex: Penguin Books, 1959), p. 52.

delusion at face value" (PV, 54). This irony is in reality a type of deception, but Kierkegaard argues it is not unethical, since in this case one is not deceiving a person out of the truth but "into the truth" (PV, 54). Thus, Kierkegaard is content to "stick calmly to Socrates," employing irony to communicate indirectly what cannot be done directly (PV, 54).

Another key weapon in the armory of the indirect communicator is humor. I shall say more about humor in connection with Kierkegaard's account of the spheres of existence, since it is designated as a crucial "boundary zone" of the religious life, and also as the outward disguise or "incognito" of the true religious person.[11] Indeed, humor may be regarded as a sphere in its own right. Here I shall only note that Kierkegaard sees all humor as rooted in a perception of a "contradiction" or incongruity. Kierkegaard believes that there is just such a contradiction embodied in a certain type of philosopher, who aspires to think, as Spinoza claimed a true philosopher should, "under the aspect of eternity." Kierkegaard thinks that there is a comical contradiction between the aspirations of such a philosopher to see the world as if he were God and his actual, finite existence.

The target of Kierkegaard's polemic is not really Spinoza, of course, but Hegel and his Danish followers. Hegel's attempt to think in this all-encompassing way makes him a difficult opponent. He tries to appropriate the insights of other philosophers, to show how their views can be understood as a partial expression of the truth that is adequately expressed only when all of reality is understood systematically. Kierkegaard thus fears that any objection made to Hegel will simply be accepted as another "moment" in this vast system; he fears becoming a "paragraph in the system."[12] The solution, embodied in the figure of Johannes Climacus as "humorist," is to draw out the inherent comedic potential in the situation of the speculative philosopher. Kierkegaard thinks the problem is not that Hegel's system is the wrong system, and thus needs to be corrected with a better one. The problem is that such a system is impossible, and it is even more impossible for such an intellectual system to produce existential wisdom. A direct attack on "the system" would not be nearly so effective as humorous satire.

The final strategy for indirect communication that I want to discuss is Kierkegaard's use of what he terms (in Danish, obviously) an *Experiment*

---

[11] See my discussion of this in Chapter 6, pp. 130–135.
[12] See CUP, 250–251, where Climacus bemoans the fate of Hamann and Jacobi, who have been reduced in this way.

(plural, *Experimenter*). The Hongs translate this term, for reasons I will discuss, as "imaginary construction," but I do not find the translation helpful. The most natural English term would seem to be the obvious cognate, but the Hongs avoid this term, for two main reasons.[13] First, the English term "experiment" is today mainly used in the context of natural science, and it has thereby acquired connotations of the detached scientist who puts his or her chemicals in the beaker or runs the rats around the lab. Certainly, this kind of experiment is far from what Kierkegaard has in mind.

Secondly, the Hongs note that Kierkegaard also uses a verbal form, *at experimentere*, and if the noun is translated "experiment" then one would think that the verb equivalent would be "to experiment." However, Kierkegaard uses the verb in the following kind of context: *At experimentere en Figur*, which would have to be translated "to experiment a character" if one translated *experimentere* in this way. However, "experiment a character" makes no sense in English without adding a preposition such as "on" or "with," and this is conspicuously missing in the Danish. Hence, the Hongs usually choose "imaginary construction" for *Experiment* and for the verb form, "imaginatively construct."

The points that lie behind this choice are sound, but still I think the translation is not a happy one, since very little is conveyed to the English reader by "imaginary construction." To begin, "imaginative" construction would be better than "imaginary," since the latter term has come to mean "unreal" or "illusory," which is very misleading. However, I think Kierkegaard does mean to talk about a kind of experiment when he uses this cognate term, something rather close to what philosophers have in mind when they talk about "thought experiments." (It is noteworthy, I think, that the Hongs themselves sometimes do translate *Experiment* as "thought experiment.") There are many famous examples of philosophical thought experiments, ranging from Descartes' well-known influential case, in which he imagines himself to be the creation of an "evil genius" who constantly deceives him, to contemporary science-fiction-inspired cases about brains in vats being electrically stimulated by super-scientist extraterrestrials. A philosophical thought experiment is obviously not an experiment in the scientific sense, but an attempt to imaginatively present a character or situation that will clarify and test our conceptual intuitions.

---

[13] For the Hongs' defense of their translation of this family of terms, see the "Historical Introduction" to *Fear and Trembling/Repetition* (FT, xxi–xxxi). I do not here completely retrace their own reasoning, but rather summarize my interpretation of the thinking that lies behind the choice.

Many of Kierkegaard's "thought experiments" are precisely of this kind: imaginatively developed presentations of possible characters and states of affairs that enable us to clarify our understanding of the basic concepts at issue. What makes this technique work as indirect communication is precisely the imaginative dimension, in which the possibilities are brought to life and presented as if they were real, rather than merely being described abstractly.

THE MAIEUTIC IDEAL AND THE LIMITS OF INDIRECT COMMUNICATION

In the previous section, my focus has been on indirect communication as an "artful" strategy, or better, a set of strategies, that Kierkegaard used to attempt to communicate to his readers. However, the English verb "communicate" can be used in two different ways, and so far as I can tell as a non-native speaker of Danish, the Danish *meddele* functions in a similar way. On the one hand, it can be used as a verb to describe someone who *attempts* to pass something on to someone. In this sense of the word, if my wife tells me not to forget to take out the trash, she has communicated something, regardless of whether I have heard her or taken notice of what she has said. However, the word is often used as what we might call a "success" verb. In this context, someone communicates only if the communication is successful, only if the communication has in some way been properly received by the one communicated to. In this sense, if I do not hear what my wife tells me, she has not communicated, though of course the blame for the failure may be entirely mine.

In the Climacus materials which have been a major source for what I have said about indirect communication so far, the claim is sometimes made that with respect to truth about existence, indirect communication is not just valuable, but essential. The person who wants to communicate about existence must employ an indirect method. It is important to note that Kierkegaard himself has second thoughts about this later in his authorship. At least insofar as the communicator is attempting to say something about a Christian view of existence, he recognizes that something more than indirect communication is required. The Christian communicator must at some point give a direct witness or testimony about what he or she believes. Kierkegaard provided this direct witness, partly in his later, non-pseudonymous religious writings, including the newspaper and magazine articles he wrote at the end of his life attacking the state Church,[14] partly in the two essays he wrote about his authorship, one published during his lifetime and the other only posthumously.[15]

In *The Point of View for My Work as an Author* Kierkegaard defends the necessity of his indirect, pseudonymous authorship, as a means of removing the delusion that his contemporaries suffer from, but also recognizes the need for more direct communication. A religious author in Christendom, he claims, "must begin as an aesthetic author and to a certain point he must keep open this possibility. But there must be a limit, since it is being done, after all in order to make aware" (PV, 53).

This is consistent with what Kierkegaard says about communication in the notes for a series of lectures on communication that Kierkegaard planned but never actually presented.[16] In these notes, Kierkegaard distinguishes between the communication of objective knowledge and the communication of what he terms "capability." The former can be communicated directly, but the latter requires indirect communication. Ethical communication is, according to Kierkegaard, primarily indirect, because human beings must be assumed, in a Socratic or Platonic fashion, already to possess the requisite knowledge of what they ought to do. The task of the communicator is to help the other acquire the ability to do what he or she knows should be done, or perhaps better, actualize an ability the person already has. Indirect communication thus serves the maieutic ideal of Socrates, the view that each person has the truth within and it is the task of the communicator to be a "midwife" who helps the other give birth to his or her own truth. This view that every person already knows about right and wrong and needs only to gain "capability" is a very optimistic picture of human nature, one that seems to underestimate the effects, good and bad, of cultural traditions and practices in the transmission of moral knowledge. The assumption is of course doubly dubious from a Christian perspective.

Still, Kierkegaard is deeply committed to this maieutic ideal, at least with respect to what he terms ethical communication, and I believe that when he claims that it is necessary to use indirect communication, he is thinking of this Socratic view of humans, one that deeply respects the

---

[14] Collected in the volume *The Moment and Late Writings*, ed. and trans. Howard V. Hong and Edna H. Hong (Princeton, New Jersey: Princeton University Press, 1998).

[15] *On My Work as an Author* was published in 1851; *The Point of View for My Work as an Author* in 1859. Both are published together in the Hong edition *The Point of View*.

[16] An English translation of these can be found in *Kierkegaard's Journals and Papers*, Vol. I, pp. 267–308.

autonomy of human persons and their responsibility as individuals to grasp the truth, at least the truth about life, for themselves. However, if we are to make good sense of Kierkegaard in this area, when he says that indirect communication is necessary, we must take him to be using "communicate" as a "success verb." For when someone successfully communicates subjectivity or passion to another, it is true that the communicator is only a "prompter." The hearer must appropriate what is communicated for himself or herself, and thus there is a necessary indirectness about the achievement.

However, indirect communication as an "art," a set of strategies or techniques, is neither necessary nor sufficient for successful existential communication. It is true that if the communicator about life conveys insights in the form of "theories" or "propositions" he may well fail to help the one he tries to communicate with. Kierkegaard is right to think that such communication may amount to the transmission of "rote knowledge" or "patter." However, the person who tries to communicate "artfully" may also fail, even if he is skillful. Since the communication will be successful only if it is received and appropriated in the right way by the hearer, no techniques or strategies, whether novelistic or ironical or experimental, are guaranteed to work. In fact, there is some reason to wonder whether Kierkegaard's own ingenious, complex tapestry of aesthetic writings has sometimes misfired, producing in the reader not serious existential reflection but only aesthetic enjoyment and contemplation.

Furthermore, the danger that a more "direct" form of address will produce "patter" and "rote understanding" is only a danger, not a necessity. Just as the artful communicator cannot guarantee success, so the person who employs a more blunt and direct form of communication may sometimes succeed in helping another, if the communication becomes the occasion for the hearer to engage in subjective reflection of the right type. If we are thinking of "indirect communication" as an art, a set of strategies for helping others think deeply about human existence, it is an exaggeration to claim that indirect communication is necessary, though it may certainly be valuable or helpful. However, if we are thinking about "communicate" as a success verb that is applicable to the kind of subject matter that requires appropriation of the communication to be successful, then communication about existence will necessarily be indirect. This is so because this type of understanding requires a "double reflection" that can be done only by the recipient of the communication. But then no particular set of techniques is either necessary or guaranteed to work in making this occur.

In any case Kierkegaard is surely right to say that when one goes beyond ethical communication to religious communication, then indirect communication is no longer sufficient. At least this is true of Christianity, since Christianity is rooted in historical events, such as the life, death, and resurrection of Jesus, that not every person already knows and must merely "recollect."[17] Christianity has content that must be communicated, though "capability" is still important as well, and thus Kierkegaard says that with respect to Christianity, "ethical-religious communication" must be "direct-indirect."[18] The "direct" communication must include the Christian's witness or testimony about Christ.

However, in a sense even the Christian who communicates directly in this way by bearing witness still honors the Socratic maieutic ideal. It is true that Christianity does not accept the Socratic assumption that the truth resides within each individual, but instead holds that human beings have forfeited the truth because of sin. However, Kierkegaard maintains that the Christian view is that the person in sin does not merely need information. Such a person also needs "capability," needs to acquire what Climacus calls, in *Philosophical Fragments*, "the condition" for having the truth (PF, 14). That condition turns out to be faith, and although faith includes beliefs, Kierkegaard describes it as a passion, a form of inwardness. Ultimately, one human cannot give faith to another; it is God's gift, freely offered. The direct testimony one person offers to another can only be the occasion for this to happen; no merely human person can give faith to another. Furthermore, the gift of faith is not forced on anyone; Kierkegaard thinks that an individual will be offended if he does not acquire faith. There is thus a sense in which even the Christian who gives direct witness to his or her faith still honors the maieutic ideal. If one takes the verb "to communicate" as a success verb, a Christian witness can communicate only indirectly, even when she bears direct testimony to her faith.

---

[17] This is a major theme of *Philosophical Fragments*, and will be discussed at length in Chapter 7, pp. 147–166.
[18] *Kierkegaard's Journals and Papers*, Vol. I, p. 308.

CHAPTER 3

The human self: Truth and subjectivity

Hegel famously begins the Preface to his *Phenomenology of Spirit* by declaiming that "everything turns on grasping and expressing the True, not only as Substance but also as Subject."[1] Although Kierkegaard is, as we have already seen, a great critic of Hegel, this memorable phrase could aptly describe Kierkegaard's own view, except that it must not be applied to "the True," an Hegelian euphemism for "the Absolute," which Kierkegaard thinks we humans lack access to, but to the human self. Hegel, as an absolute idealist, thinks that reality as a whole must be understood as a self-conscious unity. The idea is that a philosopher like Spinoza, who saw the whole of reality as one "substance," is partly right, in that reality is an interconnected substantial whole. However, Spinoza's concept of substance fails to capture the dynamic character of reality as "spirit." For Hegel a reality that is spirit is dynamic, unfolding, and self-conscious, and the concept of "substance" fails to capture this distinctive character.

Kierkegaard's view of the human self is similar in several respects. As we shall see, Kierkegaard does not want to deny that the self is a substantial reality. However, the unique character of the self is obscured if we think of it merely as a type of "entity" or "substance." To be a self is to embark on a process in which one becomes something, and there is a sense therefore in which selfhood is something to be achieved.

THE SELF IN *THE SICKNESS UNTO DEATH*: "A RELATION THAT RELATES ITSELF TO ITSELF"

While resolutely rejecting Hegel's speculative attempt to grasp the whole of reality as spirit, Kierkegaard does think of human persons as "spirit,"

---

[1] G. W. F. Hegel, *Phenomenology of Spirit*, trans. A. V. Miller (Oxford: Clarendon Press, 1977), pp. 9–10.

and his conception of spirit clearly owes a lot to Hegel. Just as Hegel wants to take Spinoza's concept of reality as Substance and make it dynamic and relational by rethinking it in terms of spirit, so Kierkegaard wants to take the dominant conception of the self in western philosophy, one which sees the self as a substance or entity, and rethink it by means of the idea of spirit.

In *The Sickness Unto Death*, the pseudonym Anti-Climacus, a Christian character Kierkegaard attributes the book to only because Kierkegaard felt personally unworthy to deliver the Christian message the book contains, says explicitly that the self must be understood as spirit (SUD, 13).[2] Anti-Climacus goes on to explain what this means in uncharacteristically (for Kierkegaard) turgid prose:

> The self is a relation that relates itself to itself or is this: that in the relation the relation relates itself to itself; the self is not the relation but is the fact that the relation relates itself to itself. The human person is a synthesis of the infinite and the finite, of the temporal and the eternal, of freedom and necessity, in short a synthesis. A synthesis is a relation between two. When regarded in this way, the human person is still not a self. (SUD, 13)

From this admittedly formidable passage, some things at least can be clearly discerned. Kierkegaard thinks that the human self is essentially relational, and relational in more than one way. First, the self is said to be a "synthesis," a uniting of contrasting elements, such as temporality-eternity and freedom-necessity. However, this duality or synthesis by itself still does not amount to selfhood. For that, the relation or synthesis must "relate itself to itself."

Here I think Kierkegaard has in mind the duality that inheres in the self as a self-conscious being. There is the self that I am conscious of, what William James famously called the "me-self," and the self that is conscious, what James called the "I-self."[3] Self-consciousness introduces other dualities into the self as well. There is the self that I am conscious of having become, the self that is constituted by a past that cannot be changed, but there is also the self that is constituted by my ideals, my

---

[2] To be precise, Anti-Climacus says that "spirit is the self." I shall assume here that Kierkegaard has no disagreements with Anti-Climacus with respect to the truth of Anti-Climacus' contentions, and that the pseudonym reflects Kierkegaard's sense of his personal unworthiness to represent Christian ideality. Though I shall identify Anti-Climacus as the author of the direct quotations, I shall freely attribute the thinking to Kierkegaard himself.

[3] See William James, *Principles of Psychology* (New York: Dover Publishers, 1890), Chapter 10, pp. 291–401. James actually talks mostly about the "me-self," since it is an object that empirical psychology can study.

sense of who I am that is constituted by who I would like to become. The fundamentally temporal character of the self here comes into view, and we can begin to see how the fundamental dualities of the "synthesis" are present as well. The self is partly finite and limited by the necessities grounded in its past. Yet it is also constituted by its ideals, which have an "eternal" and infinite character as ideals.

However, the self is not only internally relational, but is fundamentally constituted by its relations to others as well. Anti-Climacus acknowledges the abstract possibility of a self that is fundamentally autonomous and independent, and perhaps thinks that God is such a self: "Such a relation that relates itself to itself, a self, must either have established itself or been established by another" (SUD, 13). However, human selves are not autonomous selves: "The human self is such a derived, established relation, a relation that relates itself to itself and in relating itself to itself relates itself to an Other" (SUD, 13–14). We are selves whose identity is always grounded in something outside the self; we carry out the process of relating to ourselves only by relating to an "Other."

Although Kierkegaard wrote these words a half-century before Freud, his view here is consistent with one of the major insights of Freud and such followers of Freud as the Object Relations Theorists.[4] Freud was wrong about a great deal, but he was surely right to think that our sense of who we are, and thus our very identity as persons, is formed initially through our relations with our parents, and always is developed in relation to others, whether we think of those others as models to emulate or stifling standards from which we must depart or even rebel against. The self is partly a set of ideals, and these ideals do not come out of thin air but are absorbed and developed through our relations with others.

Many readers of Kierkegaard have read these words about the self being grounded in "an other" and seen only the distinction that is here drawn between Kierkegaard's Christian view of the self which sees human beings as created by God and later existentialists such as Sartre, who see human beings as autonomous beings who in one sense create themselves. In other words, it is common to see the reference to "the other" that the self relates to in order to relate to itself as a reference to God.

---

[4] For a detailed comparison between Kierkegaard, Freud, and Object-Relations Theory, see my article, "Kierkegaard's View of the Unconscious," in *Kierkegaard: Poet of Existence*, ed. Birgit Bertung (Copenhagen: C. A. Reitzel, 1989), pp. 31–48; reprinted in *Kierkegaard in Post/Modernity* (Indiana University Press, 1995), and in *Søren Kierkegaard: Critical Assessments of Leading Philosophers*, Volume II: *Epistemology and Psychology*, ed. Daniel Conway (London: Routledge, 2002).

In one sense, this reading must be correct. Kierkegaard does see
human persons as created by God and dependent on God. However, it is
important to pay attention to the abstract language Anti-Climacus uses
here. Anti-Climacus is, as I have noted, a strongly Christian pseudonym,
and he does not hesitate to use explicit theological language when he
wishes to. In the second half of *Sickness Unto Death*, Anti-Climacus
explicitly says that in the first part of the book he has developed a view
of the human self that does not take full account of the theological
dimension of the self.[5] I believe he chooses the language he does in the
first part of the book in order to express the idea that, although humans
are metaphysically dependent on God, psychologically they are often
shaped by other "powers."

Though God created human beings, and thus humans are completely
dependent on him, God has given humans the gift of freedom. "It is
almost as if God, who made the human being a relation, allows it to slip
out of his hand – that is, inasmuch as the relation relates itself to itself"
(SUD, 16). Kierkegaard certainly thinks that ideally a human self should
be centered and grounded in God; we were created for such a relationship
and cannot be fully healthy without it. However, the freedom God has
bestowed on humans as self-conscious beings means that they can and
often do ground their selves in something other than God. The fundamentally relational character of the self remains, however. We are never
free to create ourselves from nothing.

This becomes clearer in a passage from the second half of *Sickness Unto
Death*, in which the self is described by reference to its "criterion," the
ideal "other" which gives a person a way of measuring himself or herself:

A cattleman who (if this were possible) is a self directly before his cattle is a very
low self, and similarly, a slaveowner who is a self directly before his slaves is
actually no self – for in both cases a criterion is lacking. The child who previously
has had only his parents' criterion becomes a self as an adult by getting the state
as a criterion, but what an infinite accent falls on the self by getting God as a
criterion! (SUD, 7)

The cattleman whose identity is found by comparing himself with
his cattle does not thereby become a self, for his standards are too low.

---

[5] The relevant passage is as follows: "In the previous section there was continuous attention paid to
the gradation in the consciousness of the self . . . This gradation in the consciousness of the self that
we have hitherto considered is within the category of the human self, or the self whose criterion is
the human person But this self acquires a new quality and qualification by being a self directly
before God" (SUD, 79).

I cannot become a true self merely by gloating in my superiority over cows. The slave owner whose identity is grounded in his sense of superiority to the slave also lacks genuine selfhood and for a similar reason. In one sense the slaves are persons, of course, but the slave owner does not think of them as persons but as property, and thus the recognition they accord him as slave owner does not genuinely provide the status the owner craves.

A child, however, begins to become a real person by internalizing his parents' "criterion," and truly becomes an adult when the child moves into the wider world and can critically modify or even reject the parents' ideals by comparing them with the ideals that are embodied in the social order and expressed most clearly by the state. (Here we can see an echo of Hegel again.) To be sure, the self's ideals must be internalized, but Anti-Climacus thinks that we necessarily develop our "criterion," or "measuring-stick" for ourselves in and through our relation to others. Kierkegaard's "individualism" is thus very far from a view that denies the influence of other persons or society on the formation of the self. Rather, from his viewpoint, the self cannot be itself except through a relation to something outside the self. The relation to God is important because it provides a way of relativizing the influences of society and thus partly transcending them. A human self can never be completely autonomous, but a self that sees itself as "standing before God," whose identity is given to it by a relation to God, has the capacity to break with prevailing social values and "stand on its own," with God's help.[6]

"BECOMING WHAT YOU ARE": THE SELF AS SUBSTANCE AND ACHIEVEMENT

We can thus see that Kierkegaard's view of the self is complex. In one sense the self is a substantial reality, an entity created by God. In that sense, a self is something I am, something I cannot help being. However, the self that I am is a unique kind of entity, one that is composed partly of possibilities, and thus in another sense the self is something I must become. Selfhood is an achievement.

These two views of selfhood can both be found in the western intellectual tradition. A view that sees persons as substances, entities within the natural order of things, goes back at least as far as Aristotle, who famously

---

[6] See the profound discussion of how love helps the other to "stand on his own" in WL, 264–279.

defined the human self as a rational animal. This kind of view continued to prevail during the middle ages, and can still be clearly seen in Descartes' conception of the human self as a "thinking thing." Descartes even conceives of an immaterial soul in terms of "substance."

However, many contemporary discussions of selfhood and personhood describe these categories as a special status that accrues to something by virtue of some achievement. For example, Michael Tooley has famously argued that infanticide is morally permissible, because a newborn child is not yet a person with interests that can be violated because it lacks such capacities as reflective self-understanding.[7] On such a view, personhood does not refer to a type of substance but designates something as possessing a certain normative status.

Kierkegaard has, I believe, a foot in both of these camps.[8] His theistic worldview allows him to think of human persons as creatures, part of the natural order made by God. However, God has made humans with a special character; and holds them responsible for becoming what he intended them to be. Thus, to be a self is to be assigned a task.

Johannes Climacus, the pseudonymous author of *Concluding Unscientific Postscript*, expresses this thought in a whimsical and ironical manner: "Now, I understand that every human being is something of a subject. But now to become what one already is – who would waste his time on that?" (CUP, 130). The human task is to become a self in truth, a task that *seems* insignificant, because it amounts to becoming what one already is. A genuine understanding of the nature of the self reveals that this task is no triviality, however, because "what one already is" includes potentialities that must be actualized to fully become oneself.

The human self is "an existing self," in that pregnant sense of existence described in the previous chapter. Using language quite similar to that employed later by Anti-Climacus in *The Sickness Unto Death*, Climacus describes human existence almost poetically: "But what is existence? It is that child who is begotten by the infinite and the finite, the eternal and the temporal, and therefore is continually striving" (CUP, 92). This makes existence an art, and a difficult one indeed. Climacus compares the

---

[7] Michael Tooley, *Abortion and Infanticide* (Oxford: Oxford University Press, 1983).

[8] For a fuller account of this, see my article, "Who is the Other in *The Sickness Unto Death*? God and Human Relations in the Constitution of the Self," in *The Kierkegaard Studies Yearbook 1997* (Berlin and New York: Walter de Gruyter, 1997), pp. 1–15. Reprinted in my *Kierkegaard on Faith and the Self* (Waco, Texas: Baylor University Press, 2006), pp. 263–276, and as "Self and Others in Kierkegaard" in *On Being a Person: A Multidisciplinary Approach to Personality Theories*, ed. Todd H. Speidell (Eugene, Oregon: Wipf & Stock Publishers, 2003).

process of existing as a self to driving a carriage or wagon pulled by two very unequal horses, one "like Pegasus" and the other "an old nag":

And that is what existing is like if one is to be conscious of it. Eternity is like that winged steed, infinitely quick, temporality is an old nag, and the existing person is the wagon-driver, that is, unless existing is taken to be what people usually call existing, because then the existing person is not a wagon-driver but a drunken peasant who lies in the wagon and sleeps and lets the horses take care of themselves. Of course, he also drives, he is also a carriage-driver, and likewise there perhaps are many who – also exist. (CUP, 311–312)

There is a sense in which we humans cannot help but exist. To use language popularized much later by Sartre and Heidegger, we are "condemned to be free," "thrown into existence." However, most of us simply drift through life; we let the horses run where they wish. Kierkegaard wants to challenge his readers to become selves in truth.

IS KIERKEGAARD A PROPONENT OF "RADICAL CHOICE"?

But what does it mean to become a self in truth? Is there some kind of ideal for selfhood that is normative? What would this even mean? If there is such an ideal, how could someone committed to a particular view of the self defend such an ideal against rival accounts? These are difficult questions indeed, and raising them places us right in the middle of what we might call Kierkegaard's implicit epistemology.

In the next three chapters, I shall try to describe Kierkegaard's idea of the three stages or spheres of existence – life viewed aesthetically, ethically, and religiously – introduced in the previous chapter. I believe there is no doubt that Kierkegaard thinks of these spheres of existence as ranked; the ethical is superior to the aesthetic overall, just as the religious is superior to the ethical. But what makes one stage superior to another?

One answer, which we might call the "existentialist" answer, is that no stage is objectively superior to another, but that what makes one "better" is simply the choice or affirmation of the self. According to this view, Kierkegaard's ranking of the stages is simply his personal choice, and it leaves open the possibility that for others different choices would imply a different ranking or perhaps no ranking at all. On this view a person's most basic choices are what we might call "radical choices." No reasons for such choices can be given, because the choice is essentially a choice about what is going to count as a good reason for a person.

This reading of Kierkegaard has been influential, and it is rather close to the view Jean-Paul Sartre seems to endorse in his famous essay, "Existentialism," in which he affirms that the value of what is chosen as good is a function of the choice itself.[9] Since Kierkegaard is often called "the father of existentialism," it is not surprising that such a Sartrean view is sometimes read back into Kierkegaard, though I shall argue that it is not to be found there.

One influential source of this Sartrean reading of Kierkegaard is Alasdair MacIntyre's provocative book, *After Virtue*. According to MacIntyre, the Enlightenment set itself the project of giving a rational foundation for ethics to replace tradition or religion. Kierkegaard, says MacIntyre, was the first to see that this project could not succeed, and MacIntyre claims that Kierkegaard's *Either/Or* embodies this insight. What Kierkegaard essentially tried to do, on MacIntyre's reading, is to substitute a radical act of the will for reason as the foundation of ethics:

> Kierkegaard and Kant agree in their conception of morality, but Kierkegaard inherits that conception together with an understanding that the project of giving a rational vindication of morality has failed. Kant's failure provided Kierkegaard with his starting-point: the act of choice had to be called in to do the work that reason could not do.[10]

Either/Or confronts the reader with a choice between the aesthetic life, represented in Part I by the papers of "A," and the ethical life, represented in the papers of "B." But the reader is not told who is right and must choose for himself or herself, with no external "result" to confirm the rightness of the choice. MacIntyre says that Kierkegaard thinks this choice must be a radical, "criterionless" choice:

> Suppose that someone confronts the choice between them [the ethical and the aesthetic lives] having as yet embraced neither. He can be offered no *reason* for preferring one to the other. For if a given reason offers support for the ethical way of life – to live in that way will serve the demands of duty or to live in that way will be to accept moral perfection as a goal and so give a certain kind of

---

9 Sartre clearly thinks this follows from the "death of God": "My answer to this is that I'm quite vexed that that's the way it is; but if I've discarded God the Father, there has to be someone to invent values." Jean-Paul Sartre, *Existentialism and Human Emotions* (New York: Philosophical Library, 1957), p. 49.

10 Alasdair MacIntyre, *After Virtue*, 2nd edn. (Notre Dame, Indiana: University of Notre Dame Press, 1984), p. 47.

meaning to one's action – the person who has not yet embraced either the ethical or the aesthetic still has to choose whether or not to treat this reason as having any force. If it already has force for him, he has already chosen the ethical; which *ex hypothesi* he has not. And so it is also with reasons supportive of the aesthetic.[11]

This argument is far from decisive. Consider the following parallel argument. Suppose that in a political theory class I present my students with arguments for and against a libertarian view of the state, without tipping my hand as to which view I personally favor. Let us assume that prior to the class the students are not familiar with libertarian views of the state and have no settled commitments either way. Would we say in such a case that the students "can be offered no reason for preferring one position to the other"? Would we say that a student who is considering an argument for libertarianism "still has to choose whether or not to treat this reason as having any force," and if he or she does see it as having force, the student has already chosen libertarianism, contrary to the hypothesis that the student is as yet uncommitted? Clearly, it is possible for a student in this situation to find a reason compelling. There must be something wrong with an argument that the student must perform an act of radical choice in order to decide the issue, and the same flaw infects MacIntyre's argument concerning Kierkegaard.

It is not difficult to detect the flaw. The problem arises from the assumption that an individual must choose to regard a reason as having force in order for the reason to have any force for the individual. This is simply not the way reasons work. In the normal case, if someone gives me a reason for supporting or opposing a policy, the reason will or will not strike me as having force of some degree or other, and whether this is so is not under my voluntary control.

In the next two chapters I shall give a detailed account of Kierkegaard's view of the aesthetic and ethical spheres, and I will there try to show that this is exactly how Kierkegaard sees things. The argument between the aesthetic and the ethical is an argument where both sides give reasons that they believe could be appealing to the other. Both the aesthete and the ethicist are pictured as concrete individuals with desires and needs. The aesthete assumes that human beings want to satisfy their desires and avoid boredom, and tries to show that the ethical life constricts and undermines the individual's quest for a satisfying existence. The ethicist tries to show that the ethical life is superior to the aesthetic life, even when judged by

---

[11] Alasdair MacIntyre, *After Virtue*, p. 40.

aesthetic criteria, because a human life without ethical commitments turns out to be meaningless and unsatisfying. No appeal to radical, criterionless choice is made by either party.

However, does the fact that Kierkegaard gives us no "result" show that MacIntyre must be right? Does the fact that both the aesthete and the ethicist have arguments they think should be appealing to the other show that neither view is objectively superior to the other? It might appear that this is so, since Kierkegaard gives us no scorecard on which to rank the views. So far as we know, neither party to the argument is convinced. The ethicist does not succumb to temptation and have an affair; the aesthete does not repent of his scandalous ways and choose the path of marriage and respectability.

Modern western philosophy has been dominated by a certain epistemological picture that is today termed "classical foundationalism." Classical foundationalism, as I shall define it, makes two claims. First, genuine knowledge must be based on a foundation of truths that are known with a high degree of certainty. Descartes himself sets the tone in his *Meditations*: "[R]eason already persuades me that I ought no less carefully to withhold my assent from matters which are not entirely certain and indubitable than from those which appear to me manifestly to be false, ..."[12] The standard for certainty is set very high, so that even the possibility of error becomes a ground for doubt.

The second claim made by the classical foundationalist is that the only way to obtain such certainty is to become entirely objective, setting aside all emotions and other "subjective" attitudes, which are seen as sources of bias and distortion. Descartes again serves as an excellent example, as can be seen by the reasons he cites to show that he is in a favorable position to gain the certainty he seeks: "Today, then, since very opportunely for the plan I have in view I have delivered my mind from every care [and am happily agitated by no passions] and since I have procured for myself an assured leisure in a peaceable retirement, I shall at last seriously and freely address myself to the general upheaval of all my former opinions."[13]

---

[12] René Descartes, *Meditations*, in *The Philosophical Works of Descartes*, trans. Elizabeth S. Haldane and G. R. T. Ross (Cambridge: Cambridge University Press, 1911), p. 145.

[13] Descartes, *Meditations*, p. 144.

From the standpoint of classical foundationalism, the argument between Kierkegaard's aesthete and ethicist looks undecidable. For neither side in the argument seems capable of developing a proof or demonstration that will necessarily move the other to agreement. The classical foundationalist is thus tempted to see the issue as one that reason cannot decide, and perhaps something like radical choice is the only way to resolve things.

However, Kierkegaard's own perspective is profoundly different. For although Kierkegaard rarely discusses epistemological issues in a formal way, his whole outlook is a challenge to this classical foundationalist picture. Both the elements I have identified in the picture are rejected. On the one hand, the kind of absolute certainty sought by modern, western philosophy is unattainable for finite human existers. Human persons are historically situated beings, and they are incapable of thinking *sub specie æternitatis*, as Spinoza thought we should aspire to do.

On Kierkegaard's view, to have knowledge that is absolutely certain would be to have knowledge that is complete and final; it would be to have "the System," which indeed Hegel claimed to possess. Johannes Climacus surely speaks for Kierkegaard in renouncing any claims to possess a system of existence. Climacus says that a "logical system is possible" but that "a system of existence is impossible" for an existing human person (CUP, 109).[14] He does not thereby deny that there is such a thing as the final, objective truth about reality, since "existence itself is a system – for God" (CUP, 118). The problem is that we humans are not God, and thus we are not capable of seeing the world from God's point of view.

From this Kierkegaardian perspective, uncertainty is simply part of the human condition, and the aspirations of the classical foundationalist are aspirations to transcend that condition. It follows from this that the fact that neither the ethicist nor the aesthete can produce a logical proof or demonstration that makes his or her viewpoint objectively certain is not a reason to despair. We human beings find uncertainty painful, and we would like to escape it. The history of western philosophy is, as John Dewey has said, the history of "the quest for certainty."[15] However, in reality, most of us, most of the time, find ways of resolving this

---

[14] The Hongs translate this literally, but awkwardly in English, as "a logical system can be given, but a system of existence cannot be given." I have here removed Kierkegaard's original italics.

[15] See John Dewey's Gifford Lectures, *The Quest for Certainty* (London: George Allen and Unwin, 1930).

uncertainty. Despite our finitude, we develop convictions and act on the basis of commitments.

How do we do this? Here is Kierkegaard's second break with the tradition of classical foundationalist epistemology. The classical foundationalist typically sees human emotions as distorting filters and biases; the epistemological task is to somehow put these aside and become purely "rational" and objective. However, as I argued in the previous chapter, Kierkegaard sees what he variously calls "subjectivity" and "inwardness" as lying at the heart of human existence. Without desires, hopes, fears, and loves human life would be impossible because human choice and action would be impossible.

Despite our finitude, Kierkegaard does not embrace skepticism, at least with respect to what he calls "essential human knowledge," the knowledge a human person must have to be fully human and live a truly human life. It is true that we cannot stand at some impossible place of pure neutrality and objectivity and grasp the truth as a matter of pure logic. Anyone who tries to occupy what Thomas Nagel has called "the view from nowhere" will fail to grasp what human life is all about.[16] Rather, the path to truth requires us to embrace our subjectivity. The evil of cruelty cannot be recognized apart from our emotional repugnance to cruelty, just as the goodness of love cannot be perceived apart from our emotional embrace of its splendor.

However, as I have already claimed, there are emotions and there are emotions. Our task is not to divest ourselves of subjectivity, but to allow our subjectivity to be formed and developed in the right way. To explain this requires an exploration of the famous Kierkegaardian claim that "truth is subjectivity," and this will be the theme of the remainder of this chapter. This will prepare us for a deeper look in subsequent chapters at what we might call Kierkegaard's developmental psychology, his account of the "stages on life's way."

"TRUTH IS SUBJECTIVITY"

The claim by Johannes Climacus in *Concluding Unscientific Postscript* that "truth is subjectivity" is one of the most well-known and yet misunderstood Kierkegaardian claims. Climacus himself says that this claim is a "Socratic" one, and thus it is perhaps right that it should be voiced by a pseudonym rather than Kierkegaard himself. At the very least,

---

[16] See Thomas Nagel, *The View from Nowhere* (New York: Oxford University Press, 1986).

Kierkegaard the Christian writer will want to balance this Socratic claim dialectically with the apparently contradictory claim that "subjectivity is untruth," reflecting Kierkegaard's commitment to the Christian doctrine of human sinfulness.[17] However, the contradiction between the two claims is, as I shall show, only apparent, and there is little doubt that Kierkegaard himself is firmly committed to this "Socratic" thesis.

But what does it mean to say that truth is subjectivity? We can begin by saying what it does not mean. It is not an endorsement of epistemological subjectivism or some form of relativism. It does not mean, as one text-book writer has asserted, that for Kierkegaard "the belief of a Hindu that Vishnu is God, the belief of a Mohammedan that Allah is God, the belief of a Nuer that *kwoth* is God – even the belief of an atheist that there is no God – are all true; providing only that in each of these beliefs an objective uncertainty is embraced with passionate intensity."[18]

The relevant section of *Concluding Unscientific Postscript* is difficult to interpret because Climacus brings together two kinds of issues that are not usually seen as connected: epistemology and soteriology, or what theologians call a theory of salvation. He begins with epistemology by examining two classical philosophical definitions of truth. The first he calls the empiricist theory, a view contemporary philosophers would call a correspondence view of truth, which defines truth as "the agreement of thinking with being" (CUP, 189). The second view, which Climacus calls the "idealistic view," appears close to what contemporary philosophers would term a coherence theory. This view defines truth as "the agreement of being with thinking" (CUP, 189). The first sees reality as independent and objective, and regards a true proposition as one that corresponds to the way things really are. The second, inspired by idealistic metaphysics and a rationalist confidence in the power of human reason, says that ultimately reality must be what it is rational to believe, and thus reality must conform to reason.

After introducing these two accounts of truth, Climacus proceeds to give a critique of both, and so far he seems to be working on a classical philosophical problem. The problem with both views, he says, comes into focus when we clarify what we mean by "being." If we mean actual, concrete, empirical being then truth as an ideal "correspondence" must be

---

[17] Actually, Johannes Climacus himself is careful to make the point that the Christian view, while "starting" from the Socratic claim that truth is subjectivity, centers on the claim that subjectivity is untruth. See CUP, 207.

[18] W. T. Jones, *Kant to Wittgenstein and Sartre*, 2nd edn. (New York: Harcourt, Brace, 1969), p. 228.

seen as a *desideratum*, an ideal to be approximated but never finally realized, since being as concrete, empirical actuality is always in flux (CUP, 189). Not only is the world that is to be known in process, the existing being who wants to know that world is "an existing knowing spirit" that is "itself in the process of becoming" (CUP, 189). A proposition is an ideal, timeless entity and any "agreement" or "correspondence" between a proposition and actuality must be an agreement between that proposition and a reality that has been abstractly conceptualized.

So far Climacus seems to be echoing his earlier claim that there can be no "system of existence" for human knowers. Reality may be a system for God, and God's view of things may provide the ultimate truth that we aim to approximate in our own cognitive endeavors, but we must never confuse our approximations, useful and valuable as they may be, with the thing itself. Truth in this sense may be real, but it is an abstraction, not a temporal reality.

At this point Climacus makes clear his real agenda. His concern is really not with the adequacy of a philosophical theory of truth, but with the question of what it means for a human being to possess the truth. To grasp the significance of this, we must not think of truth in the way characteristic of contemporary philosophy, focusing on the properties of propositions, but in the way ancient thinkers conceived of truth. For Socrates and Plato, at least as Kierkegaard understood them, having the truth meant having the key to human life, possessing that which makes it possible to live life as it was intended to be lived. We might think, even more pertinently for Kierkegaard, of Jesus' promise to his followers that "You shall know the truth, and the truth shall make you free."[19] One might say that the possession of truth is the philosophical expression of what is termed in theology "salvation" for Christians, "enlightenment" for Buddhists.

Kierkegaard has already had Johannes Climacus begin an earlier book, *Philosophical Fragments*, with a "Socratic" puzzle about truth: "Can the truth be learned?" (PF, 9). In this work, Climacus contrasts the Socratic/Platonic view that truth is something humans already possess, and thus must merely be "recollected," with the Christian view that humans have lost the truth. According to that Christian view, God himself must reveal the truth to humans, and must transform them, recreate them so that they have the capacity to gain the truth.

[19] John 8:32.

So we should not be too surprised when Johannes Climacus suddenly switches from a discussion of philosophical theories of truth to the issue that really concerns him: How does a human being acquire the truth that makes life worthwhile? How can a human person live "true-ly"? He poses a stark alternative between "objective" and "subjective" answers to this question:

> *When the question about truth is asked objectively, truth is reflected upon objectively as an object to which the knower relates himself. There is no reflection on the relation but that what he relates himself to is the truth, the true. When that which he relates himself to is the truth, the true, then the subject is in the truth. When the question about truth is asked subjectively, the individual's relation is reflected upon subjectively. If only the how of this relation is in truth, then the individual is in truth, even if he were thereby to relate himself to untruth.* (CUP, 199; emphasis original)

Climacus attaches a footnote to this passage in which he makes an important qualification by noting that he is no longer trying to give a general philosophical definition of truth but only intends to discuss "the truth that is essentially related to existence."

In this passage Climacus does not deny the existence of objective, propositional truth, but rather presupposes there is such a thing. What he wants to know is whether a person who knows what is objectively true is thereby personally "in the truth," and whether a person whose beliefs are objectively false can nevertheless have a life that can be described as true. The answer is given through a famous thought experiment in which he compares a "Christian" of sorts with a passionate pagan:

> If someone who lives in the midst of Christianity goes into God's house, the house of the true God, with the knowledge of a true conception of God, and now prays, but prays in untruth; and if someone lives in an idolatrous land but prays with all the passion of infinity, even though his eyes rest upon the image of an idol: where then is there more truth? The one prays in truth to God though he worships an idol; the other prays in untruth to the true God and therefore in truth worships an idol. (CUP, 201)

Climacus finds no need to argue this point; he thinks his answer is "obvious for anyone who is not totally botched with the help of science" (CUP, 201).[20]

---

[20] It should be noted that the Danish term for science here, *Videnskab*, did not in Kierkegaard's day carry the implication of referring to the natural sciences, but was used by philosophers such as Hegel, as well as by theologians, who wished to claim scholarly status.

Perhaps things are not so obvious as this, but the view Climacus defends here is certainly reasonable. For if we are trying to determine what makes a human person's life "true," it seems very plausible that objectively true intellectual beliefs are neither sufficient nor necessary. Such beliefs are not sufficient, because in order for a person to live truly, it is not enough to affirm the right propositions. The person must allow his or her beliefs to transform his or her life. Climacus uses religious examples to make his point, but we could use a non-religious example also. Suppose, for example, that it is true that global warming is occurring as a result of human activity. Perhaps I believe this is so and even believe that humans ought to cut their use of fossil fuels and do other things to reduce greenhouse gases. Surely, however, it is not enough for me to have the right belief about this; what is crucial is that this belief in some way shapes my actions and leads me to change my behavior in appropriate ways.

It is just as clear that true objective beliefs are not necessary, either. Assume for the moment that the truth about human life is that the best kind of life is one devoted to compassion and loving service to others. Imagine an individual who has come to believe, perhaps by reading Nietzsche or Ayn Rand, that compassion is in fact a vice, and that truly ethical people care only about themselves. Despite this objectively wrong belief, it might be possible for this individual to respond with genuine compassion and love when confronted by actual human suffering. Whatever the ultimate ethical and religious truth may be, human persons may be better – or worse – than their theories. The Kierkegaardian view is that it is subjectivity, the inward emotions and passions that give shape to human lives and motivate human actions, that makes the difference.

LIVING THE TRUTH AND KNOWING THE TRUTH

A number of important objections to the "truth is subjectivity" thesis are likely to have occurred to readers by now, and I shall try to raise two of them and give a Kierkegaardian response. The first objection that may occur to a philosophical reader is simply that talk of a human life being true or false is inappropriate or misguided if it is taken literally. Many philosophers are inclined to say that only propositions can be true or false, and so talk of a human life as true is at best a metaphor.

This simply appears to be an act of philosophical imperialism, and it is hard to see how this restrictive view of terms such as "true" and "truth" can be justified. It is just not the case that in ordinary human language, the adjective "true" is applied only to propositions or statements. Humans talk quite commonly about "true friends," about "swords that swing true" and about "true love." What all these uses have in common is some sense of an ideal that a particular can measure up to: a friend who measures up to the ideal of friendship is a true friend. If there is an ideal for human life, a model that humans should aspire to realize, I see no reason why a human life that approximates that ideal should not be described as true, just as a proposition that approximates the way things are is appropriately described as true.

Of course the "if" clause here is controversial; perhaps many will think that no such human ideal exists. However, Kierkegaard's own religious worldview certainly leads him to think of human life this way, for Kierkegaard believes that the ideal self we should strive to become is defined by God's intentions as creator. It is even possible, I think, that the whole discussion of "truth as subjectivity" is an attempt to make sense of the claim attributed to Jesus in the Gospel of John: "I am the way, and the truth, and the life."[21] This passage at least fits well with Kierkegaard's views, for in it Christ does not claim merely to teach the truth but to be the truth, and being the truth is identified with a particular human life and "a way."

To be sure, Kierkegaard does not view the ideal self as a "one size fits all" pattern. His conception of the ideal human life is in some ways quite individualistic. Although there are universal elements to the ideal, and a universal structure to human existence, God has created all humans as unique individuals, and his intentions are for them to affirm and even celebrate that uniqueness. Despite this individuality, however, there is still something like an objective standard for every person, defined by God's intentions. If Kierkegaard is right to think that there is something like an ideal of selfhood that each of us should strive for, then it makes sense to describe our lives as representations of that ideal that can be true or false.

This brings me to the second problem I want to discuss. Even if it makes sense to talk of human lives as true or false, why think of objective, propositional truth and subjectivity as if they were mutually exclusive options? Perhaps it is right that a person can believe true things and yet live falsely, and thus it is not enough to have the right beliefs. And perhaps a person who has the wrong beliefs can still live truthfully in some ways. But is it not better to have true beliefs *and* to appropriate

21 John 14:6.

those beliefs in the right way? Can't true beliefs sometimes shape a life in the right way? And don't false beliefs sometimes hamper a person from living in a truthful manner? Would it not be better for Kierkegaard's pagan to have the "inner passion of infinity" *and* to have true beliefs about God? (Suppose, for example, he has been brought up to believe that God demands human sacrifices.) In my own earlier example, it is possible for the Nietzschean who thinks compassion is a vice to live compassionately, but it might be harder for him to do this, perhaps even impossible if he were fully committed to his Nietzschean beliefs. So it seems better for him to have both true beliefs about the value of compassion and the appropriate emotional response to those beliefs.

I think that Kierkegaard recognizes the force in this line of thinking and would concede the point. In an important journal entry, Kierkegaard himself rejects the view that Climacus does not value objectivity:

In all the usual talk that Johannes Climacus is mere subjectivity, etc., it has been completely overlooked that in addition to all his other concretions he points out in one of the last sections that the remarkable thing is that there is a "How" with the characteristic that when the "How" is scrupulously rendered the "What" is also given, that this is the "How" of faith. Right here, at its very maximum, inwardness is shown to be objectivity.[22]

Notice that in the example of the nominal Christian and the pagan, the claim that is made is only that the pagan has more truth in his life than the hypocritical Christian, not that the pagan's situation is ideal. Kierkegaard does not want to defend a sloppy relativism that holds that "it does not matter what you believe as long as you are sincere." The point is not that everything is fine so long as one is passionate about one's beliefs, so that a sincere and dedicated Nazi, or a religiously-inspired terrorist, would become an exemplar of human life. Of course the truth of our beliefs does matter, and Climacus recognizes this: "Exactly equally important as the truth, and if one of the two must be preferred still more important, is the manner in which the truth is received: it would help only a little if someone got millions to receive the truth, if these receivers precisely by their manner of reception were transformed into untruth" (CUP, 247).

The words here are carefully chosen. Subjectivity is "exactly equally important" as objective, propositional truth, and is to be preferred only if one is forced to choose between them. But when, one might ask, would

---

[22] *Kierkegaard's Journals and Papers*, Vol. IV, entry 4550.

such a choice be forced on us? The answer, I think, is that the choice is forced on us when we are told that objective truth requires the complete suppression of subjectivity, the adoption of the "view from nowhere" in which I put aside emotions and passions and resolve to believe only what can be demonstrated on the basis of objective reason.

We can now understand why this discussion of living "truly" began with a discussion of philosophical theories of truth. From a Kierke-gaardian standpoint, the person who chooses pure objectivity loses the truth both in life and in belief; the person who chooses subjectivity has a chance at truth in both areas. The quest for certainty ends up in skep-ticism with respect to beliefs and nihilism with respect to values, for humans are finite, historically situated beings who can see nothing if they adopt "the view from nowhere." Kierkegaard consistently sees the uni-versal doubt that supposedly stands at the foundation of modern phil-osophy to be impossible, and that is a good thing, since if it could be achieved it could never be overcome.[23] To see we must stand somewhere and trust that our perspective, including our emotional "take" on the world, finite and limited as it is, is one that enables us to see something.

Kierkegaard's polemic is directed against a philosophical tradition that would claim we must first settle our intellectual questions and then turn our attention to how to put our beliefs into practice. Kierkegaard believes that in one sense our questions are never "settled," since we do not have the system. Doubts can always be raised, and questions can always be asked. If we demand intellectual certainty before we begin to live our convictions we will never live at all.

The ineradicable role that uncertainty plays in human beliefs is defended at some length in an "Interlude" sandwiched in between Chapters 4 and 5 in *Philosophical Fragments* (PF, 72–88). The main purpose of this "Interlude" is to defend the claim that certain knowledge about historical religious claims, such as the Christian claim that Jesus of Nazareth is God incarnate, is impossible, and I will discuss these issues in Chapter 7. However, Johannes Climacus buttresses this claim with some general epistemological points. The general picture presented is remarkably similar to David Hume's claims about "matters of fact," which Hume says can never be known with the certainty that is possible

---

[23] See the discussion of doubt and its alleged overcoming by the Hegelian method in CUP 335–338, as well as the satirical account of those who have supposedly doubted everything and then "gone further" in FT 5–7.

for what he calls "relations of ideas."[24] Similarly, Climacus says that all beliefs of a factual character about things that have "come into existence" involve an uncertainty that corresponds to the contingency that is inherent in such facts (PF, 72–88). No judgment about what has "come into existence" can be logically certain, just as Hume claims that no "matter of fact" can be logically demonstrated. This logical gap between the claims we make and the evidence is in fact what makes skepticism possible. Ultimately, Climacus argues that skepticism is a willed life-stance. We do not overcome skepticism by reason but by willing not to be skeptics (PF, 82). Reason alone does not take us very far; we live on the basis of belief or faith (Danish has just one word, *Tro*, for both English terms.)

The upshot of all this is that we cannot sharply separate the process by which we come to have true beliefs from the process by which we try to become better persons. If we demand intellectual certainty about our beliefs before we begin to live out those beliefs, we will not make much progress on the intellectual questions themselves. With respect to what he calls "essential truth," the truth about living, progress in answering our intellectual questions goes hand in hand with progress in becoming better people. This is hardly a new idea. The idea that knowing the truth requires the knower to strive to become a better person was common in the ancient world. Even Aristotle says that it is pointless for someone who has been brought up poorly, and thus has a bad character, to study ethics.[25] Kierkegaard accepts the ancient principle that "only like knows like," and this implies that one must be good to know the good.

Thus, the answer to the charge that our beliefs matter is to agree that they do, but to argue that we cannot hope to settle questions of belief in a way that is prior to and independent of our struggle to become selves of a certain sort. Subjectivity is not only essential if we are to put our beliefs into practice, but plays an essential role in the acquiring of those beliefs.

This helps us see why Kierkegaard, though he rejects the possibility that ethical and religious truths can be demonstrated through some objective, logical method, does not see this as a failure that requires some "radical choice," or arbitrary act of will. The reasons an ethicist offer to an aesthete for becoming ethical may or may not move the aesthete. If the

---

[24] See David Hume, *An Enquiry Concerning Human Understanding*, ed. L. A. Selby-Bigge (Oxford: Clarendon Press, 1902; reprint of the posthumous edition of 1777), pp. 25–26.

[25] For Aristotle's remarks on the importance of good character and good upbringing to study what we would call ethics, see his *Nicomachean Ethics*, trans. W. D. Ross (Oxford: Clarendon Press, 1908), Book I, Chapters 3 and 4.

reasons do move the aesthete, that will be because they have made contact with the desires and hopes and fears of an actual individual. Arguments do not have to be convincing to "all sane, rational people" to be good arguments, and arguments that do move people do so by making contact with actual individuals, replete with subjectivity.

Kierkegaard does not assume, as some "postmodern" thinkers are prone to do, that the failure of classical foundationalism leads to the collapse of the ideal of truth. This kind of postmodernist is in reality much more indebted to the modern philosophical tradition than he realizes. Both the modern and postmodern philosophers are committed to the following premise: "If there is an objective truth, then there must be a method which guarantees us access to that truth." Modern philosophers, from Descartes through Husserl, accepted the premise and concluded that there must be such a method, even if they disagreed about what the method is. The skeptical postmodernist doubts we have such a method and concludes that we must give up on objective truth.

Kierkegaard, however, rejects the hypothetical premise both kinds of thinkers share. For reality is a system for God, and there is thus a way things truly are, regardless of whether I can attain the right view of things. The fact that we have no "method" that gives the foundational certainties sought by the modern philosopher is no reason to give up on objective truth. He thus thinks it is possible for the ethical life to be superior to the aesthetic life, and the religious life to be superior to the ethical life, regardless of whether it is possible to demonstrate this to a particular aesthete or ethicist. There is no escape from subjectivity and no logical techniques that will free us from the possibility of mistakes. Although Kierkegaard has faith that humans can discover what they need to know to live truly, he thinks that the process God has designed to make this possible is one that goes through subjectivity:

But truly, just as little as God lets a species of fish grow in a particular lake unless the plant also grows there which is its nutriment, just so little shall God leave in ignorance of what he must believe the person who is truly concerned . . . The thing sought is in the seeking that seeks it, faith in the concern at not having faith, love, in the concern at not loving . . . The need brings with it the nutriment . . . not by itself . . . but by virtue of God's providence. (CD, 244–245)

SUBJECTIVITY AS UNTRUTH

This optimistic assessment of the capacities of finite human knowers is, however, qualified in one respect. As I noted earlier in the chapter, as a

Christian thinker, Kierkegaard believes that humans are not only finite but sinful. Johannes Climacus, in the same chapter of *Postscript* in which he argues that truth is subjectivity, is careful to add that, from a Christian perspective, subjectivity must also be seen as "untruth." A full exploration of this theme cannot be done until we have explored Kierkegaard's account of the religious life, and his view of Christian existence, and this will be done in Chapters 6 and 7. However, the issue must at least be mentioned here.

This claim that subjectivity is untruth might appear to be a flat-out contradiction of the claim that truth is subjectivity, but it is not, as Climacus makes clear. The Christian view, he says, is one where "the discussion about 'Subjectivity, inwardness, is truth' *begins* in this way: 'Subjectivity is untruth'."[26] The meaning is this: Ideally, subjectivity is truth, in the sense that truth can enter human life only through subjectivity. Actual human selves, however, seen from the perspective of Christianity, are far from being fully truthful. The task remains but the human condition means it is a longer and more difficult task than even Socrates imagined.

---

[26] CUP, 207 (emphasis added).

CHAPTER 4

The stages of existence:
Forms of the aesthetic life

In Chapter 2 I introduced Kierkegaard's view that human lives can be usefully categorized as aesthetic, ethical, or religious, the well-known view of the "three stages on life's way." One might say that these represent different forms of inwardness or subjectivity, different configurations of caring and passion that give particular shape to human lives. In referring to these forms of human life as "stages," Kierkegaard means to speak about human existence in a developmental fashion, indicating that in some sense it is natural for human beings to begin as children in the aesthetic stage and progress to the ethical and eventually the religious stages.

However, Kierkegaard also refers to the aesthetic, ethical, and religious as "spheres of existence." So a first question is how they can be both stages and spheres. The answer lies in recalling the spiritual character of human selfhood. Human persons are partially self-determining beings who freely participate in their own development. Although Kierkegaard thinks that human persons are intended by their Creator to develop from the aesthetic to the ethical and the religious, and in that sense such development is "natural," spiritual development is never inevitable or automatic. Becoming spiritually mature is not at all like acquiring facial hair or wisdom teeth. Rather a person can become "fixated" (to use contemporary psychological jargon) in a particular stage, and if the person becomes aware of this and aware of the higher possibilities he or she is refusing, then that stage really has become an existentially-chosen sphere of existence.

The term "natural" is therefore in this context ambiguous. If by "natural" we mean what is healthy and proper, what (for Kierkegaard) is in accord with God's intentions for his human creation, then progression through the stages is natural. However, if by "natural" we mean what is "normal," what happens regularly, then this progression is not natural, since Kierkegaard believes the majority of people live their lives as aesthetes. There is of course a significant difference between the aesthetic as it appears in a child and the aesthetic as a willed life-stance in an adult. At least from the ethical perspective, the latter may appear as guilt, but this kind of critical judgment cannot be made about all who live in the aesthetic sphere.

Besides using the term "aesthetic" to refer to a stage of existence and a willed existential stance, Kierkegaard also uses the term in at least two other ways. The term is often used to characterize something that has an essential relation to the arts, particularly theorizing about the arts. So, for example, Lessing is described, in *Concluding Unscientific Postscript*, as the man who "as aesthetician" drew "a line of demarcation . . . between poetry and the visual arts" as well as providing his readers with a "wealth of aesthetic observations" (CUP, 64). In this sense, to evaluate a pastor's sermon aesthetically would be to judge it, not on the basis of the soundness of its theology or its effectiveness in renewing piety in its hearers, but on the basis of the artistic qualities of its construction, style, and delivery.

The term is also frequently used by Kierkegaard to refer to what I would term a dimension of human life. In one sense, as we shall see, the person who begins to live ethically or religiously does not leave the aesthetic behind, because it is a universal dimension of human life. The fact that it is possible to judge a sermon aesthetically shows the ubiquity of the aesthetic, for sermons can be pleasing or irritating, beautifully or clumsily expressed, amusing or boring. Part of the argument Kierkegaard provides for the ranking of the spheres depends on this point. The ethicist will argue the superiority of the ethical life on the grounds that if one chooses to live ethically, one does not have to abandon the aesthetic. In fact, as we shall see in the next chapter, in *Either/Or II* the Judge argues that the goals of the aesthetic life, what we might call the satisfaction or fulfillment of the aesthetic dimension of life, are better realized within the ethical life than within the aesthetic life.

In a similar way, the argument for the superiority of the religious life to the ethical life depends on the claim that the religious life is ethically superior to the ethical life, is better even when judged by ethical criteria. If this is right, the ethical must in some way be preserved within the religious sphere, even if it is transformed as well, just as the aesthetic must be preserved within the ethical and religious spheres.

It is good to remind ourselves that, though Kierkegaard's three stages or spheres are meant to provide a kind of conceptual "map" of the possibilities that confront a human exister, he himself does not present these ideas simply as a kind of psychological theory to be learned, because of his desire to communicate "indirectly." His goal is not to have readers who can intellectually "patter" or recite what Kierkegaard's view of the three spheres of existence is, but readers who have a kind of emotional understanding of these life-possibilities and are, to that extent, wiser. Thus, as explained in Chapter 2, Kierkegaard does not just tell us about the aesthetic life, but gives us aesthetic characters, people with whom we may identify or be attracted to, or, alternatively, feel compassion or even repugnance for.

Also, it is important to recognize that Kierkegaard gives different characterizations of the various spheres at different times, for different purposes. Some of these differences might appear to be contradictions, and perhaps they would be if Kierkegaard were giving a kind of rigid, metaphysical theory. However, the spheres of existence are each complicated and come in a variety of forms. As such, each sphere is similar to and different from others in complicated ways. Given this complexity, it is not surprising that the distinctions are spelled out differently in different contexts, because for certain purposes some similarities may be more significant than in others. At times, therefore, we find Kierkegaard emphasizing the commonality of the ethical and the religious; at other times the differences. The aesthetic is in some ways further from the religious life than the ethical, but perhaps it is closer in some ways as well.

THE AESTHETIC AS THE IMMEDIATE: LIVING FOR THE MOMENT

What all the different senses of the aesthetic have in common is some connection to what Kierkegaard calls "the immediate," a term that I shall initially take to refer to the natural, spontaneous sensations that lie at the heart of conscious human existence. (However, we shall soon see that there is more than one kind of immediacy in Kierkegaard.) The term has its roots in the Greek word for perception or sensation (*aisthesis*) from which we get the modern English term "anesthesia," designating a medical procedure that deprives a person of conscious sensations. All the various senses of "the aesthetic" in Kierkegaard are linked to immediacy in this sense. The young child is a natural aesthete because the child lives "in the moment," dominated by immediate desires. For the young child, "I want it" is a powerful argument indeed, and the ability to "defer gratification," to use the psychologists' term, is a hard-won achievement, which some people make little progress on even as adults. The arts have a connection to the immediate because the arts in some way appeal to the senses. (Contemporary "conceptual art" may appear to be a counter-example to this claim, but Kierkegaard anticipates this development and has ways of understanding it in aesthetic terms as well.) The person who inhabits the aesthetic as an existential sphere also lives "in the moment," attempts to fashion a life that is in some way satisfying. Thus, in *Either/Or II* Judge William tells us that "the aesthetic in a person is that by which he immediately is what he is . . . " (EO II, 178). The idea is simply that an aesthete is a person who takes himself as a given, complete with a set of wants to satisfy, and tries to satisfy as many desires as possible.

It may be helpful at this point to look at the relationship between Kierkegaard's concept of the aesthetic life and what philosophers call hedonism, the view that pleasure is the sole intrinsic good and therefore that a good human life is one that contains the greatest possible amount of pleasure and the least possible amount of pain, pleasure's opposite. It is natural to see a similarity, but the two concepts are not identical. Although the hedonist may be a type of aesthete, Kierkegaard's psychology is more subtle and complex than hedonism typically allows.

In describing human life as a quest for pleasure, the hedonist puts the emphasis on pleasure itself as a kind of end or goal we seek, an end that makes some ways of living more rational than others because they allow us to achieve the good we are seeking. Hedonism recognizes that humans can be irrational and self-defeating in their choices, but the basic motivation is towards a particular end: a life of pleasure.

Kierkegaard certainly agrees with the hedonist that we humans have natural desires, and a desire is by nature something that demands satisfaction, but he thinks it is misleading to characterize human desires as if they were all seeking some uniform quality we call pleasure. Our desires are incredibly varied: the masochist actually desires pain, and there are many who are not masochists who still in some way relish feelings of sadness. Some people relish complaining and only seem to be "happy" when they are miserable.

Rather than focus on some supposed end called "pleasure," Kierkegaard places the emphasis on desire itself. What the aesthete wants is simply to have what he or she wants, whatever that might be. In *Either/Or I* the pseudonym A captures this perfectly in one of the "Diapsalmata" that form a kind of "overture" to the volume: "If I had in my service a submissive spirit who, when I asked for a glass of water, would bring me all the world's costliest wines, deliciously blended in a goblet, I would dismiss him until he learned that enjoyment does not consist in what I enjoy but in getting my own way" (EO I, 31).

We could say of course that what the aesthete is seeking is happiness or satisfaction, but such a claim is completely uninformative. In some sense this is also true of the ethicist and the religious individual. The distinctive thing about the aesthete is the way happiness is linked to the satisfaction of immediate desire, however various those desires may be.

The other way Kierkegaard characterizes the aesthetic life is in terms of time: The aesthete lives in and for "the moment." It is not hard to see why this should be so, for immediate desires have just this momentary character, and to live for the satisfaction of such desires is to seek to make one's life a series of satisfying moments. The child who wants an ice cream cone wants that cone *now*, and the desires of an adult can have a similar urgency.

For Kierkegaard, each of the three spheres of existence has as its exemplar a particular relationship between the sexes. For the aesthete, the relationship is the sexual affair, burning with passion but lacking in commitment. For the ethicist, the exemplar is monogamous marriage, while the religious life is sometimes illustrated by a willingness to embrace celibacy and give up the erotic life altogether.

THE IMMEDIATE AESTHETE AND THE REFLECTIVE AESTHETE

As one can readily imagine, the aesthetic life comes in a vast range of forms, as extensive as the forms of human desire itself. Nevertheless, Kierkegaard believes that the forms of the aesthetic life can be arranged on a continuum ranging from what he calls "the immediate aesthete" to a highly developed reflective form of the aesthetic life. Each of these two forms, when taken as an extreme idealized picture, is symbolized by a mythical figure: Don Juan is the epitome of the immediate aesthete, while Faust, a highly intellectual figure, symbolizes the reflective aesthete.

One may well wonder how there can be a distinction between immediate and reflective forms of the aesthetic life, when aesthetic existence taken as a whole is characterized as a form of immediacy. Is not "reflective immediacy" a contradiction in terms, like "giant shrimp"? It is not if we recognize that immediacy comes in degrees, just as shrimp come in various sizes, and therefore it is possible for one form of existence to be *relatively* more or less immediate than another. If we look at actual human desires, we do find them differing in the character of what we might call their degree of sensuousness.

Consider the difference between the person who has been toiling in the hot sun and is desperately thirsty and the wine connoisseur who wants to sample a new pinot noir from California. Both have a desire to drink something liquid, but the resemblance ends there. The desire of the first person is rooted in the raw structure of the body, which needs and craves water. No reflection or education is needed to have such a desire. In order to appreciate the difference between a pinot noir and a cabernet sauvignon, however, it may be necessary to have a cultivated taste, with an imaginative grasp of the vocabulary used to describe the subtle "notes" of the wines.

Some forms of desire, then, essentially involve the intellect and the imagination in ways that are not true for others. While not minimizing the differences between the various forms of the aesthetic life at all, Kierkegaard wants the category of the aesthetic to extend broadly enough to capture the person who simply wants to get drunk every night as well as the person who prides himself on his refined and elegant taste in wines. Both lives are focused solely on the satisfaction of desires the person happens to have and are thus in one sense "immediate." However, the latter's desires are refined and educated, presupposing a degree of reflective awareness, since the imagination is engaged in the desire.

One may object that such a reflective aesthete cannot be simply "immediate," since such a life presupposes the kind of development provided by education. In one sense this is certainly correct; the reflective aesthete may be a highly cultured individual, with a well-schooled mind and well-developed imagination. However, though developed and therefore not immediate in one sense, Kierkegaard still wants to say that such a person is in another sense immediate, since Kierkegaard distinguishes between intellectual development and development of the self. One might say that there is one sense of "immediate" in which being immediate is contrasted with being reflective, while in another sense being an immediate person is to be contrasted with a person who is ethically and spiritually developed, a person who views his or her life as a task.

Here we must once more recall the basic view of the self Kierkegaard assumes, and which I explained in earlier chapters.[1] The self is formed through the choices it makes, and the intellect alone is powerless to make a choice. A decision requires emotional and passional involvement. However highly developed a person's intellect may be, it is possible for that intellectual power to remain at a distance from the person's life. In fact a certain kind of reflection and knowledge lends itself well to, or perhaps even requires, what we might call the stance of the spectator,

[1] See pp. 20–23, 32–35, and 50–52.

who can "make observations" about an issue without much in the way of personal involvement. For example, a person may know a great deal about ethical theory without having much in the way of ethical character. It is possible, then, for a person to be well-developed intellectually but existentially not developed at all, and therefore still in one sense immediate.

There is another, related sense in which a reflective aesthete can be said to be immediate. Hegel uses the term "immediate" to refer to that which is atomic and self-sufficient, that which has no "other" and therefore lacks the relationships that give richness and definition. Kierkegaard's reflective aesthete, as I shall show below, is precisely this kind of isolated individual who is cut off from substantive relations to others. As we saw in Chapter 3, Kierkegaard, despite his reputation as an "individualist," shares the Hegelian view that a self gains its identity through relations with others, and thus the reflective aesthete turns out to be undeveloped and "immediate."[2] Kierkegaard would certainly have been familiar with this Hegelian sense of the term "immediate" and thus it makes sense that he describes the reflective aesthete in this way.[3]

As we shall see, A, the pseudonymous author of *Either/Or I*, is a highly reflective aesthete. It is no accident, I think, that Kierkegaard chooses as his prime representative of the aesthetic life a man who is highly reflective. To begin, it seems hardly possible that an "immediate" aesthete could be reflective enough about the aesthetic life to write about it. However, even more significant, Kierkegaard believes that the reflective form of the aesthetic life is more appealing, at least to educated readers (and there are unlikely to be any other kind of readers!) and perhaps has a better chance of being successful than the immediate form. Kierkegaard wants to be honest and fair to the aesthetic life, even while ultimately showing its problems. However, although A is himself highly reflective, he writes at length about the immediate form of the aesthetic life, and in some ways shows nostalgia and longing for more vivid forms of immediacy. In the next section I will examine A's own account of the immediate aesthete.

MOZART, DON GIOVANNI, AND THE IMMEDIATE AESTHETE

While A is indeed a highly reflective aesthete, he nonetheless is obsessed with the figure of Don Juan, particularly as this mythical ideal is

---

[2] See pp. 46–50.
[3] For more on this Hegelian sense of immediacy and its use in Kierkegaard, see Merold Westphal, "Kierkegaard and the Role of Reflection in Second Immediacy," in *Immediacy and Reflection in Kierkegaard's Thought*, ed. P. Cruysbergs et al. (Leuven: Leuven University Press, 2003), pp. 159–179.

expressed in Mozart's great opera, *Don Giovanni*. Why Don Juan and this music has such appeal for A is a key question, both for understanding A and for understanding the immediate pole of the aesthetic life. A's admiration for Mozart's opera is lyrically expressed in an essay in *Either/ Or I* called "The Immediate Erotic Stages or the Musical Erotic."

The essay in some respects reads like a serious essay in aesthetic criticism; in fact at many points it employs Hegelian language and forms of argument. Nevertheless, the academic form lightly clothes a passionate love for the opera, and in the end the passion outweighs the content of the essay. A freely contradicts himself and twists his argument to make it come out right. Although he says that classic works of art cannot be ranked because they all rank "infinitely high," in the end he must show that *Don Giovanni* is not only one of these immortal classics, but deserves to be ranked first among all the great works of art (EO I, 48).

Hegel claimed that all art was at bottom an attempt to express what he called "the Idea" or "the Absolute." A views Mozart's opera as an expression of a single "Idea" as well, but the Idea in question is a most un-Hegelian idea: the idea of "sensuous genius." Don Juan is the mythical figure who incarnates this idea:

> In the Middle Ages, there was much talk about a mountain that is not found on any map; it is called Mount *Venus*. There sensuousness has its home; there it has its wild pleasures, for it is a kingdom, a state. In this kingdom, language has no home, nor the collectedness of thought, ...there is heard only the elemental voice of passion, the delight of desires, the wild noise of intoxication... This kingdom's firstborn is Don Juan. (EO I, 90)

The language of A here sounds strikingly similar to Nietzsche's later account of the Dionysiac in *The Birth of Tragedy*. Like Nietzsche, A does not want to view sensuousness in moral terms. Don Juan's kingdom is initially "not the kingdom of sin." Only when "reflection enters" does it become that, but "then Don Juan has been slain, then the music is silenced..." (EO I, 90).[4]

Music is the perfect medium for the expression of sensuousness, for it is the "language of sensuousness," and Don Juan is the perfect subject for music, since he embodies the ideal of sensuousness. Nineteenth-century aesthetic theory saw the hallmark of great art as a perfect synthesis of form and content, and so Mozart's opera is pre-eminently great. Music is the perfect medium to express the idea of Don Juan. Don Juan is the perfect

---

[4] This seems strikingly like Nietzsche's argument in *The Birth of Tragedy* that Socrates' reflective worldview led to the death of Greek tragedy by undermining the tragic perspective on existence.

subject for music. Of course A knows that this cannot be conveyed ultimately through words, but must be experienced by hearing the music itself:

Hear Don Juan – that is, if you cannot get an idea of Don Juan by hearing him, then you never will. Hear the beginning of his life; just as the lightning breaks forth from the darkness of the thunderclouds, so he bursts out of the abyss of earnestness, swifter than the lightning's flash, . . . Hear how he plunges down into the multiplicity of life, how he destroys himself against its solid embankment. Hear these light, dancing violin notes, hear the intimation of joy, hear the jubilation of delight, hear the festive bliss of enjoyment. Hear his wild flight; he speeds past himself, ever faster, never pausing. Hear the tireless craving of passion, hear the sighing of erotic love, hear the whisper of temptation, hear the whirlpool of seduction, hear the stillness of the moment – hear, hear, hear Mozart's Don Juan. (EO I, 103)

Of course no actual individual can be Don Juan. A argues that "Don Juan continually hovers between being idea – that is power, life – and being an individual" (EO I, 92). Such an elemental force can only be properly expressed through music, and A argues that literary interpretations of Don Juan, such as those of Molière and Byron, are inevitably inferior, since as soon as we try to imagine Don Juan as a particular individual (one who has supposedly seduced 1,003 women in Spain alone!) he becomes a comic figure (EO I, 92).

As the incarnation of sensuousness, it is easy to see the appeal of Don Juan as the embodiment of elemental passion. Don Juan represents a life completely free of regrets or second thoughts; Don Juan never agonizes over a decision or wonders if he is doing the right thing. All humans probably have moments in which passion simply overwhelms worry and doubt and anxiety; in such moments a person simply is what the person feels. Any highly reflective person, such as A himself, probably feels the pull of this kind of immediacy more than anyone. But however appealing this ideal may be, it is just as easy to see that an actual person cannot literally become Don Juan. There is in fact something paradoxical about the idea of *striving to become* Don Juan, for how could one self-consciously work towards a goal that requires a lack of self-consciousness? Perhaps it is possible to find strategies for becoming somewhat less self-conscious, but the ideal of Don Juan seems beyond our reach. For the truly reflective person Don Juan represents something like a lost homeland, a Garden of Eden that one never resided in but still longs to return to.

In reality a purely immediate form of the aesthetic life turns out to be a difficult project. Even if one scaled back one's aspirations to a realistic level that does not match Don Juan's exploits, a serial seducer faces many difficulties. To have any plausible chance of success, the seducer must be fortunate enough to possess good looks, charm, and money, but such assets cannot be guaranteed to last. Indeed, in the end they are almost guaranteed to be lost, and in the real world the would-be Don Juan faces the grim possibility of AIDS and other sexually transmitted diseases, not to mention potential angry and violent fathers, cuckolded husbands and fiancés, and the revenge of women who have been hurt. (In today's world, of course, one could imagine a female counterpart to Don Juan for whom the problems would be different.) From the point of view of the aesthete himself, however, perhaps the greatest problem is simply that the immediate form of the aesthetic life ultimately turns out to be boring and unsatisfying. The women (or the men) in the one-night stands run together in one's mind, and the whole project begins to appear monotonous.

It is, I believe, for this reason that the aesthete Kierkegaard presents in *Either/Or I* is not an immediate person who simply seeks to "get high and get laid" every night. Rather, A is a refined, educated person, who does not seek sheer sensuous pleasure, but always tries to find "the interesting" in life. It is time therefore to examine the other pole of the continuum of the aesthetic life, and look at A himself.

THE "ROTATION OF CROPS": A'S AESTHETIC PHILOSOPHY

A provides a witty and revealing account of his own perspective on aesthetic existence in an essay called "Rotation of Crops." The premise of the essay is that the chief human evil is boredom: "Boredom is the root of all evil" (EO I, 285). A notes that children are well-behaved as long as they are enjoying themselves, but get into trouble as soon as they are bored. We take this into account when we hire a "nursemaid," or child-care provider, in today's parlance, because such a person, besides being trustworthy, must know how to entertain children. (This need for a child-care worker who is fun to be around is well illustrated by Maria in *The Sound of Music* as well as by Mary Poppins.) A bemoans the fact that we do not take comparable account of our aesthetic needs in other aspects of life, and "only with respect to childcare does aesthetics receive what it rightfully deserves" (EO I, 286). A voices a vigorous complaint about the social practices of his day:

One would never succeed if one wanted to demand a divorce because one's wife is boring, or demand that a king be dethroned because he is boring to look at, or that a clergyman be exiled because he is boring to listen to, or that a cabinet minister be dismissed or a journalist be executed because he is horribly boring. (EO I, 286)

It is evident, I think, that contemporary western societies are much closer to A's ideals than was his own society, for we have little trouble imagining a divorce that is the result of boredom, a pastor being forced to resign because of boring sermons, or a politician losing an election because he is boring. Perhaps we have not quite sunk low enough to want to see a journalist executed because he or she is boring, but we certainly see journalists lose their jobs because they are too boring to get high ratings.

Having identified the human problem as boredom, A proceeds to analyze two alternative methods of combating boredom. In one sense all attempts to conquer boredom depend on the cultivation of variety, and A uses an agricultural metaphor to symbolize this: "the rotation of crops." There are, however, two ways to understand this. What he calls the "vulgar, inartistic" method is roughly equivalent to what one might call "slash and burn agriculture," in which there is no true crop rotation, but one simply farms a plot until the soil is exhausted and then moves on to another field. The non-agricultural application is to the person who is always looking for "something new":

One is tired of living in the country and moves to the city; one is tired of one's native land and goes abroad; one is *europamüde* (weary of Europe) and goes to America etc.; one indulges in the fanatical hope of an endless journey from star to star. Or the movement is in another direction, but still extensive. One is tired of eating on porcelain and eats on silver; tiring of that, one eats on gold; one burns down half of Rome in order to visualize the Trojan conflagration. (EO I, 291–292)

A says that this method is ultimately self-stultifying, presumably because the quest for the new in this sense itself eventually becomes boring.

The method A proposes "does not consist in changing the soil but, as in genuine crop rotation, consists in changing the method of cultivation and the kinds of crops" (EO I, 292). Recognizing the finitude of human life in terms of external stimuli, A proposes to exploit the unlimited capacity of the human imagination as an antidote to boredom. The secret is to live with intensity rather than seeking extensive experiences. The prisoner confined to solitary confinement and the school child trapped in a boring classroom provide models of how a person can accept limitation and overcome boredom through imagination. What this requires is a kind of stepping back from or disengagement from the external world, so that the experiences one has become raw material for imaginative recreation. The aesthete projects himself into the future in imagination, and from that vantage point "remembers" the current experience, thus creating a kind of experiential dissociation from it.

Every particular attempt to do this falls, A says, "under the universal rule of the relation between *remembering* and *forgetting*" (EO I, 292). The person who lives in a truly artistic manner makes his own life into a work of art, but this requires artistic freedom: "No moment of life ought to have so much meaning for a person that he cannot forget it at any instant he wants to; on the other hand, every single moment of life ought to have so much meaning for a person that he can remember it at any instant" (EO I, 293). This requires a wary discipline on the part of the life-artist; it requires that one "throw hope overboard" and guard against permanent commitments, such as friendship and marriage, that limit artistic freedom and make it impossible to do what the aesthete desires: "play shuttlecock with the whole of existence" (EO I, 294). This does not mean that the aesthete becomes a recluse and avoids contact with people; on the contrary, relations with others are often what makes life interesting. A says that human relations can even "take a deeper turn now and then," provided one still can break things off when necessary (EO I, 295–296). Presumably, such deeper relations add interest and spice to life.

Even enjoyments must be taken in moderation, so that the person does not become overly dependent upon what cannot be sustained: "From the beginning one puts a limit on the enjoyment and does not hoist full sail for any decision; one indulges with a certain mistrust" (EO I, 293). A describes the artistic aesthete as one who has the ability, even in the middle of enjoyment, "to look at it in order to remember it" (EO I, 294). One might say that the aesthete not only enjoys what other people enjoy, but enjoys himself as the one having the enjoyment.

What the aesthete really is seeking is some degree of self-sufficiency and control. I noted that the immediate aesthete, if he is a seducer, will ultimately be defeated by aging, jealous lovers, AIDS, or other factors beyond the control of an individual. However, the individual who has learned to live through imagination gains a degree of impregnability to such things, depending on his skill.

A key tactic in maintaining this freedom is the use of the arbitrary. "One does not enjoy in a straightforward manner, but enjoys something completely different that one arbitrarily introduces. One sees the middle of a play; one reads the third section of a book" (EO I, 299). A himself recounts a story of once having to endure a set of boring philosophical lectures.

Nearly in despair, I suddenly discovered that the man perspired exceptionally much when he spoke. This sweat now absorbed my attention. I watched how the pearls of sweat collected on his forehead, then united into a stream, and ran down his nose, and ended in a quivering globule that remained suspended at the very end of his nose. From that instant everything was changed; I could even have delight in encouraging him to begin his philosophical instruction just in order to watch the sweat on his brow and on his nose. (EO I, 299)

There is little doubt, I think, that the arbitrary in this sense has played a significant role in modern and contemporary art.

SEDUCING A MIND: "THE SEDUCER'S DIARY"

Volume I of *Either/Or* concludes with the famous – or infamous – "Seducer's Diary," often the first thing of Kierkegaard's translated into a foreign language. Though found in A's papers, A himself tries to disown authorship, and claims to have stolen the Diary from the actual seducer. There are, however, reasons to be suspicious of this disclaimer, as Victor Eremita, the pseudonymous editor of the whole book, says (EO I, 8–9). Victor clearly believes that A is the real author of the Diary, but that for some reason A has become frightened or anxious about his own "fiction" and attempted to distance himself from it. A certainly does appear to be uneasy about the Diary. In his introduction to the Diary, he says "I myself can scarcely control the anxiety that grips me every time I think about the affair" (EO I, 310). As evidence for the belief that A is in reality the author, Victor cites the fact that the Diary perfectly corresponds to an idea A has frequently written about in his essays, the concept of an "intensive seducer" who is the reflective counterpart to Don Juan, "where the question is not how many he seduces but rather how" (EO I, 9). Such a reflective seducer seeks not sensual pleasure per se, but lives for "the interesting."

Besides this point of Victor's, there are other reasons for thinking that A is the real author of the Diary. One is that the Seducer in the Diary seems to live in perfect accord with the "method" outlined in the "Rotation of Crops" essay, avoiding commitments, carefully controlling his enjoyment and enthusiasm so as not to lose control, and relishing the arbitrary in his quest for the interesting. (I will expand on this point below.) Also, some letters from the seduced woman, Cordelia, are included along with the Diary, and it seems suspicious indeed that A would have these in his possession if he is not the Seducer. I conclude that A's attempt to distance himself from the Diary is a hint that there are significant problems with the reflective form of the aesthetic life also, and that these show up in some way in the Diary.

The title given to the Diary by the actual author, whoever that may be, is *Commentarius perpetuus no. 4* (*Running Commentary No. 4*) (EO I, 303). It is possible that this means that this is the fourth seduction the Seducer has written an account of, but it seems more likely that the meaning is that this is the fourth version that has been written about the same series of events, for A comments that the Diary is "not historically precise or strictly narrative; it is not indicative but subjunctive" (EO I, 304). Though it appears that real life events lie at the base of the narrative, the author has used those events to fashion an imaginative story for his own enjoyment. A describes the strategy as follows:

> The poetic was the "more" he himself brought along. This more was the poetic he enjoyed in the poetic situation of actuality; he recaptured this in the form of poetic reflection. This was the second enjoyment, and his whole life was designed for enjoyment. In the first case, he personally enjoyed the aesthetic; in the second case, he aesthetically enjoyed his personality. (EO I, 305)

In effect, the Seducer has tried to make his own life into a work of art; he attempts to live poetically by distancing himself from himself, enjoying life but also observing himself enjoying life, enjoying the spectacle of his own life as if he were watching a play.

The Diary proper begins with the Seducer acting as observer, almost voyeur, making acute observations about young women and couples he sees. Then the main story begins, when he sees a young woman wearing a green cloak: "Have I become blind? Has the soul's inner eye lost its power? I have seen her, but it is as if I had seen a heavenly revelation – so completely has her image disappeared again for me" (EO I, 323). The Seducer is delighted by experiencing the rush of emotion we call falling in love, something he thought he was too jaded to feel (EO I, 324). However, from the beginning the Seducer does not honestly and spontaneously follow his heart, but rather thinks about how to use the relationship to fashion something interesting: "I have been submerged by falling in love; I have been given what swimmers call a ducking. No wonder that I am a little dazed. So much the better, so much the more do I promise myself from this relationship" (EO I, 324). So, perfectly following the strategy outlined in "The Rotation of Crops," the Seducer says that "[o]ne must limit oneself – that is a primary condition for all enjoyment" (EO I, 325).

What the Seducer really wants is not primarily sex with the young woman named Cordelia. What he wants to do is to seduce her in a particularly interesting fashion, to seduce her in such a way that it appears that the seduction was her doing. He wants to seduce her into seducing him, and this requires not merely control over her body, but control over her mind. The control, however, must be of such a nature that she is unaware of it, and in the end no one, not even the parties themselves, can be sure whether he has seduced her or she him (EO I, 308).

A's plan is simple and executed perfectly. After finally locating Cordelia and getting to know her, he proceeds to ask her to marry him. Up until this point he has not revealed his real interest in her, instead appearing to help a boring and bumbling rival suitor, who repels Cordelia and thus makes the Seducer look interesting and attractive by comparison. During the engagement itself, the Seducer does all he can to bring Cordelia to see the artificiality and boring character of middle-class engagement and marriage, so that eventually she herself begins to crave "the interesting." She decides to break the engagement and live in the moment, leading to the culmination of the affair. The Seducer's triumph seems strangely flat, however, and short-lived:

Why cannot such a night last longer? If Alectryon could forget himself, why cannot the sun be sympathetic enough for this? Yet now it is over, and I never want to see her again. When a girl has given away everything, then she is weak, then she has lost everything; for in a man innocence is a negative moment, but in a woman it is what gives value to her being. Now all resistance is impossible, and it is beautiful to love only so long as resistance is present; as soon as it ceases, love is weakness and habit. (EO I, 445)

THE REFLECTIVE AESTHETE'S EMBRACE
OF MELANCHOLY AND SUFFERING

If there are problems with the reflective form of the aesthetic life, we would expect them to show up somewhere in the Diary, as well as in other parts of A's writings. For my purposes it does not really matter whether or not A is the author of the Diary; what matters is that A's writings and the Diary offer a similar perspective on human existence, a perspective that I will call that of the "reflective aesthete," using this term to refer both to A and the Seducer.

One might think that the main problem with the reflective aesthete is the marked depression or "melancholy" he exhibits. It is difficult to determine the best English term for this psychological state. The Danish term, *Tungsindehed*, literally means "heavy-mindedness," and the Hong translation as "depression" thus seems justified. However, in contemporary society, "depression" is very much a medical term, and refers to a condition that in many cases, perhaps most cases, is physiologically caused, and this is quite different from the spiritual malaise that afflicts the aesthete. I shall speak therefore of the aesthete's "melancholy."

The tendency of the reflective aesthete to melancholy is quite evident from the very beginning of *Either/Or I*. The book begins with a series of aphoristic passages called the "Diapsalmata," and many of them express the generally downcast character of A's life: "Wine no longer cheers my heart; a little of it makes me sad – much makes me melancholy. My soul is dull and powerless; in vain do I jab the spur of desire into its side; it is worn out, … " (EO I, 41). A similar sentiment occurs a few pages earlier: "My soul is so heavy that no thought can support it, no wing beat can lift it up into the ether any more" (EO I, 29).

This melancholy certainly would be seen as a problem by many, and we shall see later that the ethicist cites it as a difficulty. However, it is not clear that the aesthete himself sees this as a problem; rather he seems to embrace his melancholy: "I say of my sorrow what the Englishman says of his house: My sorrow *is my castle*" (EO I, 21). Even more strikingly, A thinks of his melancholy as a lover:

In addition to my other numerous acquaintances, I have one yet more intimate confidante – my melancholy. In the midst of my joy, in the midst of my work, he beckons to me, calls me aside, even though physically I remain in place. My melancholy is the most faithful lover I have known – no wonder, then, that I love in return. (EO I, 20)

An understanding of the reflective aesthete's infatuation with sorrow and melancholy is one key to understanding this life-perspective.

One must begin here by remembering the reflective aesthete's project of achieving a degree of independence from life's accidents by turning inward in his enjoyments so as to achieve a kind of self-sufficiency. The reflective aesthete wants to make his own life into a work of art, one that he can enjoy as aesthetic observer. A life of sorrow and melancholy has several advantages for this project. First of all, such a life partakes of the tragic, and many people see tragedy as the greatest form of art. It is true that Shakespeare wrote both comedies and tragedies, but most people would regard his greatness as founded more on the latter than the former. Why tragedy should have such appeal for us humans may be partly mysterious, but from Aristotle to Nietzsche, it has been recognized that tragedy offers something profound as well as enjoyable. So turning one's own life into a kind of tragedy to be aesthetically appreciated makes sense, at least from an aesthetic perspective.

A second point is that suffering seems to be unavoidable in human life, and thus offers a challenge for any lifeview. Such a tragic perspective on life offers a way of dealing with, perhaps partially redeeming, this unavoidable suffering.[5] Suffering is given a kind of meaning and is no longer pointless, and this is accomplished without appeal to any doctrine of life after death with whatever consolations and compensations such life may offer.

Another advantage is that the embrace of suffering increases the independence of the sufferer and contributes to self-sufficiency. It provides a way of controlling one's own fate. This has been seen at least since the time of the Stoics in the ancient world, but it has a particular pertinence to the reflective aesthete. Some kinds of enjoyment are highly dependent on things outside of our control, but sadness seems to be one of the easiest emotions to engender and sustain. It is very hard to be deliriously joyful over a long period of time, but not so hard to be chronically unhappy. The aesthete who feels sad at least feels *something*, and thus has an object for aesthetic appreciation.

Finally, the aesthetic appreciation of melancholy provides a kind of answer to what we might call the problem of meaninglessness. It is often alleged that a life devoted to enjoyment or pleasure is ultimately one that lacks meaning; no higher sense of purpose gives unity to such a life or motivates it. A seems to accept this criticism, but once more turns the point into one that is aesthetically useful. It is true that his life lacks meaning, and many of the Diapsalmata express and even bemoan the fragmented and arbitrary character of A's life. However, such a life can ultimately be seen as tragic, and perhaps A's courage in facing this meaninglessness makes him into a kind of tragic hero. Here A anticipates Camus's treatment of Sisyphus, who pointlessly pushes the boulder up a mountain, but nevertheless maintains a kind of tragic nobility through his lucid embrace of his condition.[6]

Before jumping too quickly to criticism of this aesthetic attitude, we should recognize the attraction it has for many of us. I certainly have been

---

[5] For a good example of such a view of tragedy, see Miguel de Unamuno, *The Tragic Sense of Life*, trans. J. E. Crawford Flitch (New York; Dover Publications, 1954). Unamuno was strongly influenced by Kierkegaard.

[6] See Albert Camus, "The Myth of Sisyphus," in *The Myth of Sisyphus and Other Essays*, trans. Justin O'Brien (New York: Random House, 1955), pp. 88–91.

in many university faculty groups where there was a kind of Olympic competition for complaining; many faculty seem to get a certain satisfaction from bemoaning the sad state of the world in general and their university and department in particular. Part of the attraction of being miserable is that for many it seems a kind of proof of superiority; anyone who is truly happy must not be smart enough to recognize the true state of things. The reflective aesthete simply takes to a new level the pleasure most of us get from complaining.

DIFFICULTIES FOR THE REFLECTIVE AESTHETE: THE LOSS OF IMMEDIACY AND THE INTRUSION OF THE ETHICAL

Judge William, Kierkegaard's ethicist who is the author of *Either/Or II*, provides a full critique of the aesthetic life that I shall examine in the next chapter. However, before leaving the aesthete, I wish to note some of the limitations of the aesthetic life that show up within the aesthete's own perspective. From that perspective, the melancholy and sense of meaninglessness that pervade the aesthetic life may not be an insuperable problem, but there are other problems that cannot be evaded. In the concluding section of this chapter, I shall discuss two of them: (1) the loss of immediacy in the reflective aesthete; (2) the inescapability of the ethical.

Both of these problems show themselves, I believe, in some particular sections of the Diary of the Seducer that A (and Kierkegaard) call *actiones in distans*. These are episodes interspersed with the main plot in which the Seducer pursues Cordelia. In these "actions at a distance" the Seducer finds his attention focused on some other woman or couple. It is clear from the surviving manuscripts that Kierkegaard took particular care with these episodes, even though they are seemingly unrelated to the main story.[7] I am convinced that they play an important role in showing the problems in the aesthetic life, and I will therefore pay particular attention to them in what follows.

The loss of immediacy

The first problem is a contradiction that lies at the heart of the reflective aesthete's project. Though he seeks autonomy and liberation from

---

[7] See, for example, the passages included by the Hongs in the "Supplement" attached to EO I, 557–559. I wish to thank Karsten Harries, who first called my attention to the importance of the *actiones in distans* more than thirty years ago.

external circumstances not under his control, it is clear that the reflective aesthete is still dependent on the external world for the immediacy that is the foundation for all that is to come. This can be seen from the sense of good fortune the Seducer shows when he first meets Cordelia, the "girl in the green cloak," and is given a "ducking" by falling in love. The whole project of seducing Cordelia gets its appeal from a natural attraction that the Seducer feels for the young woman. Yet the Seducer's project of "stepping back" from himself, making his own life an object of aesthetic enjoyment rather than identifying fully with and being committed to his actions, necessarily begins to erode and undermine this immediacy. It is simply not possible to be fully in love and at the same time make one's own love an object to be analyzed and aesthetically enjoyed. The Seducer himself remarks, "How beautiful it is to be in love; how interesting it is to know that one is in love" (EO I, 334). He goes on to promise himself that he will "coddle this love as I never did my first," because he wants to "see how long it can be sustained" (EO I, 334). However, to be worried about how long a love can be sustained is already to begin to fall out of love. The Seducer's disengagement from the love he feels is already beginning to destroy that natural emotion.

At the beginning of the affair with Cordelia, the *actiones in distans* are quite rare, as the Seducer is strongly attracted to her. For example, at one point he sees a woman who attracts him, but denies the development of a possible affair because "the green cloak [Cordelia] requires self-denial" (EO I, 330). For the first sixty pages or so of his pursuit of Cordelia, there are only a few other such digressions.[8] However, in the latter part of the Diary, the *actiones in distans* become much more frequent.[9] The Seducer is beginning to lose interest in Cordelia.

It is not only the frequency of these episodes that shows his interest in the affair is lagging, but their content as well. At one point he devotes eight hours (six from his servant; two of his own) to waiting for a young woman named Charlotte Hahn. All he wants from her is a greeting, but "[h]er greeting produces in me a mood, and in turn I squander this mood on Cordelia" (EO I, 396). It appears that Cordelia herself no longer affects him strongly, so he turns to another woman to conjure up the immediacy he needs to keep the affair going. This is even more evident

---

[8] Some of the more important ones occur on pp. 354–359, and on p. 367. I will discuss these in connection with the second problem to be addressed in this section.

[9] For example, important episodes occur on pp. 385–386, 393–395, 396–397, 402–403, 405–406, 408–410, and 412–415.

in a later entry, where we find the Seducer reading Plato's *Phaedrus* to get himself sexually aroused (EO I, 418). This seems like little more than a cultured nineteenth-century counterpart to a contemporary man reading *Playboy*, or perhaps spending time on internet pornography, so as to be fully aroused on a date.

One of the most significant of the *actiones in distans* occurs on pp. 412–415. Here the Seducer speaks with a young servant woman, and leads her to believe that he is in love with her and wants to marry her. It is quite clear that the Seducer's intentions are far from honorable:

You shall be mine . . . The banns will be read from the pulpit . . . Tomorrow evening I will explain everything to you . . . up the kitchen stairway, the door to the left, directly opposite the kitchen door . . . Good-bye, my pretty Marie . . . Don't let anyone know that you have seen me out here or spoken with me. Now you know my secret – She is genuinely lovely; something could be done with her. – Once I get a foothold in her room, I can read the banns from the pulpit myself. I have always tried to develop the beautiful Greek *autoraxia* (self-sufficiency), and especially to make a pastor superfluous. (EO I, 415)

This passage is significant for a number of reasons; it is one of the places where the ethical intrudes into the life of the Seducer, and I will discuss this point below. But the bald truth here is that the Seducer has callously promised marriage to a naïve and innocent young woman to get her to go to bed with him. His affair with Cordelia is pale and bloodless, and he needs sex with a real woman, or at least the prospect of sex, to re-energize himself.

It looks as if the aesthetic life, both in its immediate and reflective forms, is afflicted with grave problems. The immediate aesthete's life is unlikely to succeed very long, dependent as it is on external circumstances and good fortune, and is certain to be defeated by old age and death eventually. Even when it appears to be succeeding it faces a law of diminishing returns, the problem of boredom incurred by repetition. The reflective aesthete seems to possess some independence of these problems, but the autonomy and control of the reflective aesthete is purchased at a cost. The disengagement and reflection that he wishes to enjoy themselves undermine the immediacy that is still required as the basis for a life of satisfaction.

The intrusion of the ethical

The second problem that appears in the reflective aesthete's life could be called the intrusion of the ethical. The aesthete does not see himself as a bad person, someone who chooses to do what is ethically wrong because he prefers pleasure to virtue. Rather, he does not wish to appraise his life in ethical categories at all. He wishes to live in what one might call a pre-moral universe. In an essay on tragedy, A reflects on the difference between the aesthetic perspective on life and the ethical: "The tragic contains within itself an infinite gentleness; from an aesthetic perspective, it is to human life what divine grace and mercy are; it is even more comforting, and therefore I say that it is a motherly love that lulls the troubled one. The ethical is strict and harsh" (EO I, 145).

In Volume II of *Either/Or* Judge William will argue that an awareness of an ethical call is fundamental to human nature, and there is at least some evidence that the reflective aesthete is aware of this ethical dimension of life, even if it is an awareness that he attempts to suppress. For example, when discussing his plan to seduce Cordelia by first getting engaged to her, and then manipulating her to break off the engagement herself, the Seducer shows some unease over the ethical implications of this kind of deception: "The cursed side of an engagement is always the ethical in it. The ethical is just as boring in scholarship as in life. What a difference! Under the aesthetic sky, everything is light, beautiful, changeable; when ethics arrives on the scene, everything becomes harsh, angular, infinitely *langweiligt* [boring]" (EO I, 367).

The Seducer proceeds to assuage his conscience by taking pride that his skills as a seducer do not require him to make false promises, and thus he does not really violate the ethical:

I have always had a certain respect for the ethical. I have never made a promise of marriage to any girl, not even in jest; insofar as it might appear that I am doing it here, it is merely a simulated move. I shall very likely manage things in such a way that it is she herself who breaks the engagement. My chivalrous pride has contempt for making promises. (EO I, 367)

There is a manifest self-deception in the Seducer at this point that becomes all the more evident later in the Diary, when he does promise marriage to Marie to get her to go to bed with him.

I will discuss only one more point where the ethical intrudes into the Seducer's life. In one of the *actiones in distans*, the Seducer is distracted by good weather. The "zephyrs," playful, exuberant breezes, beckon him outside. The Seducer follows their call, and focuses his attention on a young couple, giving particular attention to the charms of the young woman, of course. After a lengthy period of observing the two in the breeze, the Seducer concludes with a summary of the relationship of the couple, who are engaged to be married:

There goes a couple who are destined for each other. What rhythm in their step, what assurance, built on mutual trust, in their whole bearing, what *harmonia praestabilita* (pre-established harmony) in all their movements, what self-sufficient solidity. Their positions are not light and graceful; they are not dancing with each other. No, there is permanence about them, a boldness that awakens a hope that cannot be deceived, that inspires mutual respect. I wager that their view of life is this: life is a road. And they seem destined to walk arm in arm with each other through life's joys and sorrows. (EO I, 359)

There is no trace of irony in these remarks. Clearly, this engaged couple represents the ethical life, and the idea that "life is a road" perfectly expresses this, for it implies that life is a journey, and a journey has a destination – something that gives a human life both continuity and a goal. Despite himself, the Seducer finds himself drawn to the model they present. They possess something he himself does not have, and he cannot help being attracted to it.

In the end he shakes himself free of the spell, and expresses annoyance that the wind has lavished so much attention on these people: "But, you dear zephyrs, why are you so busy with that couple? They do not seem to be worth the attention. Is there anything special to notice?" (EO I, 359). Judge William will argue in the second half of *Either/Or* that the answer is yes. The Seducer's fascination with this couple and inability to resist the natural pleasure of the good weather shows the thinness of his own reflective existence, a form of life that undermines natural joys and represses the claims of the ethical, which he cannot always ignore.

CHAPTER 5

The ethical life as the quest for selfhood

In Chapter 4 I began the discussion of Kierkegaard's view of the aesthetic by distinguishing between the aesthetic as a universal dimension of human existence, and the aesthetic as a particular way of life, one of the stages or spheres of human existence. There is therefore a sense in which the aesthetic is a part of all human life, including the lives of those who live in the ethical or religious spheres. A similar distinction must be made for the ethical. In one sense the ethical must be seen as a dimension of all human lives; every human confronts questions about how life should be lived, what kinds of actions are permissible or forbidden, what kinds of character traits are desirable or undesirable, what is good and what is bad. As argued in Chapter 4, this is true even for the aesthete, for whom the ethical may appear as an unwelcome and tiresome intrusion. It is even more true, as we shall see in the next chapter, for the religious person.

However, besides the ethical as a dimension of human life, Kierkegaard also speaks about the ethical as a specific way of existing, one of the stages or spheres of existence. Even here, however, things are not simple. I claimed in Chapter 4 that the Kierkegaardian account of the "three stages on life's way" is not a rigid, metaphysical theory, since Kierkegaard characterizes each of the three spheres differently in different contexts for different purposes. This is partly because there are alternative versions of each of the three spheres; we saw this in Chapter 4 when examining the differences between the immediate and reflective forms of the aesthetic life. So it should not be surprising that Kierkegaard also gives somewhat different accounts of the ethical life in different contexts and for different purposes.

What all the forms of the ethical life have in common is what I would call the quest for identity. The ethicist sees that the aesthetic life that is lived for "the moment" ultimately reduces the self to a collection of moments. Such a self lacks coherence and in some sense fails to be a self in the proper sense at all. The ethical life is thus a struggle to become a unified self in a twofold sense. The first sense is that the self seeks to be something more than a collection of hopelessly warring desires; it seeks some degree of coherence and unity at a given point in time. The second sense is that this unified identity is one that endures over time. For Kierkegaard to be a self is to know who one is, and to know who one is one must have something to live for, commitments and "values" that permeate all one does and is and that do not change on a daily or hourly basis. As we have seen, for Kierkegaard such commitments are neither dispassionate intellectual beliefs nor arbitrary acts of will, but are embodied in enduring passions.

I shall begin with a look at the ethical life as portrayed by Judge William, the author of Volume II of *Either/Or*.[1] I shall then take a look at the picture of the ethical life presented in *Fear and Trembling*, where the ethical provides a contrast point to the life of faith. In the next chapter, I shall look at the picture of the ethical life presented by Johannes Climacus in *Concluding Unscientific Postscript*, for whom the ethical life represents a point of departure for the religious life.

JUDGE WILLIAM'S DEFENSE OF MARRIAGE

The bulk of Volume II of *Either/Or* consists of two lengthy essays, written as letters to the aesthete who is the author of the papers in Volume I, by Judge William, a middle-aged married man. The first of these, "The Aesthetic Validity of Marriage," is a vigorous defense of monogamous marriage against attacks on that institution from two different directions. On the one hand the Judge defends marriage as an ethical institution that requires a commitment against the attacks of an aesthete who finds marriage to be boring and/or stifling. The aesthete who is the target of the Judge's argument is one who is very much like A himself: someone who believes in love as an experience that makes life beautiful and interesting, but who thinks that marriage as an institution is incompatible with the freedom and spontaneity that genuine love requires.

However, the Judge by no means concedes romantic love to the aesthete. The second target of the Judge's attack are those false friends of marriage who have given up on romantic love. They defend marriage on utilitarian grounds. Such utilitarian defenses of marriage claim the institution is good because it provides such things as a greater degree of

---

[1] Judge William reappears in *Stages on Life's Way*, as do some of the aesthetic characters from *Either/Or*. However, I shall limit my discussion to *Either/Or*.

security or happiness; marriage is seen as an antidote to loneliness or poverty. Against these supposed friends of marriage, the Judge proudly raises the banner of romantic love, or what he calls "first love" (EO II, 37).

The idea of "first love" seems to stem from the romantic idea that each person can only have one genuine love, a notion that Kierkegaard himself may have believed, given his renunciation of marriage after the broken engagement with Regine, whom he clearly thought to be his one true love. Most today would certainly regard such a view as naïve, romantic in the bad sense, since few people would think that a failed early love affair, no matter how intense, would mean that they had forfeited forever any chance of happiness in love. However, I do not think that one must interpret the Judge's notion of "first love" in such a literal way. Rather, one might think about first love in the following way: Any time one is truly in love, the love appears to be unique and irreplaceable. At least from the point of view of the lovers, it is as if they had never loved before; every genuine love is a "first love."

It is not hard to see why the aesthete who lives for the moment should find marriage distasteful. Love, says the aesthete, should be of all things the most free and spontaneous, but marriage makes love a duty. However, duty describes what I must do, not what I want to do. If life is lived for the moment, it is hard to see how a lifetime commitment can be made, for no matter how deeply and passionately one may love at the moment, there are no guarantees that feelings may not change. From the aesthetic perspective, to require one to go on loving "till death do us part" is to promise what is not within one's power. To require such a promise to be kept is potentially to require someone to live a lie, to conjure up a semblance of an emotion that is no longer there.

The Judge considers one possible response to this criticism: marriage with easy divorce, for the individual who "thinks that one can probably stand living together for some time, but . . . wants to keep open a way of escape, to make a choice if a happier choice comes along" (EO II, 23). Such a view of marriage sees it as a "civil arrangement; one needs only to inform the proper authority that this marriage is over and a new one has been contracted, in just the way one might communicate that one has moved" (EO II, 23). The Judge thinks that this view is one that his age "continually threatens" to realize, but lacks the brazenness actually to carry it through. Clearly, our own age has moved in precisely this direction, and probably for just the reasons that the Judge recounts.

It would be easy to respond to this aesthetic attack by divorcing marriage from love altogether, justifying the institution on other grounds.

The grounds that could be given are many, and the Judge discusses them at length: marriage gives society stability, provides a better environment for raising children, makes possible the joys of having children, is a school for character, helps people economically, and so on.[2] Many of the claims made on behalf of marriage have factually true premises; the Judge agrees that marriage is generally good in the ways argued. However, William ultimately regards these utilitarian rationales as undermining marriage. One looks for "reasons" or "arguments" for marriage only when one is no longer in love. For the genuine lover no reason is needed but love itself.

Marriage, says the Judge, actually has the mark of a great work of art: it "has its teleology within itself" (EO II, 62). Its purpose lies within itself, in that marriage is a committed relationship that allows two lovers progressively to reveal themselves to each other. At bottom it is then a kind of communication, and the Judge says the only person who should not marry is someone "whose life is so entangled" that he is unable to "reveal himself" (EO II, 117). (It is of course very likely that this was Kierkegaard's own situation.) If we assume that human persons have a depth and complexity such that this process of self-revelation cannot be completed even in a lifetime, we can see why the Judge believes that marriage should be a lifetime commitment.

The heart of the Judge's argument is his claim that marriage is not an alien imposition on romantic love, but actually is what makes it possible for this love to endure. Marriage enables romantic love to gain a history. To be sure, romantic love is transfigured in marriage, but the change is not one that destroys or even distorts love, but rather one that completes and fulfills love's own needs. In other words, William not only argues the superiority of marriage to the love affair on ethical grounds, but on aesthetic grounds as well. The title given to the letter by the pseudonymous editor, Victor Eremita, is apt: "The Aesthetic Validity of Marriage."

The Judge makes his case for marriage by a detailed examination of the wedding ceremony, where the two lovers say their vows before God and the community. The ceremony itself is part of what scandalizes the aesthete, who wonders why such third parties should be dragged in to the intimacies of a love affair. William responds in detail by considering each element of the ceremony and arguing that what is required of the lovers is not something that will undermine love, but is rather something that love itself needs and desires. To put things in the Judge's own words, he wants

[2] For the Judge's sometimes overly-prolix arguments here, see EO II, 63–85.

to show how "first love could come into relation with the ethical and the religious without this happening by means of a reflection that altered it." Instead of being "altered," marriage draws first love up into a "higher concentricity" (EO II, 57).

I cannot take time to go through every element of this argument, but I will discuss one point to make the Judge's thinking concrete. Central to the wedding ceremony, and to marriage itself, is the vow the lovers make to each other in the presence of God and the congregation. The aesthete, says the Judge, is scandalized that "a third power wants to bind you to faithfulness to her and her to you" (EO II, 55). However, first love itself does not find this disturbing. Love itself wants security, craves some way to tie itself to the mast and ensure that love will last. As evidence for this William points out that even in the absence of a marriage ceremony lovers swear faithfulness to each other and do so in the name of something perceived as "higher" so as to bind themselves: "The lovers swear faithfulness to each other by the moon, the stars, by their fathers' ashes . . ." (EO II, 56).

There are good reasons to think that the Judge's defense of the compatibility of marriage and the aesthetic papers over some problems. Kierkegaard himself strongly suggests this is the case through the comments of his pseudonym Johannes Climacus in *Concluding Unscientific Postscript*. Climacus, in the course of a review of the other pseudonymous books, makes a terse but powerful comment about William's views on marriage, as presented in *Either/Or* and also *Stages on Life's Way*, where the Judge reappears. Climacus says that he has "read what the Judge has written on marriage" and has done so "carefully." Since Climacus sees his own task as one of "creating difficulties" he applauds the Judge for making "the matter as difficult as it is," and also for his "enthusiastic zeal for marriage." "[N]evertheless, I think that the Judge, provided I can get hold of him, when I whisper a little secret in his ear, will admit that difficulties remain" (CUP, 181). The task of combining first love and the demands of duty is even harder than the Judge imagines.

JUDGE WILLIAM ON THE NATURE OF THE SELF

The second and longer letter/essay authored by Judge William is entitled "The Balance Between the Aesthetic and the Ethical in the Composition of Personality." However, it could well have been called "Becoming a Self Through Choice," for that is the Judge's main theme. The Judge defines the aesthetic and the ethical by means of this theme of self-development through choice:

> But what is it to live aesthetically, and what is it to live ethically? What is the aesthetic in a person, and what is the ethical? To this I would answer: the aesthetic in a person is that by which he immediately is what he is; the ethical is that by which he becomes what he becomes. (EO II, 178)

A has mockingly and ironically attacked the significance of choice in *Either/Or I* in "An Ecstatic Discourse" included in the "Diapsalmata," a collection of aphorisms and remarks that forms a kind of overture to Volume I. The tone is dark and cynical:

> Marry, and you will regret it; do not marry, and you will also regret it. Marry or do not marry, you will regret it either way. . . Laugh at the world's stupidities, and you will regret it; weep over them, and you will also regret it. Laugh at the stupidities of the world or weep over them, you will regret it either way. . . Hang yourself, and you will regret it; do not hang yourself, and you will also regret it. Hang yourself or do not hang yourself, you will regret it either way. (EO I, 38)

The Judge, however, begins his letter with this appeal to A: "What I have so often said to you I say one more time, or more precisely, I shout it to you: either/or. . ." (EO II, 157).

By failing to see the significance of choice, and failing to choose responsibly, A is in danger of losing his self, even if he gains the whole world by prodigious activity (EO II, 168). Of course in one sense A, just like any other person, does make choices; he acts and by so doing excludes the alternatives. However, for the Judge everything depends upon how the choices are made. He compares the person who does not choose resolutely and self-consciously to an ocean liner that is ploughing through the water. For a moment it may appear that it does not matter whether the captain turns the wheel or not, for the port into which he intends to turn is a long way off. However, the momentum of the ship means that this period of indifference is a short one, and ocean liners do not turn on a dime. At some point the captain must take decisive action or the ship's momentum will determine its fate (EO II, 164).

Similarly, the Judge says that the person who does not choose in the decisive sense allows something or someone else to determine the choice: "The personality is already, before one chooses, interested in the choice, and if one postpones the choice, then the personality or the obscure powers within it will make the choice unconsciously" (EO II, 164). If the choice is not determined by these "obscure powers" within the self, the person will find himself or herself overwhelmed by social forces, the choice made by "the others." The crucial point for William is not the choice of the good instead of the evil, but what we might call the choice to take choice seriously. What must be chosen first is a stance in which the categories of good and evil are embraced as the framework for choosing (EO II, 168).

The Judge in fact holds a wildly optimistic view of human nature. He claims that when a person attains this moral standpoint, that person invariably chooses the good: "If one can only bring a person to the point where he stands at the crossroad, so that there is no way out for him except to choose, then he will choose the right thing" (EO II, 168). This sunny – and outrageously inflated – estimate of human capabilities is highlighted in the Preface to the book, in which Victor Eremita alludes to one of William's (whom he refers to as B) most celebrated lines: "When B maintains that out of a hundred young men who go astray in the world ninety-nine are saved by women and one by divine grace, it is easy to see that he has not counted accurately, since he leaves no room for those who are actually lost" (EO I, 11). Of course the Judge's mistake is not that he is bad at adding, but that his complacent optimism does not allow for human perversity. Throughout William's work, one finds an interesting combination: trenchant and incisive criticisms of the aesthetic life along with a serious inability to see the grave difficulties that beset the Judge's own account of the path to selfhood. The Judge often sees with clarity the problems in A's life, but fails to see his own problems.

William believes firmly in human freedom, even going so far at one point as to say that the self is freedom (EO II, 214). However, he combines this understanding of the human self as including possibilities that must be freely chosen with a firm conviction that the self has a determinate nature that requires a particular type of development if the self is truly to become itself. We have already seen that he is a bit of a depth psychologist who believes that there are "obscure powers" within the self capable of dominating it. He develops this account of the self into a full-fledged view of spiritual pathology.

Human beings are created as moral beings, agents who must choose responsibly to be happy and fulfilled. At a certain point in a young person's life, the quest for happiness can no longer be satisfied simply through the satisfaction of immediate desires. "There comes a moment in a person's life when immediacy is ripe, so to speak, and when the spirit demands a higher form, when it wants to lay hold of itself as spirit" (EO II, 188). A person who represses this need to become a self in truth will experience the consequences; a life that is devoid of ethical meaning is ultimately a meaningless life, and such a life is experienced as despair, "hysteria of the spirit" (EO II, 188).

William's view of this pathology is almost the reverse of Freud's. Freud saw the self as fundamentally biological, and "hysteria" as the result of the repression of instinctual impulses. William claims that humans have, as they mature, a fundamental need to live spiritually meaningful lives, and this requires them to possess ideals to which they are committed and which define them as selves. The repression of this fundamental need is what leads to "hysteria."

At every point the Judge appeals to what the aesthete himself desires. Marriage is defended on aesthetic grounds in the first letter/essay; it has its "teleology within itself." In his second essay, the Judge argues that genuine happiness and satisfaction require responsible commitment. We saw in the last chapter that the reflective aesthete eschews the (relatively) immediate form of the aesthetic life because he desires to control his own fate and sees that an immediate aesthete is subject to external forces outside his control. Here the Judge argues that only ethical choice allows a person the kind of control the aesthete himself seeks; if we fail to choose we will be controlled by social conformism or unconscious forces within the self that are outside our control.

TYPES OF AESTHETES: JUDGE WILLIAM'S DIAGNOSIS OF DESPAIR

Judge William develops a taxonomy of types of aesthetes as part of his argument. What he wants to show is that the aesthetic life, in all its varieties, is a form of alienation. All aesthetes, says the Judge, wish to enjoy life. (However, we will see that the Judge is aware that some people "enjoy" being miserable.) A life centered on enjoyment, however, is ultimately a life where a person's identity is something alien to the self: *"But he who says that he wants to enjoy life always posits a condition that either lies outside the individual or is within the individual in such a way that it is not there by virtue of the individual himself"* (EO II, 180, italics original). This is easier to see for some forms of the aesthetic life than others, but it is true for all of them.

The taxonomy begins with the person who lives for health, the kind of person who today might say that "If you have your health, you have everything" (EO II, 181). It requires no argument to show that good health is not something the self can always control, despite our contemporary obsession with exercise, vitamins, and organic food.

A more poetic form of the aesthetic life sees the highest value as beauty. The Judge skewers this view of life by poignantly telling the story of an aging couple, a Count and Countess whose happiness is grounded in the conviction that they are the most beautiful couple in the kingdom. The Countess clings to her illusions: "My dear William, isn't it true that my Ditlev is still the handsomest man in the whole kingdom! Oh, yes, I can see that he sags a little bit on one side, but no one can see that when I walk beside him, and when we walk together we are still the handsomest couple in the whole land" (EO II, 182).

Other forms of the aesthetic life can be found in the person who lives for money and the person who lives for "talent," by which the Judge means someone whose sense of self is tied up with having "a talent for business" or "a talent for mathematics" (EO II, 183). If properly understood such talents play a key role in the ethical life. The difference is that for the ethical person such talents become part of the person's calling, for the person asks what he or she is to do with the talent, for what purposes it is to be used. The aesthete, however, simply takes the talent as something immediately given, a gift of fortune to be enjoyed. As such, the "talent" is almost as subject to being lost as money itself.

The most common forms of the aesthetic life simply seek the satisfaction of "desire." However, the Judge notes that "desire is in itself a multiplicity, and thus it is easy to see that this life splits up into a boundless multiplicity except insofar as desire in a particular individual has from childhood been limited to one specific desire," and he mentions things such as hunting and fishing as illustrations (EO II, 183). Fortunately, says William, most of us do not have the resources and leisure to live simply to satisfy our desires, leading him to "thank God one rarely sees it [living for desire] consistently carried through because of the difficulties of earthly life that give a person something else to think about" (EO II, 184). Really to think about what such a life would be like one must turn to a figure who has unlimited power and resources, and for this purpose William turns to the Roman Emperor Nero.

William imagines Nero as a tortured soul, someone who craves enjoyment and diversion, but who, because that enjoyment and diversion is all there is to his life, becomes increasingly bored and depressed. Though he is "already familiar with every conceivable desire," he finds no real satisfaction because he refuses the demand of spirit to break through to a higher form of existence (EO II, 186). "Only in the moment of desire does he find diversion. He burns up half of Rome, but his agony is the same. Soon such pleasures do not satisfy him any more" (EO II, 187). In his boredom, Nero actually enjoys the anxiety and terror he creates in those around him, who never know whether or not a friendly glance is actually a death sentence. (At this point William's imaginative portrait of Nero brings to mind stories of the terror that Stalin inflicted on many of his comrades in the twentieth century.)

William's choice of Nero as a subject is not accidental. For Nero illustrates an aesthetic possibility that A himself has partially fallen prey to: the aesthetic life that has learned to enjoy its own misery. Nero is depressed; his life is despair. However, these negative emotions do not lead him to fundamental change but merely provide him with more material for aesthetic contemplation and "enjoyment." For what is more enjoyable aesthetically than tragedy? When one's own life has become a tragedy, the materials for aesthetic enjoyment are always at hand. We can now understand more clearly why A says in *Either/Or I* that "I say of my sorrow what the Englishman says of his house: My sorrow *is my castle*" (EO I, 21).

It might appear that such an aesthete who has learned to step back and experience his own life aesthetically as tragedy has finally secured an identity subject to his control. However, the Judge argues that such a figure is still alienated from himself, and ultimately cannot control his identity, since joy and immediate happiness may overcome such a person in the same kind of random way that an accident or illness may destroy the life of a more immediate aesthete (EO II, 235). For an example of this, one might think of the episode in "The Seducer's Diary" discussed in the last chapter, in which the nice weather enchants the Seducer and pushes him towards appreciation of a couple who typify the ethical.[3] The aesthetic life in all its forms is a life of alienation; it is the possession of a self that lacks an enduring, stable identity, but rests precariously on the whims of fortune.

CHOOSING YOURSELF: THE JUDGE'S PRESCRIPTION

Judge William has given an acute diagnosis of A as a person who is trying to make his own life into a work of art, distancing himself from himself, and treating his own life as providing the raw materials for aesthetic enjoyment, using the techniques of "remembering and forgetting," as A himself has explained in the "Rotation of Crops" essay. It is one thing to describe the illness, but another to prescribe a cure. What does the Judge

[3] See Chapter 4, pp. 88–89.

want A to do to remedy his plight? The regimen prescribed is initially surprising, even paradoxical. The Judge recognizes that A is a special case. It will do no good simply to tell him to change his ways by getting married or getting a job, even though the Judge thinks that the content of the ethical life as "the Universal" requires the individual to assume the tasks of marriage and making a living. William says that A is in despair; the cure requires A to despair (EO II, 207). But how can the sickness be the cure?

The paradox is dispelled somewhat if we recognize that the despair the Judge recommends is not identical with the despair he views as the problem. A's despair is a state he finds himself in; what he must do is take responsibility for the person he has become, to choose to be the person he is. In choosing his despair A transforms himself from immediacy to a task, for if I am responsible for who I am, then I am also responsible for who I will become. Despair is not to be chosen as an inevitable state to wallow in, but as something A has freely chosen, and which he can therefore begin to change.

The Judge's prescription, like much else in his lifeview, seems unrealistic. Perhaps he is right to think that a necessary condition for an aesthete like A to change is that A honestly recognize his condition and assume responsibility for it, much as organizations such as Alcoholics Anonymous require that those who seek help honestly admit their alcoholism and assume responsibility for the condition. However, as the experience of people in Alcoholics Anonymous shows, this admission and taking responsibility, however necessary, is insufficient for real change to take place. Merely admitting that my life is out of control and I am an addict is not enough to free me from an addiction.

The problem is that people in the grips of alcoholism (or similar forms of distress) find themselves unable to fix the problem simply by force of will. This is why "12-Step Programs" such as Alcoholics Anonymous want members to seek the help of a "higher power," however that is understood. I think Kierkegaard himself thinks that the Judge's advice is deficient in just the way this suggests. At least his philosophical pseudonym, Johannes Climacus, who so often seems to speak for Kierkegaard on such topics, says something like this is true. Judge William, says Climacus, supposes that "the ethical self is supposed to be found immanently in despair, that by enduring the despair the individual would win himself." Climacus says that this simply will not work:

When I despair, I use myself to despair, and therefore I can indeed despair of everything by myself, but when I do this I cannot come back by myself. It is in this moment of decision that the individual needs divine assistance, although it is quite correct that one must first have understood the existence-relation between the aesthetic and the ethical in order to be at this point . . . (CUP, 258)

To discover I am in despair is to discover my own bankruptcy. This is progress, but if I am really bankrupt the discovery by itself will not produce the capital I need to become the self I want to be. The problems that lie in the ethical life as the Judge describes it seem to point to something beyond the ethical, much as the contradictions in the aesthetic life point beyond it.

THE ETHICAL AS "THE UNIVERSAL": FEAR AND TREMBLING

Kierkegaard's *Fear and Trembling*, attributed to the pseudonymous Johannes de silentio, provides a picture of the ethical life that in many respects closely tracks the view presented by Judge William in *Either/Or*. However, the picture of the ethical is presented for a very different purpose. In *Either/Or* Judge William presents his own ethical lifeview as being at the same time a religious view. Just as the Judge optimistically assumes that the goals of the aesthetic life can be subsumed under the goals of the ethical life and achieved within such a life, so he also assumes a broad consistency between the ends of ethics and those of a religious existence. In *Fear and Trembling* this assumption is shattered by a vivid picture of a form of religious existence that seems to be inexplicable from an ethical perspective. The picture provided is one of the life of faith that is exemplified by the Biblical Abraham, who proved his faith in God, according to the story recorded in *Genesis* 22 and cited by the writer of the book of *Hebrews* (chapter 11), by a willingness to sacrifice his son Isaac at God's command.

Johannes de silentio (John of silence) does not claim to be a person of faith himself; to the contrary he repeatedly affirms his inability to believe as Abraham did, and expresses amazement and admiration for Abraham, but also a lack of understanding of the Biblical patriarch. There is in fact a strong hint that the message of *Fear and Trembling* may be opaque to the pseudonymous author. The motto of the book, taken from Johann Georg Hamann, deals with a story from ancient Rome: "What Tarquin the Proud communicated in his garden with the beheaded poppies was understood by the son but not by the messenger."[4] Tarquin's son had

---

[4] Here and in many places where quotations are taken from *Fear and Trembling* I have preferred to use Sylvia Walsh's translation of *Kierkegaard: Fear and Trembling*, ed. C. Stephen Evans and Sylvia

gained power in the rival city of Gabii, and had sent a messenger to his father to ask for advice. The father, not trusting the messenger, said nothing but merely walked around the garden and cut off the heads of the tallest flowers. The son understood that he should bring about the death of the leading citizens of the city. Johannes de silentio as the "messenger" may thus fail to understand what those readers who are the "sons" can grasp from the book. He presents a picture of religious faith as seen from the outside, a perspective on faith from a man who lacks faith.

Fear and Trembling is one of Kierkegaard's most-read and poetically powerful books, and it contains a great deal more than I have space to discuss here.[5] Central to the book, however, is a contrast drawn between Abraham as a person of faith and two other figures Johannes describes: the tragic hero and the knight of infinite resignation. The former is described as a paradigm of the ethical life: "the beloved son of ethics" (FT, 113). The latter may not be fully understandable in ethical terms; at least some instances of infinite resignation appear to require a kind of religious lifeview. However, the example of Judge William shows that a type of religiosity can be an important part of the ethical life also. In the next chapter I will examine more closely how a version of what Kierkegaard calls the religious sphere can grow out of the ethical life, and so I will leave a discussion of resignation for that chapter.

Fear and Trembling begins a polemic waged in many of Kierkegaard's texts against "Christendom," the assumption that in Christian countries such as Denmark, becoming a Christian is largely a matter of absorbing the values and beliefs that dominate the culture. Such a view may seem reasonable if one lives in a Christian country. The upshot of such a view is that a good Christian is simply a good representative of the values of the culture, an admirable exemplar of what is regarded as good. If we identify the ethical with the laws and customs of a people, Christendom assimilates religion to ethics. However, Kierkegaard thinks that there is no such thing as a Christian country; one should not use "Christianity" as a term for a geographical area, because genuine Christianity requires a passionate commitment that cannot simply be acquired by social enculturation.

Walsh, trans. Sylvia Walsh (Cambridge: Cambridge University Press, 2006). However, since some of the translations are my own, for the sake of consistency I have continued to cite the pagination of the Hong Princeton edition, since it contains in the margins the Danish pagination that would allow a reader to check the translation against the original Danish.

[5] For a fuller account of the book that introduces the reader to all the major themes and discusses each section of the book in some detail, see my "Introduction" to the Cambridge Texts in the History of Philosophy edition of *Fear and Trembling*, trans. Sylvia Walsh and ed. C. Stephen Evans and Sylvia Walsh (Cambridge: Cambridge University Press, 2006), pp. vi–xxx.

If Abraham is taken to be a paradigm of faith, then the story of the "binding of Isaac" makes it difficult to understand faith in ethical terms. Christendom attempts to blunt the force of the story by re-describing Abraham's act in vague language: "The great thing was that he loved God so much that he was willing to sacrifice the best to him" (FT, 28). As Johannes points out, this seems true but the vague language of "the best" hardly captures the anxiety and distress of Abraham's dilemma in being asked to sacrifice Isaac. The difficulty Abraham faces is not simply that he was asked to give up something valuable, but that what he was asked to do appeared to contradict his ethical obligations: "to the son the father has the highest and most sacred duty" (FT, 28). Abraham's greatness did not lie in his heroic realization of some universally recognized ideal, but in his willingness to go against his ethical duty as usually understood. Johannes makes a stark contrast between an ethical and religious description of Abraham's act: "The ethical expression for what Abraham did is that he intended to murder Isaac; the religious expression is that he intended to sacrifice Isaac. But in this contradiction lies precisely the anxiety that indeed can make a person sleepless, and yet Abraham is not who he is without this anxiety" (FT, 30).

It is clear that de silentio does not think Abraham's act can be understood in ethical terms. However, what conception of ethics does he presuppose in making such a claim? Many commentators have thought that Johannes understands the ethical in a manner similar to Immanuel Kant, for whom the hallmark of the ethical is the universalizability of the principles upon which we act. It is true that Johannes does use Kantian-type language to describe the ethical: "The ethical as such is the universal, and as the universal it applies to everyone, which may be expressed from another angle by saying that it is in force every moment" (FT, 54). Despite this Kantian language, I think it is clear that the conception of the ethical that is operative in *Fear and Trembling* is not that of Kant. Kant saw the ethical as grounded in a universal moral principle, the categorical imperative, valid for all cultures and times, one that individuals can know by reason a priori and directly apply to the principles of actions.

Hegel had criticized Kant's ethic as overly formal, incapable of giving guidance to human beings in particular situations. For Hegel, the individual satisfies the demands of reason, not by autonomous self-legislation, as Kant thought, but by recognizing the way in which the laws and customs of a concrete community, a people, satisfy the demands of reason. For Hegel, social morality, or what he terms *Sittlichkeit*, trumps the individual morality of Kant. The illustrations of the ethical that

Johannes gives make it clear that he has this Hegelian conception of the ethical as social morality in mind when he affirms that Abraham's act cannot be understood in ethical terms.

To make the contrast between Abraham's case and the case of the ethical exemplar clear, Johannes chooses, as his examples of the ethical, cases that bear a superficial resemblance to the binding of Isaac. Johannes describes three "tragic heroes," all of whom act to sacrifice a child but do so for reasons that are clearly ethical in nature (FT, 57–58). The first is Agamemnon, leader of the Greek invasion force against Troy, who sacrifices his daughter Iphigenia so that an angry god will relent and allow the winds to blow the Greek fleet across the sea. Jephthah, from the Old Testament, vows to sacrifice the first thing he sees on his return from battle, if God grants him a victory, and, upon his return, must sacrifice his daughter who has come out to greet him. Finally, Brutus, a consul in ancient Rome, orders the execution of his own sons when they become part of a treasonous conspiracy to restore the deposed king.

Johannes says that the actions of each of these tragic heroes is ethically defensible. Although a father's duty as a father is to protect and not harm his children, the duty to the nation trumps these familial obligations: "The tragic hero still remains within the ethical. He lets an expression of the ethical have its telos in a higher expression of the ethical" (FT, 59). In other words, one's normal ethical duty is suspended because of a higher ethical duty.

Abraham's case is different, however. Abraham has no state, and participates in no social institution higher than the family. He is willing to sacrifice Isaac simply because God has asked that he do so as a test of his faith. No higher ethical duty is present. If Abraham is justified in being willing to sacrifice Isaac, it must be because there is something higher than the ethical. Johannes calls such a case "a teleological suspension of the ethical."

It is clear that the conception of the ethical that this whole discussion presupposes is the Hegelian one of *Sittlichkeit*, or social morality. To be ethical is to fulfill the social responsibilities assigned to one as a participant in various social institutions, such as the family and the state, with the state as the highest of these institutions. And this conception of morality is in some ways very much like the one defended by Judge William in *Either/Or*, where there is also great stress on the fulfillment of social roles such as husband, wife, parent, citizen, conscientious worker, etc.

Such an ethical way of life, while not "religious" in the Kierkegaardian sense to be discussed in the next chapter, does not have to be secular. The

Judge himself, as we have seen, thinks of himself as a religious man, and the Hegelian conception of the ethical often appropriates religious language, for Hegel thinks of *Sittlichkeit* in religious as well as ethical terms. Hegel himself thinks of modern society, with its stress on freedom and reason, as in some sense divine, the concrete realization of what religious people are looking for when they seek "God." Johannes de silentio recognizes the way that the ethical can think of itself as religious, but he wants to distinguish this type of religiousness from the faith that Abraham exhibits: "The ethical is the universal and as such in turn the divine. It is therefore right to say that every duty, after all, is duty to God, but if no more can be said, then one is saying as well that I really have no duty to God" (FT, 68). On this kind of ethical conception of God, God does not come into focus as a personal being who might make surprising demands on an individual, but is simply a personification of the social morality that the individual comes to know in becoming a part of society. "If I say then in this connection that it is my duty to love God, I am really only stating a tautology insofar as 'God' here is understood in an entirely abstract sense as the divine, i.e. the universal, i.e. the duty" (FT, 68).

If there is no teleological suspension of the ethical, if there is nothing higher than social morality, then it also follows that there are no special duties to God. God and the ethical become synonymous: "The whole existence of the human race rounds itself off in itself as a perfect sphere and the ethical is at once its limit and its completion. God becomes an invisible vanishing point, an impotent thought, his power being only in the ethical, which completes existence" (FT, 68). The conclusion that Johannes draws from these claims is hypothetical. *If* there is no teleological suspension of the ethical, Abraham is morally beyond the pale and should be regarded as a murderer. If there is no such thing as an absolute duty to God, then Abraham's act cannot be justified. To the Christendom that Johannes (and Kierkegaard) believe is perfectly expressed in the Hegelian ethics of *Sittlichkeit*, Johannes poses a dilemma. Either you must recognize that there is something higher than the ethical as *Sittlichkeit*, or else you should stop venerating Abraham as the father of faith and instead condemn his actions. Which view is right Johannes does not say, but his own admiration for Abraham clearly points him towards the view that there is something higher than the ethical.

A similar point is argued in connection with another "problem" that Johannes discusses: whether Abraham was "ethically justifiable" in keeping silent and not explaining his actions to his wife, to Isaac and others

(FT, 82). Johannes says that "the ethical" is simply what can be explained and defended to others, and one can only defend and explain what makes sense in terms of the given ethical practices of a culture. In the twentieth century, Ludwig Wittgenstein taught his followers that "to imagine a language is to imagine a form of life," and Johannes seems to have a similar conception of the relation between language and social practices. To justify an action to others one must appeal to accepted standards of right and wrong, and those standards are themselves embodied in a language. It follows from this that a fundamental challenge to "the ethical" that is encapsulated in that language cannot justify itself by appealing to the standards that it wishes to call into question.

From this perspective, although Abraham may be justified in his silence, he cannot be *ethically* justified, for his actions are based on a word from God that is not mediated through the established linguistic and social practices of his society. He can only be justified if there is something higher than the ethical, and that something must necessarily be something different than the ethical standards of *Sittlichkeit*, the social morality that is embodied in the institutions and practices of a given society. Once more there is a dilemma: either there is something higher than the ethical which makes Abraham's silence justifiable, or Abraham should be morally condemned.

THE LIMITS OF THE ETHICAL: ABRAHAM AS "THE GUIDING STAR THAT RESCUES THE ANGUISHED"

What is at stake here? Why does it matter what judgment we make about Abraham? Why should we not simply condemn Abraham and be done with him?

Johannes does not answer these questions as clearly as we might like. Perhaps he cannot do so, since he is a person who lacks faith himself and does not understand faith. However, he does give us some very powerful hints. Early on in the book he contrasts an ethical version of Abraham with the Biblical Abraham who exemplifies faith. If Abraham had doubted God, according to Johannes, he "would have done something different," but still "something great and glorious, for how could Abraham do anything else but what is great and glorious!" (FT, 20) Here is how an Abraham without faith would have acted:

He would have set out for Mount Moriah, he would have chopped the firewood, lit the fire, drawn the knife – he would have cried out to God: "Do not disdain the sacrifice, it is not the best I have, that I know very well, for what is an old man compared with the child of promise, but it is the best I can give you. Let Isaac never come to know it, that he may take comfort in his youth." He would have thrust the knife into his own breast. (FT, 20–21)

Such an Abraham would have been an ethical hero, and his actions "would have been admired in the world, and his name would not be forgotten" (FT, 21). However, Johannes says, enigmatically, that "it is one thing to be admired, another to become a guiding star that rescues the anguished" (FT, 21). Who are the anguished and how can Abraham's example rescue them?

In the course of his discussion of whether Abraham was justified in keeping silence about his intended act (Problem III), Johannes discusses several characters who seem to be anguished souls. One is the merman taken from the legend of "Agnes and the merman," a popular Danish folk tale. In Johannes' version of the story, the merman has a "human consciousness" and has become a merman because of "a human pre-existence in whose consequences his life was ensnared" (FT, 96). The merman meets Agnes and falls in love, but because of his previous sins, he cannot simply "follow the universal" and marry her. Although Abraham is, unlike the merman, a righteous man, there is a similarity between the merman and Abraham. Abraham's identity as a person of faith is not derived simply from society, but from his trust in a transcendent God who addresses him as an individual. In a similar manner, Johannes says, the merman must "have recourse to the paradox" (FT, 98). Such a person cannot simply be told to "be like the others," because his sinfulness blocks any immediate achievement of selfhood: "For when the single individual by his guilt has come outside the universal, he can only return to it by virtue of having come as the single individual into an absolute relation to the absolute" (FT, 98).

Sin, Johannes informs us, is not to be identified with our natural human life; it is not "the first immediacy" but "a later immediacy" (FT, 98). Citing the Kantian principle that "ought implies can," Johannes says that a figure such as the merman is already higher than the universal, "because it is a contradiction for the universal to want to require itself of one who lacks the necessary condition" (FT, 98). Sin is then a problem for "ethics" in the sense of *Sittlichkeit*. If such an ethic ignores sin, it is "a futile discipline," but if it tries to take sin into account, "it runs aground precisely upon repentance, for repentance is the highest ethical expression but precisely as such the deepest ethical self-contradiction" (FT, 98n.).

Johannes makes a similar point about the figure of Gloucester in Shakespeare's *Richard III*. Gloucester seems to be a moral monster, full of resentment at the pity others have extended to him because of his own physical deformity. Once more Johannes says that "ethics" has little to offer Gloucester: "Natures like Gloucester's cannot be saved by mediating them into an idea of society. Ethics really only makes a fool of them" (FT, 106). Johannes seems to think that there are at least a few individuals, like the merman and Gloucester, who simply are incapable of becoming full human beings by absorbing the values and habits of their societies. For such tormented people, the example of Abraham provides hope that there is another path to selfhood.

Johannes seems to see Gloucester and the merman as exceptional individuals, "people who have been placed outside the universal by nature or historical circumstance" (FT, 106). However, are such figures really that exceptional, or do they not represent a possibility that every person can understand to some degree? Do any of us become authentic selves simply by "accomplishing the universal," assuming our assigned social tasks? Do I become my true self merely by finding "my station and its duties," to use the phrase associated with Hegel's great disciple, F. H. Bradley? Certainly, from the perspective of Christian theology, sin is not merely a characteristic of a few deformed individuals, but a pervasive part of all human existence. Anyone who believes in original sin (or "inherited sin" as translated literally from the Danish *Arvesynd*) will believe that every human being is in need of the transforming healing that comes through an identity that comes from a direct relationship with God. Even secular thinkers who do not accept this Kierkegaardian solution will recognize the problem posed by the pervasiveness of evil in human life and the feebleness of *Sittlichkeit* as the answer. Such secular thinkers may well look for analogues to Abrahamic faith, a path to selfhood that does not deify the established ethical order.[6]

In any case it is no accident that Kierkegaard's own next book after *Fear and Trembling* was *The Concept of Anxiety*, a book that examines the psychological condition that makes sin possible. *The Concept of Anxiety*, by the pseudonymous Vigilius Haufniensis (a Latin name that roughly can be translated as "the watchman of Copenhagen"), does not try to explain the actuality of sin. That is impossible, since sin "lies outside of

---

[6] For examples of such secular analogues to Abraham's faith, see Edward Mooney, *Knights of Faith and Resignation: Reading Kierkegaard's* Fear and Trembling (Albany, New York: State University of New York Press, 1991).

any science" (CA, 16). Instead, Haufniensis tries to explain the possibility of sin, which lies in the psychological condition of anxiety, the emotion in which humans become aware of their freedom and their responsibility. In the Kierkegaardian literature, anxiety is not, as it is in Freud, simply a symptom of some repressed biological urge. Rather, anxiety is a fundamental part of the human condition.

Fear and Trembling and *The Concept of Anxiety* show the limits of *Sittlichkeit*. They point us towards a different kind of ethic in the Kierkegaardian literature, one that applies to individuals as individuals, and points those individuals in the direction of what Kierkegaard calls "the religious sphere" of existence. In the next chapter I shall turn towards this higher understanding of the ethical life by an examination of *Concluding Unscientific Postscript*.

CHAPTER 6

Religious existence: Religiousness A

The concept of the ethical is, as we have seen, central to many of Kierkegaard's early pseudonymous writings, including *Either/Or* and *Fear and Trembling*. However, the concept of the ethical is also important in what may be Kierkegaard's most important philosophical work, *Concluding Unscientific Postscript to Philosophical Fragments*, attributed to the pseudonymous Johannes Climacus, though with Kierkegaard's own name on the title page as editor. *Postscript* (as I shall abbreviate it) is, as the title claims, a sequel to an earlier book, *Philosophical Fragments*, also attributed to Climacus with Kierkegaard as editor.

Fragments (again to use an abbreviated title) takes the form of an extended thought-experiment in which Climacus first develops what he calls the "Socratic" view of the Truth and how the Truth can be acquired, a view that draws on the Platonic view that humans have an inborn knowledge of "the Forms," so that what we call learning is actually "recollection." This Socratic view seems to stand for any human philosophy that views the Truth as something immanent to human nature, something humans can access through their own rational efforts. Climacus then pretends to invent an alternative to this view, using the tools of logic and the imagination. The alternative, however, looks suspiciously similar to Christianity, since it centers on the idea that human beings have lost the Truth and can only regain it through a Teacher who is both divine and human, an incarnate deity. The Truth on this view must come to humans through a special kind of divine revelation, rather than through any human philosophy.

At least on its surface, *Fragments* does not argue for the superiority of either the Socratic view or the Christian-like alternative, but merely tries to show their logical dissimilarity. I shall not discuss *Fragments* any further in this chapter, since the real interest of *Fragments* centers on Christianity, which will be the major topic of Chapter 7, and thus it makes more sense to discuss it at length in that context.

Postscript purports to be a sequel to *Fragments*, in which the disguise of the invented thought-experiment is dropped, and the problem is "clothed in its historical costume" by bringing Christianity directly into the picture (CUP, 10). This description is roughly accurate for the first section of *Postscript*, but it does not do justice to the great majority of the book. As Climacus himself says, the "historical costume" can be provided merely by mentioning the word "Christianity" (CUP, 17), and so the task hardly requires a book of the length of *Postscript*, which is many times longer than the *Fragments* for which it is supposed to be a kind of footnote.

It is not surprising, then, that *Postscript*, at least for most of the text, in reality deals with an altogether different problem. If we assume that *Fragments* is correct to show that the Socratic and Christian views of the Truth are incompatible, the question can still be raised as to what we humans can do to acquire the Truth that Christianity claims to offer. *Fragments* describes the alternative to the Socratic view as one where the Truth must be given to humans as a gift by God, not something that can be gotten by human reasoning or willing. However, even if the Truth is not something that humans can achieve on their own, is there anything that we humans can do that will help us towards that goal? Climacus tries to answer this question by taking himself as the subject of a thought-experiment:

> I, Johannes Climacus, a native of this city, now thirty years old, an ordinary human being as are the majority of people, assume that a highest good, called an eternal happiness, awaits me just as it awaits a housemaid and a professor. I have heard that Christianity is the condition for acquiring this good: now I ask how I may enter into a relation to this doctrine. (CUP, 15–16)

Climacus proceeds to pursue this question for hundreds of pages. The answer, it turns out, is consistent with the message of *Fragments*, which is that genuine Christian faith must be a gift from God and is not a human achievement. However, the answer given in *Postscript* does considerably complicate the moral of *Fragments*. For we learn that although we cannot produce Christian faith, there are humanly achievable qualities that are necessary preconditions for such faith. *Postscript* is an extended series of reflections on those qualities and how they can be acquired.

The picture presented is that there is a natural form of the religious life, one that Climacus calls "Religiousness A," that humans are capable of. This "Socratic" form of the religious life, while not something that Christianity can be reduced to, does turn out to be something that Christianity presupposes. And this Socratic form of the religious life has its origins in a version of the ethical life.

THE ETHICAL AGAIN: DISCOVERING GOD

In *Postscript*, then, Kierkegaard offers us, through the thinking of
Johannes Climacus, yet another picture of the ethical life. Here ethical
existence is not so much something to be contrasted with religious
existence as it is the point of departure for a genuine religious life. We
have seen that the "ethical," in both *Fear and Trembling* and *Either/Or*, is
understood primarily as a kind of socially mediated ethic, in which an
individual is defined by the roles assigned by his or her place in a given
society. In these works the ethical is understood in a manner similar to
Hegel's notion of *Sittlichkeit*. However, in *Postscript* the ethical is precisely what allows an individual to escape from such a network of socially
assigned roles. For me to discover the ethical is to discover myself as
something more than a social ensemble.[1]

Climacus first describes the ethical task in an Aristotelian fashion as
one of self-actualization: "Ethics focuses upon the individual, and ethically understood it is every individual's task to become a complete
human being, just as it is the presupposition of ethics that everyone is
born in the condition of being able to become that" (CUP, 346). We can
infer from this quote that, although the task seems Aristotelian in form,
there is a deontological note in the ethical life as Climacus understands it.
The picture given is at least as Kantian as it is Aristotelian. For Climacus
(and I will later argue for Kierkegaard as well), self-actualization is not
merely a good to be desired, but rather a task, something human persons
have been assigned to do and which they will be held responsible for
achieving or failing to achieve.

Of course not everyone is aware of this ethical task. Climacus says that
a great many people drift through life, "managing with custom and
tradition" in their respective cities (CUP, 244). Such people live their lives
in a way similar to the way children who have not been taught table
manners might get by at a fancy party: "[W]atch the other polite children and behave as they do" (CUP, 244). Someone who lives life this
way lacks what Kierkegaard regularly terms "*Primitivitet*," a term the
Hongs translate as "primitivity" but which could also be translated as

---

[1] For a fuller account of this conception of the ethical than I can provide here, see "The Ethical Task
as the Human Task," Chapter 4 of my book, *Kierkegaard's Ethic of Love: Divine Commands and
Moral Obligations*, pp. 85–111. Also see my "Existence and the Ethical," Chapter 5 of *Kierkegaard's
Fragments and Postscript: The Religious Philosophy of Johannes Climacus* (Atlantic Highlands, New
Jersey: Humanities Press, 1983), pp. 73–93. This book has been reprinted by Humanity Books, an
imprint of Prometheus Press.

"authenticity" or "originality." Such a person "would never do anything first and would never have any opinion unless he first knew that others had it" (CUP, 244).

Climacus says that such a person has never discovered God, and the reason this is so is that he has never received any "impression of the infinitude of the ethical." It now becomes clear how closely the ethical and the religious are linked for Climacus, and why "[i]t is really the God-relationship that makes a human person a human person" (CUP, 244). For God simply is identical with the one who assigns human persons the ethical task. God creates each person as an individual and in effect says to each human being: "Become yourself, be the person I made you to be." Although Climacus is a non-Christian pseudonym, his thinking is at this point completely consistent with views found in Kierkegaard's explicitly Christian writings that will be examined later.[2]

The self that I am called to actualize is a human self, and as such, there are universal dimensions to that self that are necessary to its becoming what it is. Thus, Kierkegaard is an "essentialist," someone who believes there is a universal human nature. One cannot be a human self without thought, imagination, and emotion, and thus to become a "whole" human being, the individual must develop all these aspects of the personality. "The true is not higher than the good and the beautiful, but the true and the good and the beautiful belong essentially to every human existence and are united for an existing person not by thinking but by existing" (CUP, 348).

However, these universal dimensions of the self do not exhaust its identity. Unlike in the animal world, where "the particular animal is related directly as specimen to species," human beings are created by God as individuals (CUP, 345). This individuality does not contradict our essential nature as humans, but it means that our generic human nature does not exhaust our identity. The individuality partly makes itself manifest in the way the universal dimensions of human nature are actualized, for such qualities as "the true, the good, and the beautiful" are highly abstract and it is up to individuals to refine and interpret them in

---

[2] In Chapter 8 I discuss *The Sickness Unto Death*, where Kierkegaard's Christian pseudonym Anti-Climacus defines despair as either a failure to be the self God created us to be or a defiant will to be some other self than the self God wills us to be, and then says that this despair is identical with sin when the person exists "before God." I will also look at *Works of Love*, where Kierkegaard vigorously claims that our fundamental obligation to our fellow humans is to love our neighbors as ourselves, and vigorously argues that this duty stems from a divine command. It is rooted in our status as God's creatures, subject to God's authority.

relation to their own situations. But the task of self-realization also includes the development of those "differential" or "accidental" qualities that distinguish individuals from each other. Some people are highly gifted in music; many are not. If I have musical gifts, Climacus would say that I must not take these qualities simply as "immediate" gifts of fortune to be enjoyed, but I must ask myself how these gifts are to be developed and used. (At this point Climacus' views sound very much like Judge William's.)

This understanding of the ethical helps us understand what is usually called Kierkegaard's "individualism." In one sense, as was discussed briefly in Chapter 3, Kierkegaard has, like Hegel, a very social view of the self.[3] There are no self-made humans; all of us are who we are because of the relationships that define us. However, for Kierkegaard God is a real person, and the relation to God is a real social relationship, one that can and should "trump" the roles that human relationships assign to an individual. The person who is conscious that he lives "before God" thus gains the possibility of an identity that is not exhausted by human relations. Such a person is not forced simply to live like "the others," but has the potential to say, "I need to live my life this way, since it is what God desires for me, even if it means that I have to break with my society's accepted ways of doing things."

The ethical task as Climacus describes it is therefore the task of becoming the person God created one to be. He does not say a great deal about why God has the authority to make such a demand on a person, but it is clear he recognizes God as having this authority by virtue of being the creator. This view of God as the foundation of the ethical life helps us understand why Climacus and Kierkegaard seem to have so little interest in the questions that have dominated philosophy of religion in the west since the Enlightenment, such as how one can know God's existence, or explain the occurrence of evil if God has created the world. Kierkegaard's writings pay little attention to such questions; in fact there is often downright hostility to apologetic arguments, whether philosophical or historical.[4]

---

[3] See Chapter 3, pp. 46–50. This view of the self developed in *The Sickness Unto Death* will be discussed at greater length in Chapter 8.
[4] However, I do not think Kierkegaard's opposition to apologetics is absolute, but rather is directed to one type of evidential argument. See my article, "Apologetical Arguments in Kierkegaard's *Philosophical Fragments*," in *International Kierkegaard Commentary* volume on *Philosophical Fragments* (Macon, Georgia: Mercer University Press, 1994), pp. 63–83. Reprinted in my *Kierkegaard on Faith and the Self,* pp. 133–150.

If God is the source of the ethical "ought," then anyone who is aware of the moral task already has an implicit awareness of God's reality, even if the individual does not recognize that it is God who is addressing him.[5] Thus, someone who is concerned about the existence of God is either a comic figure who ignores a reality that is present to him, or else shows by his worry about God's reality that he has ignored the ethical demand placed upon him:

> To demonstrate the existence of someone who is present [*er til*] is the most shameless assault, since it is an attempt to make him ludicrous, but the trouble is that one does not even suspect this, that in dead seriousness one regards it as a godly undertaking. How could it occur to anyone to demonstrate that he [God] exists unless one has allowed oneself to ignore him; and now one does it an even more lunatic way by demonstrating his existence right in front of his nose. (CUP, 545)

In *Upbuilding Discourses in Various Spirits*, written only a little later than *Postscript* and published in the next year, Kierkegaard gives an account of the ethical life in his own voice that is substantially similar to that given by Climacus. In the first part of *Upbuilding Discourses in Various Spirits*, which has also been translated and published separately in English under the title *Purity of Heart*, Kierkegaard also presents the idea that the ethical life is rooted in a person's relation to God as Creator. In this work Kierkegaard argues that a person who is pure in heart must have a unified will, but that only a commitment to "the Good" allows a person to achieve such unity and avoid "doublemindedness." However, "the Good" turns out not to be some external end, but simply the achievement of the task the individual has been assigned by God:

> [A]t every person's birth there comes into existence an eternal purpose for that person, for that person in particular. Faithfulness to oneself in relation to this is the highest thing a person can do, and as that most profound poet has said, "Even worse than self-love is self-contempt." (UDVS, 93)

The person who is truly committed to the Good is a person who lives according to conscience, but to have a conscience is simply to have a "relationship in which you as a single individual relate yourself to yourself before God" (UDVS, 129).

---

5 For an explanation of how someone can be aware of God's existence and still be an atheist, see my "Can God Be Hidden and Evident at the Same Time? Some Kierkegaardian Reflections," *Faith and Philosophy* (23, 3: July 2006), pp. 241–253.

The ethical life therefore, as conceived by both Climacus and Kierkegaard himself, turns out essentially to involve a kind of awareness of God, understood as the source of the moral task of becoming the unique self one is intended to be. One interesting implication of this conception of the ethical life is that it turns out to be deeply egalitarian in character. One might think that this is not the case, since people have very different life situations; some are brought up in highly ethical families and encouraged to care about the good, while others are less fortunate. Both Climacus and Kierkegaard take such differences into account. The ideal self that each person should become is relativized, so to speak, to take account of the potential that is inherent in their genetic and environmental situations. We might say that when God forms his expectations of an individual, he takes into account the difficulties that face that particular individual. Each of us has in one sense the same task, the task of becoming the selves we were intended to be, but the differences in our individual situations allows for a kind of equality:

However great or small the task is makes absolutely no difference, God be praised, in relation to the highest. Oh, how merciful the eternal is towards us human beings! The eternal has no knowledge of all the corrupting strife and comparison that condescends and insults, that sighs and envies. Its requirement is equal for everyone, the greatest who has lived and the lowliest. (UDVS, 81)

THE ORIGIN OF THE RELIGIOUS LIFE: THE QUEST FOR ETERNITY

In *Postscript* the transition from the discussion of the ethical life to the religious life is made by equating the concept of the "highest good," an important concept in classical ethical theory, with the religious concept of an eternal happiness. As we have seen, in one sense the ethical life as Climacus understands it is already religious in character, in that the ethical individual has a kind of awareness of God and relation to God. It would therefore be a mistake to think that a person who inhabits Kierkegaard's ethical sphere must be someone who lacks religious beliefs. The difference between the religious person in the full-fledged sense and the ethical person for Kierkegaard is not simply that the religious person believes in God while the ethical person does not. Rather, the difference lies in the attitudes towards God found in the two figures. The person who exists ethically has a kind of self-confidence in her relation to God; she sees herself as someone who can achieve the ethical task assigned to her. The religious individual in the more distinctive sense is someone who has made discoveries about the difficulties of becoming an integral self, someone who is no longer confident of the God-relation as a goal to be achieved through action. Rather, the religious person sees herself as in some way broken, and finds in the God-relationship grounds to hope that the self can be made whole again.

What I wish to do at this point is show how the religious life in this full-blown sense emerges from the ethical life. How is it that Climacus manages to identify the ethical concept of the highest good with the religious concept of eternal happiness? On the surface, the identification is problematic, for the same reasons that Kant's account of the highest good is often claimed to be problematic, because it seems to assume that the quest for morality must be motivated by a reward. After Kant has argued that morality requires people to do their duty because it is their duty and not for the sake of a reward, he claims that the highest good, the final end of all moral action, must be understood as a world where people are morally good, and also happy, with their happiness contingent upon their virtue.[6] Kant famously argues that this requires the morally good person to believe in God, since I cannot hope to make progress towards the achievement of this good by moral actions, unless the world is governed by a moral providence that will ultimately ensure that moral goodness is rewarded with happiness.[7]

Critics of Kant argue that this undermines Kant's contention that a morally good person must do what is right simply because it is right, without considering whether morally good action will be rewarded.[8] In a similar way, critics may wonder whether the picture of the ethical life presented in *Postscript* does not undermine the deontological character of the ethical life, if the highest good sought by the ethical turns out to be a person's own eternal happiness. Does such a view imply that the ethical person is simply a shrewd individual, who cares more about his own happiness than moral goodness, but is clever enough to realize that moral goodness is the surest way to gain that happiness?

Climacus recognizes this potential problem and works strenuously to head it off. To begin, we should note that the term for happiness he uses is *Salighed*, which can also be translated "blessedness." It refers to the

---

[6] See Immanuel Kant, *Critique of Practical Reason*, trans. Lewis White Beck (New York: Macmillan Publishing Co., 1985), pp. 111–126.

[7] See Kant, *Critique of Practical Reason*, pp. 128–136.

[8] For an excellent discussion of Kant's views here and a defense of him against this criticism, see Allen Wood, *Kant's Moral Religion* (Ithaca, New York: Cornell University Press, 1970). Also see Chapter 2 of my *Subjectivity and Religious Belief* (Grand Rapids, Michigan: Wm. B. Eerdmans, 1978).

distinctive kind of happiness that is attained by the saint or the sage, not the happiness gained from wealth, renown, or other worldly goods (Danish *Lykkelighed*) that is so largely conditioned by fortune. If the eternal happiness that the ethical person sought consisted of such goods, or something similar in the afterlife – virgins in paradise, streets of gold, etc. – then the purity of the ethical life would indeed be compromised. The eternal happiness that is the highest good must not be conceived in terms of particular aesthetic goods. It is thus quite in order that the eternal life that is the goal of the ethical life lacks aesthetic content and is in fact aesthetically unappealing:

> Ethically it is entirely consistent that the highest pathos of the essentially existing person corresponds to what aesthetically is the poorest conception, and that is an eternal happiness. Someone has said, correctly (aesthetically understood) and wittily that the angels are the most boring of all beings, eternity the longest and most boring of all days, since even one Sunday is boring enough, an eternal happiness perpetual monotony, and that even unhappiness is to be preferred. (CUP, 393)

Instead of conceiving of an eternal happiness in aesthetic terms, Climacus says that "eternal happiness, as the absolute good, has the remarkable quality that *it can be defined only by the mode by which it is acquired*" (CUP, 427; italics original).

We can understand these claims of Climacus if we reflect on the difference between two kinds of rewards. Many thinkers have noted the difference between a reward that is internal and intrinsic to an activity and a reward that is extrinsic. Think, for example, of two aspiring musicians, both of whom are talented and work hard at becoming great performers through long hours of practice. The first musician, we may imagine, simply loves music and is primarily motivated by the desire to become a better musician and produce more beautiful music. Imagine that the second musician primarily cares about becoming rich and famous, and views music simply as a means to this end. In the second case, we would regard the motivation of the musician to be somewhat tainted, because there is no intrinsic connection between being a good musician and being rich and famous. The first musician clearly also is motivated by a reward, and will be happy if she achieves the goal of being a fine musician. However, in this case the happiness that is sought does not tarnish the activity, because the happiness is grounded in a genuine love for music.[9]

---

[9] For an excellent argument for this view that there are types of rewards that do not sully motives, see C. S. Lewis, *The Problem of Pain* (London: Centenary Press, 1940), pp. 132–142.

Climacus is clearly saying that something like this is true for the eternal happiness that is sought by the ethical person. The "mode of acquisition" for achieving this happiness is simply ethical striving itself. However, the happiness that is sought in this case is not some extrinsic reward that is tacked on to the ethical life; it is simply the opportunity to become the person one is required to become. The happiness that motivates the ethical quest is the happiness enjoyed by the person who truly loves the good.

But why should we think of this happiness as eternal in character? There seems little doubt that some secular people today would agree that the ethical life can be rewarding in the way that Climacus assumes, but argue that we humans must limit our hopes for happiness to this life. It is only when we think of the happiness that motivates the ethical life as more than merely temporal happiness that we seem to have a hope that is clearly religious in character.

To answer this criticism I should first note that there is an interpretation of Kierkegaard in which his view of eternal life is not so different from this secular perspective as one might think. Some philosophers have thought that talk of "eternal life" in Kierkegaard's writings should not be understood to mean a literal life beyond the grave.[10] Rather, to speak of eternal life is to speak of a new quality or dimension of life that can be enjoyed now, so to speak. On such a view to enjoy eternal life is to see one's life as rooted in values that are eternally valid, or to see one's life as having a meaning that will not die, even though a person's conscious, bodily life will cease. At least a minimal religious character can still be seen if this meaning is linked to God, as when a person thinks of eternal life as God's eternal love and appreciation for what one has achieved. To be remembered eternally by God is at least to ensure that one's life will never be reduced to oblivion.

This interpretation of Kierkegaard's understanding of eternal life has several points on its side. First, it is clearly right that eternal life for Kierkegaard is not a mere extension of this life. It is not merely living forever, but the attainment of a new quality of life. Furthermore, this reading of Kierkegaard connects his thought to the Christian teaching that eternal life is not simply something to be enjoyed after death, but is something the Christian believer can possess immediately.[11] Besides these

---

[10] See, for example, the brief discussion of Kierkegaard in D. Z. Phillips, *Death and Immortality* (London: Macmillan, 1970), pp. 47–49.

[11] This is a consistent theme in the Gospel of John, for example, where the author frequently claims that eternal life is something possessed already by those with faith in Christ. See John 3:16, 4:13, 5:25, and many other passages.

points, there are some passages in Kierkegaard that emphasize the terrible finality of death.[12]

However, this interpretation of eternal life simply as a quality of life to be enjoyed in time is not a plausible reading of Kierkegaard, all things considered. It is true that eternal life is far more than a mere extension of temporal existence, but we have very good reasons to think that Kierkegaard himself would have seen eternal life as including life after death. The alternatives of "mere unending life" and "new quality of life in time" are not mutually exclusive; there is also the possibility of a new quality of life that extends beyond the grave, even if it is also something to be enjoyed here and now. To see this, we can begin with Kierkegaard's own selection of a text for his gravestone from a hymn by Brorson. Freely translated from Danish, the text expresses a fervent confidence in a robust life after death:

> In a little while
> I will have won.
> The entire battle
> Will at once be over.
> Then I can rest
> In paradise
> And talk unceasingly
> With my Jesus.

There are many statements in Kierkegaard's published writings that reflect a similar view of eternal life as involving a literal victory over death. Climacus in particular is critical in *Postscript* of philosophers such as Hegel who, when asked about whether individual humans possess immortality, respond by changing the subject and talking about the immortality of our ideals or the human spirit (CUP, 171). Rather, Climacus (and Kierkegaard) seem much closer to the spirit of Kierkegaard's later follower, Miguel de Unamuno, who was obsessed with the question of life after death, and spoke powerfully of his own longing for eternal life: "I do not want to die – no; I neither want to die nor do I want to want to die; I want to live always, always, always. And I want this I to live – this poor I that I am and that I feel myself to be here and now,

---

[12] For example, see Kierkegaard's discourse "At a Graveside," in *Three Discourses on Imagined Occasions*, trans. and ed. Howard V. Hong and Edna H. Hong (Princeton, New Jersey: Princeton University Press, 1993), pp. 69–102. Also, see "The Work of Love in Recollecting One Who Is Dead" (WL, 345–358).

and therefore the problem of the duration of my soul, of my own soul, tortures me."[13] Kierkegaard extends such a literal hope for life after death to non-Christians, noting in *The Point of View for My Work as an Author*, that although Kierkegaard is well aware that Socrates is not a Christian, he is "convinced that he [Socrates] has long since become one" (PV, 54).

In any case, it is hardly idiosyncratic of Johannes Climacus to think that the goal of human life is in some way bound up with the defeat of death. Virtually every human culture seems to have had beliefs about some kind of life after death, and many have developed elaborate rituals and customs designed to ensure a happy or peaceful afterlife. It is true that in contemporary western cultures, there are many individuals who are committed to what they would call a scientific view of the world that leaves little room for such hope. However, it is arguable that even such people at some points must wonder whether death is the final chapter of human life. In any case, Kierkegaard seems to have little concern for the kind of epistemological stance that denies the possibility of life after death. Rather, his attitude about eternal life parallels his attitude with respect to God's existence. In neither case do we have objective proof that is sufficient to ground belief. However, in both cases the individual who is gripped by the proper kind of passion will naturally believe in God and seek eternal life. The proper worry is not whether there is such a thing as eternal life, but whether *I* am the kind of person who will gain eternal life.

Again, Socrates provides a model for Climacus. Socrates offers no objective certainty, but he embodies in his life the kind of subjectivity that gives human persons the truth they must have:

But Socrates! He poses the objective question as problematic: if there is an immortality. He was therefore a doubter, compared with one of the modern thinkers with three proofs? By no means. He stakes his whole life on this "if" ; he dares to die, and with the passion of the infinite he has so ordered his life that it might be found acceptable – *if* there is an immortality. Is there any better proof for the immortality of the soul? (CUP, 201)

The ethical quest for the "highest good" is therefore interpreted by Climacus as the quest to become the true, authentic self one is meant to be, and to be that self eternally.

---

[13] Miguel de Unamuno, *The Tragic Sense of Life*, trans. J. E. Crawford Flitch (New York: Dover Publications, 1954), p. 45.

ETERNAL LIFE AS A RELATIONSHIP TO GOD

If it seemed dubious for Climacus to interpret the ethical quest for the highest good as a quest for eternal life, it might seem even more far-fetched to understand both of them as essentially identical to a relationship with God. However, some reflection shows that once the first two are understood as Climacus does, identifying them with a God-relationship makes perfect sense. We have already seen that for Climacus the ethical life in its highest form involves a relation with God as the one who creates every person and assigns each of them the task of becoming the self he or she was created to be. In this sphere of "immanent" religion, in which God is known through moral experience, God simply is the reality that stands behind our experience of moral obligation.

Nor it is implausible to think that a relation with God is identical with the eternal happiness that is the motivating goal of the ethical life. We have seen that such an eternal life must be conceived as a reward that is internal to the moral life, a reward that will only be recognized as a reward by those who are committed to the good. A relation with God fits this description perfectly. Since God is the ground of morality, a person who is morally developed is a person who has the right kind of relation to God. Climacus says that God cannot be seen in world history because "as it is seen by humans God does not play the role of Lord; as one does not see the ethical in it, therefore God is not seen either" (CUP, 156). This clearly implies that within the ethical life God can be recognized. Such a relation to God is rewarding, because what can be more satisfying to a good person than to have the opportunity to achieve goodness and thereby have a relationship with that reality that is itself supremely good?

Still, one might wonder why such a reward, even if it is a form of happiness, must be seen as eternal, unending life. The answer, I suspect, lies in the nature of the ethical quest for the good. The person who truly desires to achieve the good desires to *be* a certain kind of person. But why should one who wills this, and understands the value of what is willed, not will this eternally? Why should a person not will that something of such surpassing value endure eternally?

These claims of Climacus are of course not novel, but are rooted in a long Christian tradition that has viewed the highest good as the "beatific vision," a knowledge of God that Christians regard as the highest bliss and the intended destiny of human persons. However, it is important to see that Climacus makes no appeal to Christian revelation in describing this natural form of the religious life. The kind of ethical religiousness he wants to describe "could exist in paganism" even if it has not, since "it has only ordinary human nature as its presupposition" (CUP, 559). He is attempting to give an account of the religious experience of human beings, and although his own account certainly reflects a Christian perspective, it still should be judged by its ability to interpret and make sense of human religious experience in general. Climacus sees that experience as marked by a quest for ethical character and eternal life, and he sees those goals as intertwined.

It is worth noting that the account that Climacus gives of the religious life in *Postscript* coheres in many ways with the account Kierkegaard gives under his own name in the early *Upbuilding Discourses*. These early devotional writings of Kierkegaard, while religious in character, do not have the specifically Christian and polemical character of much of his later writings. Many of these essays develop the theme that the development of genuine "inwardness" in a person is a process that also involves the development of a knowledge of God and a relation to God. To cite just one example, in "To Need God Is a Human Being's Highest Perfection" Kierkegaard tries to show how a person who truly comes to know himself, and understands his complete dependence on God, thereby must know God as well. The person who comes to know God in this way can acquire a "decisive certitude that God *is*" (EUD, 322).

RELIGIOUS LIFE AND THE NEGATIVITY OF EXISTENCE

We have already seen that the transition from what Kierkegaard calls the ethical life to the religious life hinges on the recognition of brokenness and a need for healing in the self. The ethical life from the beginning involves a kind of implicit awareness of God. However, God is known in a different way when the self comes to understand itself not merely as striving to become the self God requires one to be, but as a self that needs God's help to carry out the task. Climacus gives an account of what he calls "Religiousness A" which is basically the story of how that deeper form of religiousness emerges from the ethical task.

In general the religious life sketched is a progressive deepening of the individual's quest for the highest good, an eternal happiness, or God-relation. (As we have just seen, these are all equivalent for Climacus.) Climacus proceeds to discuss three "moments" of this deepening religious life, characterized as the "initial," "essential," and "decisive" expressions of the religious life, and these turn out to be, respectively, resignation, suffering, and guilt. I will proceed to discuss each of these in some detail, but first one may ask why the religious life is described in such apparently negative and gloomy terms.

The short answer is that the negativity is demanded by the structure of human existence itself. I have at several points discussed the idea that for Kierkegaard human existence is a never-finished (in this life) process in which a person attempts to synthesize the temporal and the eternal.[14] One way the unfinished character of human existence manifests itself is precisely by negativity. A human exister who is fully "positive" would be a person who has completely arrived at the goal of existence and has no room for improvement, but no actual human being may dare to be at such a place. There is always a gap between our ideals and our actuality, a gap that demands a continual negation of the status quo and a willingness to move further towards the ideal. Thus, Climacus says that "*[in] his existence-relation to the truth, the existing subjective thinker is just as negative as positive, . . . and is continually in a process of becoming, that is, striving*" (CUP, 80; italics original).

This is true of existing human life as a whole but it is particularly true of religious existence. It is true that religious existence contains a kind of positivity, a new pathos, a higher form of "immediacy." However, this positivity is distinguished from the passion of the aesthetic life by the way it is conditioned by the negative: "[R]evelation is recognizable by mystery, blessedness by suffering, faith's certainty by uncertainty, easiness by difficulty, truth by absurdity; if this is not held fast, then the aesthetic and the religious run together in a common confusion" (CUP, 432a). Climacus uses a memorable if somewhat repugnant image to drive this point home. The existing individual must not allow the "wound of existence" to scab over, but must "keep the wound open" to make spiritual health possible (CUP, 85).

RESIGNATION: THE INITIAL EXPRESSION OF RELIGIOUS PATHOS

There is a certain formal character to the description of the religious life that Climacus provides in *Postscript*. Although most of his examples are taken from the Christian culture he knows, it is important to recognize the abstract character of the categories he uses. This abstractness entails the possibility of giving examples taken from other cultures with different religious traditions. Climacus certainly seems to think of "the absolute" as

---

[14] See pp. 47–52.

God, for example, but the highest good might well be understood differently in a non-theistic context. It is an open question how well the categories work when applied to these other religious traditions, but it is clear that Climacus wants to leave such possibilities open.

The religious life begins, as we have seen, with the task of seeking a "highest good" or "absolute telos." The person who is seeking such a good is described by Climacus as having "an absolute relation to the absolute" while maintaining a "relative relation to the relative" (CUP, 387). This formula could in fact be used as a general description of the natural religious life for humans.

But what does this mean? Climacus says that the test for whether a person is in fact absolutely committed to the absolute is what happens when there is a conflict between the absolute and some relative good that the person is committed to. A person who is unwilling to give up a relative good for the sake of the absolute thereby shows that he or she is not absolutely committed to the absolute. Thus, his "initial" description of the religious life uses the category of "resignation."

The contrast to resignation is a term taken from the Danish followers of Hegel: mediation. Mediation represents a "revolt of the relative ends against the majesty of the absolute, which is supposed to be dragged down to the level of everything else, and against the dignity of the human being, who is to be made a servant solely of the relative ends" (CUP, 419). Climacus here tells us that the mindset associated with mediation wants an absolute relation to the absolute but wants it to be included as "one more thing." Such a person wants to be successful in business, to be recognized as talented, to have a happy and comfortable family life, and *also* to be religious.

One might ask what is wrong with such a view? After all, human beings do care about such things as careers and families and homes. Why should a person not want such things *along with* a relation to God (or whatever the absolute telos is understood to be)? After all, there seems no reason to think that an absolute good will necessarily conflict with such relative goods.

Climacus does not assume that an absolute telos will necessarily conflict with any particular relative good. It is for that reason that the task of resignation is described hypothetically: it is a willingness to give up the relative for the sake of the absolute when this is called for. The possibility of such a conflict is important to him, however, since a person can only show that he or she has the right kind of relation to the absolute through a willingness to renounce the relative for the sake of the absolute.

Mediation is a Kierkegaardian term for the kind of perspective on decision-making that informs modern economic theory, or what is sometimes called "rational-choice theory." Time, energy, and economic resources are always finite, and the rational person, on this kind of economic model, allocates those resources appropriately. The assumption that lies behind such a model is that there is a qualitative similarity between the goods that are being compared, an assumption that is made explicit when a monetary value is assigned. Imagine a married couple who decide not to have children because the expense of raising a child would not allow them to buy the kinds of autos they wish to have or travel to the kinds of places they wish to travel. With respect to goods that are truly relative, Climacus believes that such decision-making is permissible and even unavoidable (CUP, 400). However, a person who lives only in this fashion has no real identity as a self; he or she is literally for sale, since there is no commitment that could not be undone if sufficient compensation were offered.

It is for this reason that Climacus thinks that mediation robs human beings of dignity. Our sense of who we are as human selves requires some commitments that cannot be bartered in this way, some things that a person simply would not do for any price. Some of the things we value are "pearls of great price" that are simply incommensurable with other goods and cannot be put into some kind of calculus that assumes some common scale of values whereby they are to be ranked.

The idea here is related to one contemporary philosophers have discussed under various labels, which is that it is a distinctive characteristic of human beings that they do not merely have desires but are capable of evaluating the worth of those desires and ranking them qualitatively. Harry Frankfurt, for example, distinguishes between first-order desires and second-order desires.[15] An alcoholic may have a first-order desire to have a drink, but also may have a second-order desire not to have that desire to drink. He wishes to be free of the powerful desires that he sees as enslaving and degrading. Frankfurt labels a person who lacks such second-order desires as a "wanton."

Similarly, Charles Taylor distinguishes between what he calls strong and weak evaluation.[16] A weak evaluator has desires and makes choices on

---

[15] Harry Frankfurt, "Freedom of the Will and the Concept of a Person," *Journal of Philosophy* 67:1 (Jan. 1971), pp. 5–20.

[16] Charles Taylor, "What is Human Agency?" in *Human Agency and Language: Philosophical Papers Volume I* (Cambridge: Cambridge University Press, 1985), pp. 15–44.

the basis of those desires, and even has the ability to make calculative judgments about the most efficient way to achieve those desires over the long run, forgoing short-term satisfactions for greater long-run happiness. However, a strong evaluator is someone who takes into account the qualitative worthiness of the desires themselves, and Taylor argues that strong evaluation is what distinguishes human beings from other animals. The rejection of mediation in *Postscript* is simply an emphatic version of such a view, one that holds that "strong evaluation" requires that there is some good that simply cannot be considered as one good among others. This requires that there be some things that a person simply would not do for any price.

Mediation, in addition to taking the form of a finitizing of the absolute, can also take the form of making the absolute into an abstraction with no content, an empty phrase that merely sanctifies a person's existing relative commitments by regarding them as the expression of the absolute:

Mediation either allows the relation to the absolute telos to be mediated into relative ends, whereby it becomes relative itself, or it allows the relation to the absolute telos as an abstraction to exhaust itself in relative ends as the predicates, whereby the majesty of the absolute relation is reduced to something meaningless, becomes an ostentatious introduction to life that nevertheless remains outside life, like a title page that is not included when the book is bound. (CUP, 405)

Unless the absolute telos has some content it will be just such an abstraction. If it does have some content, then the possibility of a conflict between this good and other goods is necessarily present, and this possibility will reveal whether the absolute is really absolute.

SUFFERING: THE ESSENTIAL EXPRESSION OF RELIGIOUS PATHOS

Resignation is the task that defines whether an individual truly has an "absolute relation to the absolute and a relative relation to the relative." However, to describe the task as one of resignation is to give a kind of idealized description of it. Actual human beings, according to Climacus, are not ideal beings however. In reality we are all captured by relative ends; our lives are dominated by our desires for such things as good health, successful careers, satisfying families, desirable material possessions. We are so attached to such things that we are unwilling to resign them for the sake of the absolute good when this is required. Therefore, actually achieving resignation requires individuals to loosen the hold that these relative goods have on them. Climacus describes this process as "dying to immediacy" or "dying to self" and he recognizes that this is painful for creatures such as ourselves. The religious life is thus essentially a life of suffering.

It is easy to misunderstand what this means. Religious suffering must be distinguished from aesthetic suffering, just as eternal happiness (*Salighed*) must be distinguished from aesthetic unhappiness (*Ulyksalighed*). Religious suffering thus must not be identified with the person who has had the misfortune to suffer illness, loss of loved ones, financial disaster, or other such things. Rather, religious suffering is a task that is universal. Ordinary human sufferings can contribute to this task, if a person understands the sufferings rightly and responds to them correctly; to that degree Climacus recognizes the common view that religion can be fostered by ordinary human suffering and can be a way to give meaning to such suffering.

It is not surprising that the shock of losing a job or experiencing a life-threatening illness can give a person a new perspective on the value of the relative things that fill our lives. A country and western song popular in the United States, sung by Tim McGraw, expresses this idea perfectly. The singer, who has been diagnosed with a terminal illness, suddenly gains a new perspective on life and actually wants his friends to share this new perspective: "I hope that you someday will have the chance to live like you were dying." However, merely enduring ordinary suffering is not the same as the achievement of religious suffering.

Nor should religious suffering be identified with self-punishment or ascetic practices that are often associated with religion. "Suffering as dying to immediacy is, therefore, not flagellation and things like that; it is not *self-torment*" (CUP, 463). Explaining why this is so gives a good deal of insight into what Climacus has in mind by "dying to self." To give the explanation we must give some attention to the meaning of the Danish term for suffering (*Lidelse*).

Lidelse has as its root the verb *at lide* ("to suffer"), just as is the case for the corresponding English terms. The Danish verb *at lide* has, however, a double meaning that "to suffer" originally also had but has now largely lost. *At lide* means not only to suffer in the sense of having a painful experience, but "to let, to allow, to take up a passive attitude towards something." Thus, in Danish one says that one likes something by saying that one "kan lide" it, literally meaning that one can suffer it, can accept it or receive it. At the time of the King James Bible, the English "to suffer" had the same range of meanings, as in Mark 10:14: "Suffer the little

children to come unto me." This is of course translated in more contemporary versions as "Let the little children come to me."

Thus, when Climacus says that the religious task is one of suffering, he
does not merely mean that it involves pain, though it does, but that it
requires a person to recognize the limits imposed by their creatureliness,
to understand what is within a person's power and what must be accepted
as something one cannot control. At this point the theistic context Climacus presupposes becomes more prominent. Though human persons
may have the illusion that they are autonomous, "self-made men," in
reality we are all completely dependent on a reality outside and beyond
ourselves that we cannot control. Climacus expresses this by saying that
the religious task is to learn that "without God a person can do nothing."
I cannot simply by willing guarantee that my body will not be paralyzed
in the next moment or that the air I need to breathe will continue to be
healthy and pure. If we are the creations of God it is literally true that
without God's creative and sustaining power human beings would not
exist, would be nothing at all. The recognition of my nothingness before
God and complete dependence upon God is essentially to recognize that
God is God and I am not. It is in fact a form of worship, since worship is
at bottom a recognition and affirmation of the greatness of God.

We can now understand why religious suffering is not equivalent to
some kind of ascetic self-torture, whether the self-torment is physical or
psychological. The person who thinks that he or she can achieve something of real value through such activity is still under the illusion that he
or she has some kind of autonomous power. Such a person has not
learned that genuine religious suffering is simply identical with an
understanding of one's complete dependence on God.

Climacus adds an extended discussion of monasticism at this point,
since that is a form of life within Christian culture that attempts actively
to achieve a form of resignation through disciplined practices, often of an
ascetic character. Climacus is critical of monasticism, on the grounds that
it is misguided to think that any particular form of "outward life" can
adequately express religious suffering. He sees the monastic life as a
"desperate attempt" to find a way to express religious passion in a superior
form of life (CUP, 492–493). It is worth noting, however, that this
criticism is accompanied by genuine respect; the middle ages, he says, at
least showed passion by their embrace of monasticism, something that the
"mediation" of contemporary "Christendom" notably fails to exhibit.

That Climacus is trying to emphasize the recognition of one's
dependence on God as the heart of religious suffering is made clear in

several ways. First, there is a long (perhaps too long) discussion of an individual who is considering going for an outing in the Deer Park, a park north of Copenhagen that includes an amusement park called Bakken (CUP, 467–497). This seems an innocent-enough diversion, but the difficulty of the task stems from the fact that it is just such situations that tempt us humans into the illusion that we are autonomous creatures who can do quite a lot of things by ourselves. The religious hero for Climacus is an individual who recognizes his human need for such a diversion, overcomes the illusion that this is something he can do all by himself, and nevertheless manages to do it, because the recognition that a person can do nothing apart from God goes hand in hand with an understanding that with God's help there are indeed things that can be done. Furthermore, the religious individual does not shrink from such things as innocent amusements:

> Our religious person chooses the way to the Deer Park, and why? Because he does not dare to choose the way to the monastery . . . "But he does not enjoy himself," someone may say. Yes, he does indeed. And why does he enjoy himself? Because it is the humblest expression of the God-relationship to admit one's humanness, and it is human to enjoy oneself. (CUP, 493)

Paradoxically, the religious life of suffering turns out to be a life that can encompass enjoyment.

The other paradox Climacus highlights is that the "passivity" inherent in religious suffering turns out to be a form of activity:

> Now, to act (*at handle*) might appear to be just the opposite of to suffer (*at lide*), and to that degree it might seem strange to say that the essential expression of existential pathos (which is acting) is suffering. But this is only apparently so, and once more the religious sphere's recognizable characteristic – that the positive is distinguished by the negative – shows itself: . . . that to act religiously is marked by suffering. (CUP, 432)

The religious life is marked by a painful recognition of one's finitude and acceptance of dependency, but the achievement of this recognition in a "pathos" (something we would probably today call an emotion) is nevertheless an active achievement.

IRONY AND HUMOR IN THE RELIGIOUS LIFE

As noted above, Climacus rejects monasticism because he does not think that the religious life necessarily expresses itself in any specific outward form. Instead, he defends what he calls "hidden inwardness," a religious stance about which Kierkegaard himself later expresses suspicion.[17] Nevertheless, Climacus does think that the religious person may be recognizable through what he calls "humor," which can function as the "incognito" or "outward costume" of the truly religious person. In a similar way, irony functions as the incognito of the ethical individual for Climacus. Before completing my discussion of the description of the religious form of existence, I would like therefore to pause to consider the nature of humor and irony in *Postscript* as well as Kierkegaard's writings more generally.[18]

Climacus describes irony and humor in connection with his account of the three spheres of existence: "There are three existence-spheres: the aesthetic, the ethical, the religious. To these there correspond two border territories: Irony is the border territory between the aesthetic and the ethical; Humor the border territory between the ethical and the religious" (CUP, 501–502). Irony and humor are for Kierkegaard existential standpoints, rather than merely something to be found in literature or expressed in jokes. Furthermore, they are transitional standpoints, perspectives where an individual sees the problems with one lifeview and thus has another lifeview open up as a possibility.

These standpoints have something peculiarly intellectual about them. Both irony and humor presuppose a certain degree of reflection on the part of an individual, and thus are only possible for a person who has a certain level of education and cultural formation. Irony therefore requires a kind of superior standpoint, and this feature of it is captured in the ordinary literary sense of irony as speech in which one says something that actually undermines the surface meaning of what is said. Kierkegaard does not use "irony" to refer only to a mode of speech, however, but a mode of existence which characteristically expresses itself in ironical speech.

It is important, however, to distinguish the existential ironist from what Kierkegaard calls relative irony. Existential irony, for instance, as the "border territory" between the aesthetic and the ethical, is rooted in a

---

[17] See Chapter 8, pp. 191–193, for a brief discussion of this.

[18] For a fuller account see my "Irony and Humor: Some Boundary Situations," Chapter 10 of *Kierkegaard's* Fragments *and* Postscript: *The Religious Philosophy of Johannes Climacus* (Atlantic Highlands, New Jersey: Humanities Press, 1983), pp. 185–205 (reprinted by Humanity Books, an imprint of Prometheus Press). Also, see my "Kierkegaard's View of Humor: Must Christians Always Be Solemn?" *Faith and Philosophy* (4,2: 1987), pp. 176–186, reprinted in *Kierkegaard on Faith and the Self* (Waco, Texas: Baylor University Press, 2006), pp. 81–91. John Lippitt gives an excellent book-length treatment in *Humour and Irony in Kierkegaard's Thought* (Basingstoke: Palgrave Macmillan, 2000).

kind of knowledge of the ethical. An "ironist" in this sense is a person who sees through the relative value of the things that captivate most people, by comparing them to the ethical ideal, and thus might speak ironically about the things that most people value absolutely. This kind of ironist should be distinguished from the "relative ironist," who undermines the values and perspectives of one social group on the basis of another, supposedly higher group, as when a person from a large city, such as Dallas, looks down on the values of someone from a small Texas town. Such a relative ironist can of course in turn be looked down upon by an inhabitant of a yet more cosmopolitan city such as New York or London. The true ironist is someone who sees through the pretensions of all such relative values. Climacus comments on the way this irony will be reflected in the speech of this kind of individual: "The irony appears by continually placing the particulars of the finite beside the infinite ethical requirement and allowing the contradiction to come into existence" (CUP, 502).

The "contradiction" referred to here is the basic incongruity that Kierkegaard describes in all his writings as present at the heart of human existence. I shall here continue to exposit this theme as it appears in *Postscript* but I could easily make the same points by discussing such works as *The Concept of Anxiety* or *The Sickness Unto Death*. It is obvious that Climacus does not mean to refer to a logical contradiction here, in which the same proposition is both affirmed and denied, but rather to a tension that lies at the heart of human experience.[19] Human existence is described as a never-finished attempt to synthesize the infinite and the finite, the eternal and the temporal, the possible and the necessary. Since the synthesis is never fully realized, the union of the two contrasting elements is never complete; some tension or "contradiction" always remains, and an awareness of this tension is the mark of the existential ironist.

One might say here that irony is a kind of intellectual recognition of the demands of the ethical and the inadequacy of aesthetic immediacy. Such a recognition makes possible a transition to ethical existence. However, for Kierkegaard existential growth is never something purely intellectual, but requires the engagement of the passions.[20] Thus, we can understand the

---

[19] It is very important to keep in mind this usage of the term "contradiction" when we go on to discuss Kierkegaard's view of the incarnation as "the absolute paradox" which involves a "contradiction." I will discuss this in Chapter 7.

[20] See Chapters 2 and 3, pp. 32–35 and 46–52, for fuller discussion of this point.

"in-between" character of irony as an intellectual standpoint on the verge of ethical commitment. Since existential development is not a "once-for-all" kind of thing but the kind of achievement that must be renewed to be sustained, we can also see why irony remains a constant possibility for the ethical individual; we can always find ourselves with a degree of understanding that is not embodied in our actual lives.

Climacus describes irony as a form of "self-assertion," and it is therefore something that separates individuals as individuals, unlike humor, which is said to be "sympathetic" and therefore something that binds people together (CUP, 553). Irony is "separative" in the sense that it allows an individual to distinguish herself from the immediate values that a person absorbs simply by being socialized into a particular culture. One might go so far as to say that irony is a way of discovering the self as an individual rather than simply a product of the social order.

How does such an ironist differ from the humorist? Somewhat surprisingly, Climacus thinks that there is a close connection between humor and the religious life. This is surprising because our culture tends to stereotype religious people as dour and joyless, but Climacus thinks that this is not correct. Just as irony represents a kind of intellectual recognition of the ethical demands of the eternal, humor represents a kind of intellectual recognition of a religious standpoint. And it is worth pointing out that Climacus' view here is shared by Kierkegaard himself, who says in his *Journals* that "the humorous is present throughout Christianity" and that Christianity is the most humorous view of life to be found in world history.[21]

The concept of humor is explicated in terms of the related concept of the comic. A humorist is a person who has mastered the comic; this is so because humor "has the comic *within itself*" (CUP, 521; italics original). The comic is in turn explained by contrasting it with the tragic. Both the tragic and the comic contain a recognition of the "contradiction" that lies within human existence, but *"the tragic is the suffering contradiction, the comical the painless contradiction"* (CUP, 514; italics original). Both a tragic and a comic apprehension of life see the incongruity between the ideals we humans strive for and the actuality of our lives, but the former experiences this tension as painful while the latter does not.

Climacus goes on to illustrate his account of the comic by a lengthy footnote going on for several pages that consists almost wholly of jokes

---

[21] *Søren Kierkegaard's Journals and Papers*, 7 vols., ed. and trans. Howard V. Hong and Edna H. Hong (Bloomington, Indiana: Indiana University Press, 1967–78), Vol. II, entries 1681 and 1682.

and descriptions of comic situations. My favorite is the story of the German-Danish clergyman who, confused by the false cognate between the German *Fleisch* (flesh) and the Danish *Flæsk* (pork), mounts the pulpit and solemnly announces, on the basis of the first chapter of John's Gospel, that the "Word has become pork" (CUP, 514n–519n). Many of these situations, like this one, might well have been painful rather than funny at the time, especially for some individuals, such as the clergyman in the above example. However, this fact actually supports what Climacus wants to maintain about the comic. In order to experience a contradiction as painless and therefore comic, a person needs some way of canceling the painfulness of the situation. Climacus says such a person must have "a way out," must be able to distance himself from the pain by occupying a "higher standpoint" (CUP, 520).

We can now understand why humor is associated with religious existence by Climacus (and Kierkegaard). We have already seen that the religious life is linked to suffering, and in the next section I shall look at the religious life as providing an answer to the problem of guilt. But suffering and guilt are simply forms of passion that embody an understanding of what Climacus calls "the contradiction" in human existence. Insofar as religion provides a "healing word" for these passions it offers us a way of reconciling ourselves with the pain of that existence. Climacus thinks that all forms of human religiousness are attempts to provide such a healing word. The person who has a kind of "knowledge" of the religious view thus stands on the boundary of the religious life, much as the ironist who has a knowledge of the ethical stands on the boundary of the ethical life.

We can also understand why humor, in contrast to irony, is "sympathetic." It brings individuals together rather than pulls them apart, because the humorist sees all human beings as having a common plight. "We all get equally far," says Climacus (CUP, 450), and the relative differences in our achievements are insignificant. All of us fall short of the ideal, but the religious person nevertheless has hope that there is some way in which the problem of guilt can be resolved. A knowledge of this resolution allows one to smile at life and not simply see it as tragic or absurd.

Such a humorist can never take himself too seriously. Climacus, who describes himself as a humorist, illustrates this by a claim that the humorist always "revokes" the significance of what he does (CUP, 447). However strenuous his ethical-religious efforts, such a person still embodies a kind of playfulness, and Climacus, in a manner quite consistent with this playfulness, "revokes" what he has written at the end of *Postscript* (CUP, 617–623).[22]

This humoristic perspective is the "incognito" of the truly religious individual, because such an individual rejects any prideful assertion of his or her superiority to others. Regardless of what I have achieved, the healing of the contradiction that allows me to affirm my existence in a way that transcends tragedy is not due to my own efforts, but to the religious solution to the problem of guilt. Here "the eternal" is not merely the ethical demand, but is in some way also that which provides a way for us to be reconciled to that demand.

Since humor may be both the stance of a person who is on the border of the religious life as well as the "incognito" of a truly religious person, it is legitimate to ask whether the two characters can be distinguished. At least from a third-person perspective, it is hard to see how this is possible. And if that is the case, one may well wonder whether the self-description of Climacus as a humorist means that he is on the edge of the religious life, or whether the humor he displays is a costume that hides a genuinely religious person who modestly refuses to present himself as such.

GUILT: THE DECISIVE EXPRESSION OF THE RELIGIOUS LIFE

The description of religious life as "Religiousness A" that Climacus offers is one that has a "backward" direction. He begins with the ideal account of religious existence as resignation, in which a person seeks an absolute relation with the absolute and a relative relation to the relative. However, the person who embarks on such a task finds that the religious life requires the achievement of "suffering," because the person is enmeshed in the relative and must "die to immediacy" and recognize the absolute dependence on God or the eternal. Once more, however, the individual who embarks on this task will discover new failures. All of us fail in some ways to achieve the proper standpoint in relation to the eternal. If we understand this theistically, as Climacus does, it means that we fail to acknowledge our dependence on God and succumb to the illusion that we are autonomous individuals.

What is the nature of the guilt that an honest religious person confronts? Before answering this question, I shall first try to say why

---

[22] For a good discussion of what this "revocation" does and does not mean, see John Lippitt, *Humour and Irony in Kierkegaard's Thought*, pp. 47–71.

Climacus thinks humans are in fact guilty. Climacus does not present arguments that all humans are guilty; rather he assumes that all of us are and that the evidence for this is the consciousness of guilt found in each of us. He does not mean that feelings of guilt are always reliable indicators of actual guilt about particulars; it is possible for a person to feel guilty for something that the individual is not really responsible for or which is not genuinely a failing. However, even if feelings of guilt sometimes are inaccurate, the fact that we have an awareness of guilt itself shows that, taken as a whole, our lives are not innocent. Hence, even an attempt to justify oneself with respect to some particular act reveals an acquaintance with guilt that a truly innocent person would not possess (CUP, 528).

The judgment that human existers are guilty is for Climacus a "qualitative" rather than a quantitative claim. Guilt for him is not a matter of "more or less" but reflects a kind of verdict: guilty or not guilty. Either we measure up to the standard or we do not, and he thinks that our existential awareness of guilt shows that each of us understands the truth at some level, though this does not mean we have a correct understanding of the nature of our guilt.

It is now time to say something about the nature of that guilt. Climacus begins by distinguishing a proper religious conception of guilt from lower, inadequate conceptions. The way in which a person understands her failure to realize some ideal obviously depends on the nature of the ideal. There is therefore a temptation for humans to do what John Hare has called "reducing the demand."[23] Climacus ranks various conceptions of guilt by looking at what they accept as a solution to the problem, what counts as "making satisfaction" for guilt.

Someone who thinks of civil punishment as the proper solution for guilt obviously makes the moral-religious standard too low, for it is easy for a person to fail to break the laws of a state and still fail miserably to be what he should be as human being (CUP, 541). A second inadequate conception is what Climacus calls the "aesthetic-metaphysical" conception of guilt, in which it is assumed that people "get what is coming to them," and thus such things as natural disasters are deserved punishments (CUP, 541–542). It is pretty obvious that such a perspective on guilt is mistaken, since it is empirically evident that such misfortunes happen to the good and the bad.

---

[23] John Hare, *The Moral Gap* (Oxford: Clarendon Press, 1996), pp. 142–169.

A somewhat higher conception of guilt is expressed in the practice of "penance," in which there is some self-inflicted punishment. Here what Climacus says parallels his earlier discussion of monasticism. In comparison with the complacency of contemporary Christendom, Climacus praises the practice of penance, both within and outside of Christendom, as "a childlike and enthusiastic venture in greatness" (CUP, 542). Nevertheless, in the end he claims that the highest religious conception of guilt is one that understands that there is no "solution" within our human powers. There is ultimately nothing humans can do that perfectly repairs their relation to God, and therefore their relation to their own task.

This impossibility again tempts us to excuse ourselves by confounding guilt with finitude. Climacus says that since guilt is embedded in the actual way a human being exists, it is tempting for a person "to shove the guilt away from himself onto existence, or onto the one who placed him in existence, and so be without guilt" (CUP, 528). Such a maneuver confuses guilt with suffering, which does indeed have its basis in the ontological gulf between creature and creator. Guilt, however, is not simply finitude; it stems from the way we live our finitude, and Climacus thinks that none of us can have any assurance that we have properly lived up to the ideal, however that may be understood.

One might think that if guilt is universal and pervasive, and if there is nothing humans can do to make satisfaction for guilt, then the outcome would be despair. However, Climacus says that despair is "the infinite, the eternal, the total in the moment of impatience," and it is thus a kind of "ill temper" (CUP, 554). The recollection of guilt in the religious individual is yet another example of the way in which in the religious life "the positive is recognizable by the negative." In some way the religious individual's honest recognition of guilt, in which he understands how far removed he actually is from an eternal happiness (or the God-relation that is the realization of this happiness), nevertheless is at the same time the basis of a relationship to that good. "No, the eternal recollection is a mark of the relation to an eternal happiness, as far away as possible from being a direct mark, but nevertheless always sufficient to prevent the shift to despair" (CUP, 554).

The guilt-consciousness of Religiousness A has only "an obscurely sensed possibility" that there is some solution to the problem of guilt, a possibility that rests in the "underlying immanence" in which the individual grasps the eternal (CUP, 541). Religiousness A here seems to resemble the religion of reason described by Kant in *Religion Within the Limits of Reason Alone*, in which the individual must hope that God will in some way do what is necessary to resolve the problem of guilt even if we do not know what that is.[24]

Climacus once more makes it clear that this account of the religious life, though it fits the experience of many within Christendom, is intended to apply outside of Christianity as well:

Someone existing religiously can express his relation to an eternal happiness (immortality, eternal life) outside Christianity, and this has certainly happened, since one must say about Religiousness A that even if it had not been present in paganism it could have been, because it has only common human nature as its presupposition. (CUP, 559)

This is most emphatically not true for Christianity, however, and it is to Kierkegaard's understanding of Christian existence that I will turn in the next chapter. However, it is now clear why his quest to understand what can be done to become a Christian has taken him on this tour through the religious life. The person who is in the grip of Religiousness A and understands his life as guilty seems perfectly placed to hear the proclamation of the Christian gospel of forgiveness.

---

[24] Immanuel Kant, *Religion Within the Limits of Reason Alone*, trans. Theodore M. Greene and Hoyt H. Hudson (New York: Harper and Row, 1960), p. 134.

CHAPTER 7

Christian existence: Faith and the paradox

In Chapter 1 of this book I argued that Kierkegaard's claim that his authorship should be understood as one devoted to the service of Christianity is defensible, and that this provides a valuable standpoint for reading that authorship. However, I also claimed that for Kierkegaard the primary problems that modern intellectuals have with Christian faith stem from a failure to understand the nature of human existence, and thus Kierkegaard saw the need to tackle once more the basic questions about existence. Christianity is itself a way of existing, and it is an answer to questions posed by human existence. Those who do not understand the questions will not grasp the significance of any purported answers to those questions. So, even though Kierkegaard's own motivation may have been in the service of Christianity, the descriptions Kierkegaard offers about the structure of human existence as well as the "spheres" of existence are of interest to those who do not share his Christian faith.

Much of what Kierkegaard has to say is therefore interesting to different people for different kinds of reasons. For example, his description of the natural religious life that I examined in the previous chapter will be interesting to people who want to understand the phenomenon of religiousness, regardless of their own religious standpoint. However, Kierkegaard's pseudonym Johannes Climacus presents his own analysis of "Religiousness A" as part of a general quest to understand how it is possible for an individual to become a Christian and what this might mean.

The main difference between Religiousness A and Christianity, which Climacus calls "Religiousness B" in *Postscript*, is that Religiousness A is a religion of "immanence," presupposing only the natural concepts and emotions that are possible for human beings on the basis of their own reason and experiences. Christianity, on the other hand, is supposed to be a religion of "transcendence," meaning that it claims to be rooted in a revelation from God that humans could not have discovered or invented using their own powers. Climacus makes the point by saying that

Christianity has a "dialectical" element that is lacking in Religiousness A (CUP, 556). In clearer language this is simply a claim that Christianity has a particular kind of intellectual content that stems from the revelation that is its basis.[1] Religiousness A is also said to be dialectical, in the sense that it can and should inspire reflective thought about human attempts to relate to an eternal happiness (CUP, 559). However, Christianity (or "Religiousness B") is dialectical in a new sense, in that "the eternal" in Christianity is itself dialectically qualified. In Christianity humans must not only think hard about how to relate to an eternal happiness, but the eternal happiness to which they must relate is intellectually qualified in ways that create new problems for thought, although the task is not primarily intellectual but one of developing an existential pathos for living that is qualified by this dialectical content (CUP, 556).

The particular way in which Kierkegaard understands Christianity (assuming as I do that Climacus' descriptions of Christianity are ones that Kierkegaard himself endorses) gives his discussions of it genuine philosophical interest, even to those who may be followers of other religions or who have no religious faith at all. Clarifying the nature of Christian faith requires Kierkegaard to examine the nature of human reason and to inquire as to whether there are limits to human reason. It also requires him to think hard about the nature of an alleged divine revelation and how a genuine revelation might be recognized. This issue turns out to be closely related to the question of the relation between the dominant ways of thinking and behaving in a particular society and a dissenting individual.

However, the fact that Christianity has intellectual content and requires thought about such questions does not mean that Christian faith is understood in Kierkegaard's writings as a primarily intellectual phenomenon. On the contrary, Christian faith is understood to be a passion, a new or higher "second" form of immediacy, what Kierkegaard sometimes calls an "immediacy after reflection," meaning that it is not simply a natural or spontaneous form of immediacy but a quality that must be developed, and that the individual has some role in developing.[2] The

---

[1] Kierkegaard's use of the term "dialectical" is influenced by Hegel at certain points. Hegel uses the term to refer to an intellectual attempt to hold together two opposites without resolution, with the resolution being called "speculation." See Hegel's discussion of this in the *Encyclopedia Logic*, ed. T. F. Geraets, W. A. Suschting, and H. S. Harris (Indianapolis, Indiana: Hackett, 1991), paragraphs 79–82. In Kierkegaard's case, the opposites are often temporality and eternity. My thanks to Merold Westphal for help with this point.

[2] For example, see the description of faith as a "later immediacy" in FT, 82. For a clear description of the immediacy that precedes reflection and that which presupposes reflection and thus is higher, see

person who is a Christian does think differently about herself and her world than the non-Christian, but that is far from the only difference. For Kierkegaard the Christian also has a different emotional configuration; she hopes, fears, and loves different things as a result of being a Christian.

In our culture, one sometimes encounters a simplistic dichotomy between emotion and reason, or between cognition and what psychologists call "affect." From this perspective one might have difficulty understanding how Christian faith could be described as a "passion" or form of immediacy and yet have the intellectual content it has. However, Kierkegaard simply does not see human thinking and emotion as bifurcated in this way. For him our emotions have content; they possess the quality that philosophers call "intentionality," which is the ability of a mental state to refer to or be directed to some object or state of affairs. We do not simply love; we love someone who has particular qualities. When we fear, we fear something or somebody. When we hope, we hope for some particular state of affairs. From this perspective it is not surprising that Christian faith transforms a person's emotional outlook; nor is it odd that a person who experiences Christian emotions necessarily has a different set of beliefs than the person who has other emotions.

Johannes Climacus describes the process by which Christian faith is acquired as one in which the "pathos" of Religiousness A, which Christianity presupposes, is "mixed" with the dialectical content of Christianity to form a new pathos (CUP, 555). In other words, Christianity presupposes the presence of a certain set of emotional concerns in a person, but transforms those concerns by introducing a new way of thinking. In this chapter I shall primarily be concerned with that new way of thinking, and the intellectual problems that Christian faith raises, for this book is an introduction to Kierkegaard as a philosopher. However, it should be kept in mind that for Kierkegaard himself Christian faith is a passion, a new master set of concerns that both gives continuity to a person's life and enables a person to bring some unity to the discordant elements that characterize human existence.

My discussion of Kierkegaard's treatment of Christian faith will be divided into three sections. First, I shall discuss the idea of Christianity as a "religion of transcendence," a religion based on a revelation that is not a merely human product. Second, I shall look at the specific content of that revelation, which for Kierkegaard centers on the incarnation of God in

---

TA, 111. Kierkegaard uses the term "enthusiasm" here rather than "immediacy" but what is referred to is clearly the same.

Jesus of Nazareth, understood as an "absolute paradox" that human reason cannot understand. Finally, I shall look at the question of what it means for a human person to accept Christianity. How does Christian faith arise in a person and what differences are present in a person whose life is shaped by such faith?

CHRISTIANITY AS A REVEALED RELIGION: *THE BOOK ON ADLER*

It is of course a commonplace that Christianity is a "revealed religion," one that claims, like Judaism and Islam, to rest on a revelation from God. Furthermore, Christian theologians and philosophers have long held that not only is Christianity originally the result of a revelation, but that genuine Christian faith is a response to that revelation. Thomas Aquinas, for example, holds that faith is a matter of believing what God has revealed because it is God who has revealed it.[3] In a similar manner, John Locke defines faith as "the assent to any proposition, not thus made out by the deductions of reason, but upon the credit of the proposer, as coming from God in some extraordinary way of communication."[4] As we shall see, Kierkegaard accepts this traditional view of faith, differing from such thinkers as Locke and Aquinas mainly with respect to the question as to whether reason can defend the claim that a particular revelation does indeed stem from God.

Kierkegaard's own characteristic way of expressing the traditional Christian view is to say that Christianity is a religion of "transcendence" and not "immanence." The terms "transcendence" and "immanence" here do not refer to the being of God, but to how God is known by humans. A religion or religious perspective that holds that God can be known through human reason and experience is one that is "immanent," while a religion or perspective that affirms that God must be known through a special revelation in history is "transcendent" because God is known "beyond" or "outside" natural human experience and reflection.

Although this view of faith as acceptance of what God has revealed because God has revealed it is indeed a commonplace in the Christian tradition, by Kierkegaard's day it could no longer be taken for granted, and Kierkegaard recognizes the claim as one that is threatened by modern

---

[3] See *Summa Theologiæ* , trans. Mark D. Jordan (Notre Dame, Indiana: University of Notre Dame Press, 1990), 2–2, 2 A. 1 (pp. 65–68); 2–2, 2, 2 (pp. 69–70); 2–2, 3, A. 1 (pp. 95–96).

[4] John Locke, *An Essay Concerning Human Understanding* (Amherst, New York: Prometheus Press, 1995; originally published 1693), p. 583.

thought. In *Religion Within the Limits of Reason Alone*, Kant had argued that although the truths of religion may originally have been known through a historical revelation, at least a subset of those truths can be known through reason, thus making it unnecessary to hold those truths because they were revealed.[5] Schleiermacher had set himself the task of showing that the insights found in the Bible that stemmed from the religious experiences of ancient peoples could be verified by appealing to the experience of modern people.[6] On such a view the Bible's authority seems subordinated to the authority of the contemporary's experience. Most relevant to Kierkegaard is Hegel's attempt to show that the content of religion, while accessible to faith, is essentially identical to the content of philosophy.[7] On such a view, at least the philosophical intellectual no longer has to be content with faith, but can know that the content of faith is certified by reason.

Kierkegaard's thinking about this issue is seen most clearly in *The Book on Adler*. Adolf Peter Adler was a pastor in the Danish Lutheran Church who claimed to have had a revelation dictated by Jesus, and as a result was eventually removed from his pastorate and pensioned. Kierkegaard was fascinated by the case and thought that the chief problem of the modern age, namely its abandonment of religious authority, could be clearly seen by examining Adler's situation. Kierkegaard produced no fewer than three versions of a book about the case, though he never published any of them, chiefly due to concerns over their effect on Adler as a human being. (Kierkegaard did publish some sections of the book, revised so as not to make any references to Adler, most notably "The Difference Between a Genius and an Apostle.")[8] However, discussions of the importance of divine authority (and the closely related topic of the authority of an "apostle" as someone given authority by God) are by no means limited to *The Book on Adler*, but are pervasive in Kierkegaard's writings.

As Kierkegaard sees things, the attempt by modern philosophy to give rational support to Christian doctrines actually undermines genuine

---

[5] See Kant, *Religion Within the Limits of Reason Alone*, trans. Theodore M. Greene and Hoyt H. Hudson (New York: Harper and Row, 1960), pp. 100–105, and also Kant's "Preface" to the second edition.

[6] See Friedrich Schleiermacher, *The Christian Faith*, ed. and trans. H. R. Mackintosh and J. S. Stewart (Edinburgh: T. and T. Clark, 1928), where throughout Christian doctrines are explained by reference to the "consciousness" or "self-consciousness" of the believer.

[7] See G. W. F. Hegel, *The Christian Religion: Lectures on the Philosophy of Religion, Part III*, ed. and trans. by Peter C. Hodgson (Missoula, Montana: Scholars Press, 1979), especially pp. 289–293.

[8] For a fuller account of Kierkegaard's work on the book and what he did publish, see the "Historical Introduction" by Howard and Edna Hong (BA, vii–xix).

Christianity. If I believe what God has revealed only because I myself have independently investigated matters and found that the doctrines revealed are true, then my belief does not stem from trust in God and thus does not count as genuine faith. Adler, who claimed to have had a revelation, had confusedly argued that his claim was inoffensive because the contents of his revelation were consistent with orthodox Christianity. However, for Kierkegaard, the fact of a revelation claim is decisive on its own, regardless of the contents of the revelation: "the one called by a revelation, to whom a doctrine is entrusted, argues on the basis that it is a revelation, on the basis that he has authority. I am not obliged to listen to Paul because he is brilliant or matchlessly brilliant, but I must submit to Paul because he has divine authority" (BA, 177).[9]

It is of course one thing to claim to speak for God; another actually to possess such divinely delegated authority. How can someone know whether a person who claims to have such authority really does have it? Because of Kierkegaard's aversion to the views of the modern philosophers whom he sees as having undermined divine authority, he says that there is no way for human reason to determine the truth of such revelation claims in any conclusive way. It looks as if a decision to accept or reject a claim to authority has no rational basis at all: "But how, then, can the apostle demonstrate that he has authority? If he could demonstrate it *physically*, he would simply be no apostle ... An apostle has no other evidence than his own statement, and at most his willingness to suffer everything joyfully for the sake of that statement" (BA, 186). In such a situation, it appears that whether a person accepts or rejects a revelation would be completely arbitrary.

However, a closer look shows that Kierkegaard does not really think that there are no criteria to help in recognizing a genuine apostle who possesses divine authority, for in his discussion of Adler, he gives a number of criteria that he claims enable us to recognize the fraudulence of Adler's claim.[10] The first criterion is implicit in the above quote, and it is simply that the one who makes the revelation claim has a clarity about the implications of such a claim and does not confusedly ask for belief on the basis of the brilliance of his argument or the profundity of his rhetoric, thereby confusing a claim to apostolicity with a claim to genius.

---

[9] Since *The Book on Adler* is not contained in Kierkegaard's *Samlede Værker*, I will take all direct quotations from this work from the Hong translation rather than providing my own translations.

[10] All of these are discussed in more detail in my article, "Kierkegaard on Religious Authority: The Problem of the Criterion," *Faith and Philosophy* (17, 1: January, 2000), pp. 48–67.

A second sign of a genuine revelation would be that the bearer of the revelation will rest his case on God's providence, specifically spurning any attempt to use worldly power or influence to insure the success of his cause. Though a genuine apostle might have "power in the worldly sense," meaning that he "had great influence and powerful connections," if he actually used this power "he *eo ipso* would have forfeited his cause" (BA, 186). The genuine apostle has no need to have the support of a human majority; as a person who has been called by God he trusts completely in God's providence for the outcome (BA, 160). He believes that "if everything is in order with his relation to God, his idea will surely succeed, even if he falls" (BA, 157).

Both of these two criteria (which Kierkegaard thinks Adler fails to pass) have more to do with the messenger than the message. However, Kierkegaard also thinks that there is one characteristic of the content of a revelation that one might expect a genuine revelation to possess, and that is that the content of such a revelation would be paradoxical, something that human reason finds baffling, even impossible to understand. That an apostle is sent by God is a paradoxical fact, but the content of the message is essentially paradoxical as well (BA, 187). Odd as it may sound, Kierkegaard takes the fact that the content of a revelation is something reason cannot make sense of to be evidence (rational evidence?) of the genuineness of the revelation.

In the next section I will give a fuller analysis of Kierkegaard's understanding of the Christian revelation as paradoxical. But there is no doubt that he regards paradoxicality as a good and not a defect. That paradoxicalness actually provides support for the genuineness of a revelation is obscured by Kierkegaard's emphasis on the tension between human reason and the paradox, another theme that will be explored later in this chapter. However, in the "Appendix" to Chapter 3 of *Philosophical Fragments* Johannes Climacus makes the point with style that paradoxicalness is a sign of the genuineness of a revelation. This Appendix, titled "An Acoustic Illusion," personifies human reason (called "the Understanding") and revelation (called "the Paradox") and describes the two figures as having a nasty argument that degenerates into name-calling (PF, 49–54). The Understanding dismisses the Paradox as absurd because it cannot understand it. However, the Paradox calmly replies that the fact that the Understanding finds the Paradox absurd is in reality evidence of the genuineness of the Paradox. In fact, the claim made by the Understanding is really an echo of what the Paradox itself has proclaimed. So when the Understanding calls the Paradox absurd, the Paradox responds with its own invective:

> When the Understanding wants to take pity upon the Paradox and help it to an explanation, the Paradox does not put up with it but finds it quite in order for the Understanding to do that, for is that not what our philosophers are for – to make supernatural things ordinary and trivial? When the Understanding cannot get the Paradox into its head, this is not something the Understanding discovered, but rather the Paradox itself, which is paradoxical enough not to be ashamed to call the Understanding a clod and a dunce who at best can say "yes" and "no" about the same thing, which is not good theology. (PF, 53)[13]

The claim that the opacity of a revelation to reason is itself a mark of the genuineness of the revelation is not unique or original to Kierkegaard. For example, Thomas Aquinas offers as a criterion for the genuineness of the Christian revelation the fact that it contains "truths that surpass every human intellect."[11] We would expect a genuine revelation to have such a character, according to Aquinas, because we only know God truly "when we believe him to be above everything that is possible for man to think about him."[12] Such a claim is not as odd as it may initially appear. After all, if a revelation contained only what humans could learn on their own, it might appear to be superfluous. It seems reasonable to think that a genuine revelation from God would contain something that humans could not know without that revelation, perhaps something they cannot fully understand even after it has been revealed.

Kierkegaard also mentions one other criterion, one that he places little weight on, but that has played an important role traditionally in arguments for the authenticity of a revelation. This criterion concerns accompanying miracles, which have often been regarded as the best sign of such authenticity. Kierkegaard puts little stress on miracles, primarily because he claims that since a miracle itself requires faith to accept, miracles cannot provide an epistemic ground for faith. One can only believe in a miracle if one already accepts the miracle as an action coming from God.[13]

I conclude that Kierkegaard's own attempt to provide criteria for the recognition of the genuineness of a revelation shows that reason is not

---

[11] Thomas Aquinas, *Summa Contra Gentiles*, ed. and trans. Anton C. Pegis (Notre Dame, Indiana: University of Notre Dame Press, 1975), p. 72.

[12] Aquinas, *Summa Contra Gentiles*, p. 70.

[13] Kierkegaard's thinking here clearly needs unpacking to be convincing, and I doubt that when unpacked it will be decisive. See my discussion of this issue in "Kierkegaard on Religious Authority," pp. 60–62.

completely shut out of the process, since it is clear that these criteria can only be applied by the use of reason. However, the criteria Kierkegaard offers, even if they are sound, are clearly not going to be decisive in all cases. One can see how they might function well as a negative test; some alleged revelations, such as that of Adler, will fail the tests and thus be shown to be inauthentic. However, it seems very possible for a purported revelation to pass these tests and still not be genuine. One can easily imagine someone who sincerely claims to be a prophet or apostle, but who is deluded. Such a person might well assert divine authority and ask for belief on that basis, rather than reason, and such an individual might offer as the alleged revelation a doctrine that seems paradoxical and opaque to reason. As Kierkegaard himself asserts, commenting on Johannes Climacus' discussion of the paradoxicalness of Christianity, "not every absurdity is the absurd."[14]

So it seems reasonable to think that even if there are criteria that might play some useful role in determining whether an alleged revelation is genuine, satisfying those criteria would be far from a decisive proof. One might think that in the end something like a non-rational choice is necessary, and that is how Kierkegaard is often read. However, such a conclusion would be hasty. To recall the discussion of Kierkegaard's epistemological views from Chapter 3,[15] if we assume the classical foundationalist epistemology dominant in modern philosophy, it looks as if a decision to accept a revelation cannot be made on rational grounds. However, as we saw in that discussion, Kierkegaard brings an entirely different epistemological perspective to these issues. From that perspective, it will turn out to be the case that faith in a revelation is not the kind of thing that is produced by evidence at all, and so the lack of decisive evidence may not be as troublesome as might seem to be the case. To understand Kierkegaard's view of faith and its relation to reason we must give more attention to the content of faith, and thus I shall proceed to look at Kierkegaard's view of Christian faith as centering on the incarnation, understood as "the absolute paradox."

THE INCARNATION AS THE OBJECT OF FAITH: *PHILOSOPHICAL FRAGMENTS* AND THE "ABSOLUTE PARADOX"

Kierkegaard's understanding of the incarnation as "the Absolute Paradox" is developed at some length in *Philosophical Fragments*. *Fragments* is

---

[14] *Kierkegaard's Journals and Papers*, Vol. I, entry 7.   [15] See pp. 55–61.

attributed, as we have noted, to the pseudonymous Johannes Climacus. Again, as noted in Chapter 6,[16] the book takes the form of a thought-experiment, in which Climacus first lays out the logical structure of what he calls the Socratic view of the Truth and how the Truth can be acquired, and then proceeds to "invent" an alternative view, using both the tools of logic and of the imagination.

The logical scaffolding of the two views is laid out in Chapter 1. Since on the Socratic view, humans possess the truth already and only need to "recollect" it, the alternative must deny that humans possess the truth or even the ability or "condition" to gain the truth on their own. On the Socratic view the teacher who helps me understand the Truth turns out to be merely an occasion, a "midwife" who helps me to give birth myself, since what such a teacher helps me to understand is that essentially I possess the Truth already and thus cannot be fundamentally in debt to any other human being. The alternative must then posit a fundamentally different kind of teacher and a fundamentally different relationship between learner and teacher. On the alternative, which we may call the "B hypothesis," the Teacher must be someone who not only brings me the Truth that I lack but fundamentally transforms me by giving me the condition to grasp the Truth. Such a Teacher, according to Climacus, must be God, since such a transformation is equivalent to a re-creation of my being and requires a Creator. Furthermore, if I acquire the Truth from such a Teacher, my relationship to the Teacher will be one in which I am fundamentally dependent on the Teacher. If the God re-creates me and gives me the Truth and the condition for grasping the Truth, the Teacher will not be merely a midwife, but the one to whom I owe everything.

The logical scaffold is filled in with imaginative details in Chapter 2, "The God as Teacher and Savior," subtitled "A Poetical Venture." Here Climacus sketches a story as to how and why "the God" might become the Teacher posited by the B hypothesis in Chapter 1.[17] Since the God does not need human beings, any action to become our teacher must be motivated by a kind of selfless love on the God's part. Once the situation has been characterized as a love affair, Climacus fully engages his imagination by making analogies with human love affairs, though he cautiously warns that these analogies must not be pushed too far, since "no human situation can provide a valid analogy" to the God (PF, 26).

---

[16] See pp. 110–111.

[17] Through the book, Climacus uses the distinctive phrase "the God" (Danish "Guden") to refer to the deity, echoing the way Plato refers to God in his dialogues.

A love affair between unequals is inherently problematic even for human lovers. We understand how difficult it is for a love affair to be successful when one party is rich and one is poor, or one is educated and the other uneducated, or one is powerful and one is powerless. Such inequality is problematic because love demands a kind of equality, in which both parties love the other freely. However, such human inequality cannot even be compared with the inequality between Creator and fallen creature, the one who gives the Truth and the one who is bereft of the Truth. Nevertheless, Climacus uses a human analogy "to awaken the mind to an understanding of the divine" (PF, 26).

The story he uses is the familiar tale of the powerful king who falls in love with a humble maiden. The king has the wealth and power to ensure a match, but he is troubled by a worry "whether the girl would be made happy by this, whether she would win the bold confidence never to remember what the king only wished to forget – that he was the king and she had been only a poor maiden" (PF, 27).

It is not hard to understand the king's worry here. Essentially, it concerns the motivation of the woman to love him. If she marries him out of fear of his power or out of a desire to enjoy his riches, then the king will realize that she does not really love him as a person, but fears his power or loves his resources. Somehow, he must communicate his love to her in a way that allows her to come to know what he is truly like, and that allows her the freedom to respond or to fail to respond. All of us know what the king's solution to the problem will be; he must go and woo the young woman in disguise, putting aside his royal robes and appearing in the form of a peasant on her level. In a similar way the God must descend to the level of the humans he wishes to teach if he wants to consummate his love for them. The difference, according to Climacus, is that the God does not merely put on a disguise, as the king does, but actually takes on human form:

For this is love's unfathomableness, not in jest but in earnestness and truth to will to be the beloved's equal; and resolute, omnipotent love is able to do what neither the king nor Socrates were capable of, which is why the roles they took on were still a kind of deceit. (PF, 32)

Of course the reader will long since have realized that Climacus' "invention" is far from his own creation, but has a suspicious resemblance to some of the central features of Christianity. In case any readers miss this obvious feature, Climacus highlights it by interspersing the comments of an imagined reader, a figure often called "the interlocutor," who interrupts the argument at the end of each chapter. At the conclusion of both of the first two chapters, the interlocutor accuses Climacus of pla- giarism, of putting forth as his own invention something that "any child knows about" already (PF, 35). Climacus responds to this charge with mock shame, but freely concedes the ironical form of the book by admitting that his invention is not his at all. In fact, he goes so far as to suggest that his "poem" is not a human invention at all, but a miracle that comes from the God (PF, 36).

It is transparent that the literary device of "inventing" something that suspiciously resembles Christianity is one that Climacus uses to make points about Christian faith, and he finally admits this straightforwardly at the end of the book. I have already discussed Kierkegaard's own worry that "direct communication" is problematic in cases where moral and religious truth is at stake, since it is so easy to confuse knowledge of propositions with the kind of existential understanding that is at stake. Even though Christian faith does have propositional content, there is an analogous worry here when dealing with Christianity, namely that a scholarly debate about what Christianity is and its relation to philosophy will endlessly postpone the decisions that must be faced by an individual.

Climacus affirms what we might call the uniqueness of Christian faith, which wants to ground the salvation (or "eternal consciousness") of an individual in a relation to particular historical events. Christianity is not merely a set of philosophical doctrines, nor an imaginative mythology, nor a bare set of historical facts (PF, 109). Rather, it is an attempt to view a certain set of historical events as having more than merely historical interest. This Christian idea is one "that has not originated in any human heart" (PF, 109).[18]

The uniqueness of this Christian claim can easily be lost in a com- plicated scholarly discussion about the nature of Christianity:

> The monks never finished narrating the history of the world because they always began with the creation of the world. If in discussing the relation between Christianity and philosophy we begin by narrating what was said earlier, how shall we ever – not finish but even manage to begin, for history just keeps on growing. (PF, 109)

Climacus' solution to the problem is to extract what he takes to be the essential core of Christianity that makes it unique, and present it in the

---

[18] Climacus here alludes to I Corinthians 2:7–9, a passage that Kierkegaard quotes frequently in his writings.

form of a thought-experiment. That the content of the invention is "what every child knows" is a good thing, because it implies that his view of what lies at the core of Christianity – which is that it rests on a story of God becoming a human being in history, an event regarded as decisive for human salvation – is non-controversial. His pretended invention of an alternative to the Socratic picture really does capture something distinctive and essential to Christianity.

THE NATURE OF THE ABSOLUTE PARADOX: WHY IT IS NOT A LOGICAL CONTRADICTION

Kierkegaard is often accused of being an irrationalist on the strength of what he and his pseudonyms (such as Johannes Climacus) say about the incarnation as "the Absolute Paradox." The incarnation understood in this way is called "a contradiction," and belief in such a paradox is belief in "the Absurd." The very encounter with the Paradox brings with it "the possibility of offense," through which an individual must pass to become a Christian. It is not hard to see why such claims have been interpreted as implying that belief in the incarnation is something that is contrary to reason. Herbert Garelick is typical of many commentators who see things this way: "This Paradox is the ultimate challenge to the intellect, for all attempts to understand it must conform to the laws of judgment and discourse: identity, contradiction, and excluded middle. Yet the Paradox violates these laws ... Rationally, the statement 'God-man' is a nonsensical statement."[19]

However, there is also a long and distinguished tradition of commentators who have rejected this reading of Kierkegaard and seen him as claiming that the incarnation is something that is not contrary to reason, but above reason, a mystery that reason cannot comprehend.[20] On such a view, tensions between reason and faith are possible, but there is no inherent or inevitable opposition between them. I shall try to show that

---

[19] Herbert Garelick, *The Anti-Christianity of Kierkegaard* (The Hague: Martinus Nijhoff, 1965), p. 28.
[20] See David Swenson's classic *Something About Kierkegaard*, revised edition (Minneapolis: Augsburg Publishing Co., 1945). Also see Alastair MacKinnon's "Kierkegaard: 'Paradox' and Irrationalism," in *Essays on Kierkegaard*, ed. Jerry Gill (Minneapolis, Minnesota: Burgess Publishing, 1969), pp. 102–112, and his "Kierkegaard's Irrationalism Revisited," *International Philosophical Quarterly*, ix (1969), pp. 165–76. Classic essays by Fabro and Søe can be found in *A Kierkegaard Critique*, ed. Howard Johnson and Niels Thulstrup (New York: Harper and Row, 1962).

this second tradition of interpretation is essentially correct; Kierkegaard is not an irrationalist and in the most important sense he does not think Christian faith is something that is contrary to reason. However, there is an important insight contained in the first type of interpretation as well. Though there is no necessary opposition between faith and reason in Kierkegaard, there is something like a natural tension between them when reason is understood in a certain way. What I shall try to do is to explain how this tension arises, but also try to show how Kierkegaard thinks it is possible for faith and reason to be on good terms.[21]

The view that Kierkegaard thinks that belief in the incarnation is contrary to reason usually rests on an interpretation of the paradoxicalness of the incarnation as resting on a logical contradiction. Clearly, if belief in the incarnation is belief in a formal contradiction, or a belief that entails a formal contradiction, it would indeed be contrary to reason. And Kierkegaard himself, as well as his pseudonym Johannes Climacus, does indeed describe the incarnation as the Absolute Paradox, and explains this by saying it involves a contradiction.

However, it is simply not the case that in Kierkegaard's writings the term "contradiction" (Danish "*Modsigelse*") generally refers to a logical contradiction. We saw in Chapter 6 that Climacus says that both the comic and the tragic have at their root a contradiction, with the comic being a "painless" contradiction and the tragic a "suffering" contradiction (CUP, 514).[22] It is obvious that the tensions and incongruities Climacus has in mind here are not formal contradictions, since contradictory logical formulas are neither funny nor sad. Rather, the "contradictions" in mind here are things like the tension between a young woman's hopes for true love and the deceit of her lover (a tragic contradiction) or the incongruity between the upward gaze of a comedian and his downward ascent when he takes a pratfall (a comic contradiction).

The contradiction found in the incarnation is the contradiction that something that is eternal has become temporal. Very significantly, in *Postscript* Climacus describes human existence itself as embodying this very contradiction: "Existence itself, existing, is a striving and is just as pathos-filled as it is comic; pathos-filled because the striving is infinite, . . . comic because the striving is a self-contradiction" (CUP, 92). A couple of paragraphs later Climacus goes on to explain that the

---

[21] For a fuller account than I can give here, see my "Is Kierkegaard an Irrationalist?" *Religious Studies* 25:3 (1989), pp. 347–62. Reprinted in *Kierkegaard on Faith and the Self*, pp. 117–132.
[22] See pp. 132–134.

contradiction in question is precisely the tension between eternity and temporality in human life: "But what is existence? It is that child who is begotten by the infinite and the finite, the eternal and the temporal, and therefore is constantly striving" (CUP, 92). Ultimately, this structural parallel between the incarnation and human existence is profoundly significant. It helps us understand why Climacus says the incarnation seems to us humans to be "the most improbable" of all things (PF, 52). The claim that Christ is fully God as well as fully human is a claim that a human being as a temporal being can fully embody the perfection of eternity, and that is a claim that all our experience seems to undermine. For all of *us* experience a constant gap, a never-fully-resolved tension, between the eternal ideals we strive for and the reality of our temporal lives, and it is this experiential evidence that helps explain the tension between reason and belief in the incarnation.

However, although our experience gives us inductive, empirical evidence that it is impossible for something to be both eternal and temporal, this evidence is not logically decisive. It may simply reflect the limitations of our human experience. It may appear to us that it is not possible for God to become a human being, but our understanding of what is possible and impossible is relative to the clarity of our conceptual understanding. To know that the concept of the "God-man" is logically contradictory, like the concept of a "square-circle," we would have to have a reasonably clear conception of what it means to be God and what it means to be a human being. Clearly we do have a reasonably clear understanding of what it means for something to be a circle and for something to be a square, and for that reason we can understand why it is not possible for anything to be both. However, Climacus explicitly affirms that we do not have a clear understanding of either God or human nature. Chapter 3 of *Philosophical Fragments* is an extended argument that humans do not have any philosophical knowledge of God. Climacus not only rejects any proofs of God's existence, but even rejects the idea that God can be known negatively by reason as that which is beyond reason. If something is genuinely beyond the limits of reason, then reason simply cannot grasp it.

However, this is true not only for God but for human beings as well. Climacus compliments Socrates for his discovery that human nature itself is paradoxical:

Although Socrates devoted himself with all his power to gather knowledge about humans and to know himself – yes, even though he has been praised for centuries as the person who certainly knew the human – he nevertheless confessed that the reason he had no tendency to think about the nature of such creatures as Pegasus and the Gorgons was that he still was not quite clear about himself, whether he (a person acquainted with the human) was a monster stranger than Typhon or a friendlier and simpler being, by nature sharing something divine (see *Phaedrus*, 229e). (PF, 37)

There is thus a paradoxicalness not only in the incarnation, but in human nature itself. Our ignorance about both God and human nature means that we must be cautious in claiming to know what is possible, especially what is possible for God. Our experience suggests that what is temporal cannot fully realize the perfection of eternity, but it would be rash for us to claim to know this with certainty, since we do not really understand God or what it would be like to be God, nor do we have enough understanding of our own nature to be confident about our intuitive judgments about what is possible and what is not possible for human beings. It may seem or appear to us that an incarnation is impossible, but that is far from a Cartesian "clear and distinct" intuition.

In one crucial passage, Climacus actually distinguishes two different senses of "contradiction," one of which is clearly a formal or logical sense of the term, and asserts that the incarnation is not that kind of contradiction (PF, 101). The passage deals with the question of how faith in the incarnation arises and what a person of faith who is a contemporary of the God's appearance can and cannot do for a person who comes later. Climacus claims, in strict consistency with Christian theology, that faith is a gift from God that no human can give to another. The contemporary who has been given this gift can offer testimony to a person who comes later but cannot directly pass this gift of faith on to another, which must always come from God. The hypothesis that the contemporary could pass along this faith is, according to Climacus, a piece of "meaninglessness," that is "unthinkable *in a different sense* than our stating that that fact [the incarnation itself] and the single individual's relation to the God are unthinkable" (PF, 101; emphasis added). Climacus goes on to explain why this hypothesis is meaningless and unthinkable: "it produces a self-contradiction: that the God is the God for the contemporary, but the contemporary in turn is the God for the third party" (PF, 101). In contrast, the incarnation itself is not logically contradictory: it is true that humans experience it as "the most improbable of all things" and "the strangest of all things," but despite that fact, it is something that "thought is free to preoccupy itself with" (PF, 52; 101).

THE LIMIT OF REASON: FAITH AND OFFENSE
AS RESPONSES TO THE INCARNATION

It might seem that even if the incarnation is not a logical contradiction it is still contrary to reason, given its character as something that appears exceptionally improbable and strange. One might think that what I have called our inductive, experiential evidence that the eternal and temporal cannot be united is enough to show that belief in the incarnation is irrational. However, that is not the way Climacus views things in *Philosophical Fragments*, and it is not the way Kierkegaard himself views the matter. There are a number of significant entries from Kierkegaard's *Journals* in which he identifies the view of Climacus as his own and clearly asserts that the incarnation is above but not necessarily against reason:

The *Absurd*, the *Paradox*, is composed in such a way that reason has no power at all to dissolve it in nonsense and prove that it is nonsense; no, it is a symbol, a riddle, a compounded riddle about which reason must say: I cannot solve it, it cannot be understood, but it does not thereby follow that it is nonsense.[23]

For Kierkegaard, the Paradox is something that lies beyond the limits of reason, but just because it is beyond the limits of reason, reason cannot pronounce upon it. "This is what I have developed (for example, in *Concluding Unscientific Postscript*) – that not every absurdity is the Absurd or the Paradox. The activity of reason is to distinguish the Paradox negatively – but no more."[24]

The argument Climacus develops in *Fragments* centers around this notion of a boundary or limit to reason. The question of whether reason has limits and what those limits might be is itself one of the main questions of philosophy. Immanuel Kant had famously argued that the limits of reason could be recognized by the "antinomies" or apparent contradictions that reason falls into when it exceeds its proper limits.[25] For Kant, reason necessarily forms an Idea of God and seeks to think about the world from this perspective. However, theoretical knowledge is limited to the world of experience, and God transcends such experience, so when we try to gain knowledge of God we find ourselves enmeshed in apparent contradictions, which can only be resolved when the limits of

---

[23] *Kierkegaard's Journals and Papers*, Vol. I, entry 7.
[24] *Kierkegaard's Journals and Papers*, Vol. I, entry 7.
[25] See Chapter 2, Second Division, of Immanuel Kant, *Critique of Pure Reason*, trans. Norman Kemp Smith (London: Macmillan and Co., 1933), pp. 384–484.

reason are acknowledged. The problems reason falls into when it exceeds these limits, says Kant, are "the most fortunate perplexity into which reason could ever have become involved" because it helps us recognize the proper sphere of reason.[26] Kant is careful to argue that reason can form no judgment, positive or negative, about what lies beyond the boundary.[27] It cannot prove the existence of God but this provides no basis for the judgment that God does not exist.[28]

For Climacus the Absolute Paradox seems to function in much the same way. It is the boundary or limit of reason, and when reason attempts to comprehend this limit it finds itself enmeshed in apparent contradictions. However, reason does not necessarily take a negative view of such a limit. Rather, there is what we might call a fundamental ambivalence in reason's attitude toward such a boundary. On the one hand, insofar as the limit is something reason cannot understand, the discovery of such a limit appears to be a defeat for reason. However, Climacus argues that the restless desire to understand and explain that is characteristic of human reason can be viewed as a quest for such a limit. Whenever reason encounters something it does not understand, it is goaded to try to explain and make sense of it. One might say that each time reason encounters something unknown, it tests it to see if it is truly the boundary of reason. There is no natural limit to this imperialistic expansion of the scope of reason, unless reason does encounter something that is truly beyond its capacity to grasp. Climacus argues that such an encounter could be viewed as the fulfillment of reason's quest, and not simply as a defeat, because "the ultimate paradox of thought" is "to discover something that thought itself cannot think" (PF, 37). It is the passionate quest to find this limit that lies behind reason's restless and relentless search.

The end result of the encounter between reason and the Paradox is a kind of natural ambivalence on the part of reason. When reason encounters the incarnation, there is a tendency to take a negative stance:

The understanding certainly cannot think it [the Paradox], cannot on its own even imagine it, and when it is proclaimed, the understanding cannot understand it and merely notices that it is likely to be its downfall. To that extent, the understanding has much to object to . . . (PF, 47)

[26] Immanuel Kant, *Critique of Practical Reason*, trans. Lewis White Beck (Indianapolis: Bobbs-Merrill, 1956), pp. 111–112.
[27] Kant, *Critique of Pure Reason*, p. 531.
[28] Kant goes so far as to say that his critical philosophy implies that "all objections to morality and religion will be forever silenced, and this in Socratic fashion, namely, by the clearest proof of the ignorance of the objectors" (*Critique of Pure Reason*, p. 30).

However, this tendency towards a negative response is not the whole story, because "on the other hand, in its paradoxical passion the understanding certainly wills its own downfall" (PF, 47). This other tendency on the part of reason is one that allows for the possibility of a "mutual understanding" between the understanding and the Paradox. When this mutual understanding is present there is a "happy relationship" between reason and the Paradox, one in which "the understanding gives itself up" while the "Paradox gives itself" (PF, 54). Later, Climacus expresses the same thought, using a slightly different image: A happy understanding between reason and the Paradox is possible when "the understanding steps aside and the paradox gives itself" (PF, 59). This condition, in which the two are on good terms, Climacus calls "faith." It is significant that it is reason which itself "steps aside." The situation is not an irrational refusal to meet the standards of reason, but rather a recognition by reason itself that there are limits to reason.

Actually, Climacus does not merely assert that it is possible for reason and the Paradox to be on good terms; he goes further and argues that when this happens in some way reason finds fulfillment. He explains the idea through an analogy with erotic love. The relation between reason and faith is similar, he argues, to the relation between self-love and love:

Self-love lies at the basis of love, but at its peak its paradoxical passion wills its own downfall. This is what love wants as well, and therefore these two forces have an understanding with each other in the moment of passion, and this passion is precisely love. (PF, 48)

The initial motivation for love is one's own happiness. If I fall in love I want to be with the other person because that person makes me happy. However, Climacus thinks that when love reaches its highest peak, this self-love paradoxically transcends itself. I find my greatest happiness when I place the happiness of the other above my own happiness. Self-love is dethroned, but somehow fulfilled as well. In the happy relation between reason and the Paradox something similar occurs; reason recognizes its limits but at the same time is fulfilled. Climacus eventually decides to call the happy passion in which this occurs "faith" (PF, 59).

Of course things do not always turn out so well, either for love or faith. Sometimes, in the case of love, a person is too selfish to open himself or herself to real love for the other. Such a person "shrinks from love" and "can neither grasp it nor dare to venture it" (PF, 48). Such a person may rail against love and be actively embittered, but Climacus says that in fact this unhappiness is a kind of suffering, in which self-love misunderstands itself (PF, 49). I think the idea is that the selfish person at some level understands that love would offer genuine happiness, and that this is what he genuinely desires. However, his selfishness cuts him off from love, and he envies and resents the situation of the person who possesses this happiness.

The analogous passion to this unhappy form of self-love is termed "offense." For faith to be present in a person, reason must be willing to recognize its limits and accept the revelation God offers in the incarnation. When what I have just called the imperialistic character of reason becomes dominant, reason insists that whatever it cannot understand is absurd. Climacus argues that this reaction on the part of reason is understandable but far from rational, since it stems from a kind of misunderstanding. In fact, the claim of reason that the Paradox is absurd is really just an echo, "an acoustic illusion," of what the Paradox claims about itself. Offense, far from offering a decisive objection to faith, indirectly provides a kind of confirmation of the claims of revelation. The offended reason tries to attack the Paradox, but the Paradox calmly replies that the attack is actually support: "Now what is so surprising? It is exactly as you say, and the surprising thing is that you think it is an objection, but the truth in the mouth of a hypocrite is dearer to me than to hear it from an angel and an apostle" (PF, 52). It is true that the Paradox is "the most improbable thing of all," but the Paradox is unfazed by this: "Comedies and novels and lies must be probable, but how could I be probable" (PF, 52).

The main point I believe is to affirm what I have called the "no neutrality" thesis.[29] Many philosophers have viewed reason as a kind of neutral, impartial judge with respect to issues of religious belief. This implies that if reason judges faith to be absurd, then faith is something that a rational person must reject. However, Kierkegaard simply does not see human reason as capable of neutrality with respect to religious issues. When we humans encounter the incarnation, we necessarily respond either with faith or offense. Both faith and offense are passions; neither stems from a neutral, objective standpoint. Kierkegaard sees faith as a humble stance in which reason recognizes its own limits; offense is the arrogant stance of the reason that refuses to admit the reality of anything beyond its capacity. The one thing that is not possible is indifference.

We can now understand why Kierkegaard thinks that faith is fundamentally faith in something that is above reason, something that

---

[29] For a fuller account of the "no neutrality" thesis, see my *Faith Beyond Reason* (Edinburgh: Edinburgh University Press; Grand Rapids, Michigan: Eerdmans Publishing Co., 1998).

transcends reason, and yet we can also explain why there is a natural tension between faith and reason. Fundamentally, the incarnation is a mystery, something that transcends human reason, since it is the action of a God who transcends our human ability to know God. However, a prideful reason that refuses to recognize anything that transcends its ability will surely clash with such a mystery. The incarnation understood as "the Absolute Paradox" will be "against" that kind of reason and not simply above reason. Of course it is a long-standing part of the Christian faith that humans are a fallen race, shaped by sin, and many theologians have viewed the heart of human sinfulness to lie in pridefulness. Climacus himself insists that our inability to understand God is grounded in the fundamental "unlikeness" between ourselves and God (PF, 47).

One might think that this unlikeness simply lies in the gulf between Creator and creature, but Climacus insists, somewhat surprisingly, that the Creator–creature relationship is one in which there is some similarity or resemblance, not an absolute unlikeness (PF, 46–47). The absolute difference between God and humans stems from our sinfulness. Thus, it is sin that lies at the ground of the tension between reason and faith. It is true that God, as the infinite Creator, transcends our human finite minds. One might say that human finitude is the ground of the mysteriousness of the Paradox, which would be a Paradox even for an unfallen race. However, this mysteriousness would not be, for unfallen creatures, a problem, but would be recognized as a confirmation of the unsurpassable greatness of God.

In addition to pride, theologians have often claimed that selfishness or self-centeredness lies at the heart of human sin. If this is so, we have an additional reason why there should be a natural tension between human reason in its current form, and the incarnation. For the incarnation, if it occurs, must be a manifestation of selfless love, since God does not need anything from his creatures. Since we have no other experience of such love it is natural for us to doubt its reality, unless and until we have experienced this love ourselves. The analogy between selfish self-love and offense turns out to be rather close.

FAITH AS GOD'S GIFT, HISTORICAL TESTIMONY AS THE "OCCASION" FOR FAITH

We have looked at the argument Climacus gives for seeing the para-doxicalness of God's revelation as being what we might call a con-firmatory characteristic rather than a problem. However, we still have not given a concrete account of how faith comes into existence in a person. Why do some people opt for faith, while others are offended?

One might think that faith or belief[30] in the God's appearance in human form must be based on historical evidence, for that is true for most historical beliefs. However, Climacus (and Kierkegaard) do not think this is so in the case of belief in the incarnation. In the "Interlude" between Chapters 4 and 5 of *Fragments*, Climacus gives an epistemological analysis that undergirds this claim. He begins by arguing that in a strict sense historical evidence by itself never is the basis for historical belief. All beliefs about what has "come into existence" are infected with contingency; whatever has come into existence could have been otherwise, and what could have been otherwise cannot be logically proven. The realm of logic is the realm of necessity, and what is not necessary cannot be proven. This is true even for beliefs about the natural world, but it is doubly true for history in the strict sense, since human history involves a "coming into existence within a coming into existence" (PF, 76). There is a double contingency that affects human history, which is partly constituted by human actions. Such actions are part of the natural world, and thus are contingent. But human beings are a special part of the natural world, and contain within themselves possibilities which must be chosen. Thus, human history "could have been otherwise" in a double sense and is even less susceptible to proof. No matter how strong the evidence, there is always some possibility that things could have happened differently than the evidence suggests. Climacus makes these points, drawn partly from the history of Greek skepticism, not to argue that we should be skeptics, but to claim that skepticism is overcome, not by logical evidence, but by faith or belief (PF, 81–85). Skepticism is rooted in the will, he argues; the logical gap between evidence and belief is merely what makes it possible for the skeptic to achieve what he wills to achieve. Ultimately, those of us who are not skeptics are what we are because we do not want to be skeptics, and choose not to be skeptics. Faith is thus fundamental to our epistemic lives.

All of this is true for what Climacus calls "ordinary faith" (PF, 87). Faith in the incarnation is faith in "the eminent sense" (PF, 87). The object of faith in this case, the God in time, includes all the uncertainty that attaches to any historical event, plus the special uncertainty that accrues from the fact that the event in question is the Absolute Paradox, something reason cannot comprehend and that runs counter to our

---

[30] Danish has just one word "*Tro*" for both faith and belief.

expectations about what can and will happen. The latter type of uncertainty makes questions about the quality of the historical evidence unimportant. "Lawyers say that a capital crime absorbs all the lesser offenses – it is like that with faith as well: its absurdity absolutely absorbs minor matters. Discrepancies, which otherwise would be disturbing, do not disturb here and do not matter" (PF, 104).

Hence, it is not surprising that Climacus argues that no amount of historical evidence is sufficient to produce faith in an individual. Imagine, he says, an individual who combined "a tyrant's power" with "a tyrant's passion" and who does all he can to determine the historical facts, interrogating the surviving witnesses, even starving and locking them up so as to force them to get things right (PF, 92). Such a person would have achieved all that could be achieved through historical research, but would not necessarily become a disciple of the God, according to Climacus.

Nor is any particular amount of historical evidence necessary for faith. Climacus imagines a contemporary of the God who only comes into contact with him on the day the God dies, leaving no time to discover much about the God's teaching or life. This historical ignorance would not necessarily prevent this encounter with the God from being decisive for that individual, if he is thereby transformed and becomes a disciple (PF, 60). Notoriously, Climacus goes so far as to say that, as far as historical evidence goes, if the contemporary generation of the God's appearance had only left behind a scrap of paper, with the words, "We have believed that the God in the year such and such appeared in the humble form of a servant, lived and taught among us, and then died," then the contemporaries would have done "what is necessary" for those who come later; indeed this would be "more than enough" (PF, 104).[31]

If historical evidence is neither sufficient nor necessary, then how does faith come into existence in a person? The answer is that the historical encounter with the God, whether this happens by way of the experience

---

[31] It is important to recognize that this does not imply that the content of a revelation about the God's life is unimportant to the believer. Climacus here speaks from within the "frame" of his thought-experiment, not as a believer, but as a kind of philosopher. The point is the logical point that only a bare minimum of historical information would be strictly necessary for faith in his sense to be possible. However, since the believer holds that a particular person is in reality the God, the believer naturally would desire knowledge of the character of the God as revealed in that life, and thus would value more than this bare minimum of knowledge. Climacus affirms this too by claiming that "for the disciple the external form (not its detail) is not inconsequential" (PF, 65). We can thus understand why Kierkegaard himself puts great emphasis on understanding the character of Jesus' life, so as to be able to imitate him. For more on this, see Chapter 8, pp. 191–193.

of an immediate contemporary or by means of testimony that has been handed down to those of later generations, must be a life-changing encounter. The "condition" that makes it possible to grasp the truth about the God is faith, and faith is a passion produced in the individual by God when the individual encounters the God in time. Faith is simply a gift of God and nothing that a human being can achieve by ordinary human efforts, either intellectual or volitional (PF, 62).

If faith is completely a work of God, it might seem at this point that Climacus is moving towards a doctrine of predestination in which some individuals are simply given the gift of faith and others are not. However, it turns out that there is one thing humans can do or fail to do, and that is to accept the fact that they can do nothing to acquire faith on their own. The one thing human beings can do to achieve salvation on this view is to recognize that they can do nothing to achieve salvation. This recognition is essentially a recognition of sinfulness, an acceptance of the fact that we do not possess the Truth or the condition for gaining the Truth. If faith is "the condition" for having the Truth, then we could call the consciousness of sin the condition for the condition, for Kierkegaard himself consistently holds that what motivates a person to believe in Christ is the consciousness of sin. For example, the reason why historical knowledge by itself is not sufficient to produce faith is that such knowledge by itself "does not develop the deepest self-reflection in the learner," which is "the consciousness of sin as the condition for understanding" (PF, 93). It is, I believe, the presence or absence of the consciousness of sin that determines whether an individual responds to the encounter with the incarnation in faith or offense.

Strictly speaking, even the consciousness of sin is not something a human can achieve on his or her own. Climacus says that we only really understand the depth of human sinfulness by revelation; the consciousness of sin is something "only the God can teach" (PF, 47). It is something that is acquired when we meet the God and recognize the difference between the God's love and our own selves, and see to what lengths God must go for our salvation.

However, though an encounter with the God is necessary for us to discover our sinfulness, it is not sufficient. We must be willing to accept this insight, and thereby come to understand the ways in which our reason is limited. This is something we must do for ourselves, and it provides, according to Climacus, the one and only point of agreement between his presentation of Christianity in the form of a "thought-experiment" and the Socratic view of the Truth, in which the Truth is something every person possesses already and the teacher is only a mid-wife. "To this act of consciousness [the discovery that one lacks the Truth] the Socratic principle is valid: the Teacher is only an occasion, whoever he may be, even if he is a god, because I can discover my own untruth only by myself" (PF, 14).

KIERKEGAARD'S VIEW OF FAITH AND EXTERNALIST EPISTEMOLOGY

In Chapter 3 I briefly discussed classical foundationalism, the epistemological perspective that dominates modern western philosophy and still plays an important role in our broader culture.[32] From this perspective, knowledge requires certainty; a person only knows when he has the ability to know that he knows. Certainty is acquired by taking a standpoint of objectivity that requires us to put our emotional lives out of play. The foundational certainties lie at the basis of our epistemic lives and provide evidence for other beliefs. Classical foundationalists give various accounts of belief, but at least some follow John Locke, who held that beliefs that do not rise to the level of knowledge may still be rational. However, such rational beliefs that fall short of knowledge still must be based on evidence. Such a Lockean account of beliefs, which holds that we should only believe what the evidence supports, with the strength of our beliefs proportionate to the evidence, is still popular among contemporary philosophers.[33]

From such a perspective the Kierkegaardian account of Christian faith seems unacceptable, since faith is not based on evidence at all. However, we have already seen that Kierkegaard mounts a challenge to this epistemological perspective, especially with respect to moral and religious beliefs. From his perspective, certainty is unattainable: a logical system may be possible, but a system of existence is impossible for human beings, though not for God (CUP, 109). The truth that we can gain is achieved, not by distancing ourselves from our emotions and becoming purely objective, but by acquiring and developing the right emotions, the right kind of "subjectivity." This challenge to the forms of epistemology

---

[32] See pp. 55–57.

[33] This is the case both for defenders of religious belief as well as critics. For an example of a defender, one could take almost any of the works of Richard Swinburne. See his "Principles for Weighing Evidence" in *The Resurrection of God Incarnate* (Oxford: Oxford University Press, 2003), pp. 9–31.

dominant in modern philosophy continues in Kierkegaard's account of faith or belief.

Modern epistemology has typically ignored the knower and focused only on questions about evidence. From Kierkegaard's perspective, this is an error; what we can know is conditioned by the kinds of people we are. One development on the contemporary epistemological scene is called "virtue epistemology," which argues that an adequate account of knowledge must pay attention to the knower and the qualities good knowers have.[34] One cannot expect people who are unethical to have a deep and penetrating understanding of ethical truth. From this perspective, it seems less odd to hold that a person's ability to grasp some religious truth might turn on the acquisition of a quality such as humility more than the possession or lack of possession of evidence.

Another challenge to classical foundationalist epistemology can be found in a contemporary epistemological view called "externalism." Externalism is best explained by contrasting it with the "internalism" that is part of classical foundationalism. The internalist holds that it must be possible for someone to determine whether knowledge or rational belief is present by examining the contents of the mind. Thus, knowledge and rational belief depend on what is internal to consciousness. The classical foundationalist by and large sees it as the task of epistemology to evaluate our claims to knowledge and rational belief and see if they measure up; the underlying assumption is that this can be done by examining our own minds. When we have access to the right kind of evidence, then knowledge and rational belief are present.

Such an epistemology aspires to give our knowledge claims a kind of rational backing, a certificate of authenticity one might say. Armed with this epistemological machinery, the philosopher hopes to vanquish the skeptic and sort out genuine from spurious knowledge, rational belief from irrational belief. One might call this program that of "ambitious epistemology."[35] However, not all philosophers agree that this program can be carried out.

Is there an alternative? Perhaps it is beyond the power of philosophy to refute skepticism and give our knowledge and beliefs the kind of

---

[34] For a good example of virtue epistemology, see Robert C. Roberts and W. Jay Wood, *Intellectual Virtue: An Essay in Regulative Epistemology* (New York: Oxford University Press, 2007).

[35] For a more detailed account of ambitious epistemology and what I call "modest epistemology," see Chapter 9 of my *The Historical Christ and the Jesus of Faith* (Oxford: Oxford University Press, 1996), pp. 202–230.

guarantee that ambitious epistemology would like to give us. Perhaps whether humans have knowledge or rational belief depends on our relation to the external world and not solely on factors that are present within our own minds. It is possible that we are all brains in vats, part of the Matrix, but with our brains being stimulated so as to produce the experiences we would be having if we were not in the Matrix. If so, we are deceived and will never discover the truth. From the perspective of externalism, knowledge is a matter of being rightly related to the external reality we think we know. If our faculties are reliable, if they are functioning properly in the right kind of environment, then perhaps we can have knowledge and reasonable beliefs, but we have no guarantees that we can determine whether these conditions hold.

Externalist epistemology has been inspired by two radically different kinds of influences. On the one hand, evolutionary thinkers have focused on knowledge and belief as natural abilities that must have evolved so as to enable us to deal with the environment.[36] Other philosophers have been more influenced by religious perspectives, which hold that our human faculties are gifts of God and thus cannot be inherently deceptive or unreliable.[37] Both perspectives emphasize the finitude of human knowers. We are creatures, animals who must begin by trusting our faculties and our environment, not godlike beings who have the right to demand a guarantee before employing their faculties.

From the perspective of externalism and virtue epistemology, Kierkegaard's account of Christian faith makes more sense than it does on a classical foundationalist view. For the heart of externalism is the claim that knowledge is a matter of being rightly related to the external world, and the related claim that whether this is the case is not always something that we can be assured about. Our ability to relate rightly to that reality depends partly on the qualities we possess as human beings. When we do know or rightly believe, this is made possible by trusting the processes

[36] For influential examples see Alvin Goldman, *Epistemology and Cognition* (Cambridge, Massachusetts: Harvard University Press, 1986) and Fred Dretske, *Knowledge and the Flow of Information* (Cambridge, Massachusetts: MIT Press, 1981).

[37] See in particular the work of Alvin Plantinga, the pre-eminent "Reformed epistemologist." The relevant major works are *Warrant and Proper Function* (New York: Oxford University Press, 1993) and *Warranted Christian Belief* (New York: Oxford University Press, 2000). The work of Plantinga and the other Reformed epistemologists is clearly indebted to Thomas Reid, who emphasized the necessity of trust in our God-given faculties. For a good account of Reid by an outstanding Reformed epistemologist, see Nicholas Wolterstorff, *Thomas Reid and the Story of Epistemology* (Cambridge: Cambridge University Press, 2001).

that enable us to "track" that reality. Kierkegaard wants us to see how the development of a certain kind of subjectivity, called the "consciousness of sin," enables us to track the reality of God. He does not think that philosophy can give us any guarantees that we are indeed tracking that reality properly. However, if classical foundationalism is a failure perhaps this will be true of any answer to fundamental human questions.

CHAPTER 8

Kierkegaard's dual challenge to the contemporary world

As a Christian philosopher, Kierkegaard presents a dual challenge to the contemporary world. On the one hand, he forcefully presents a picture of Christian existence as offering the highest possibilities for fulfillment for human beings. Such a view of human life is clearly a challenge in the contemporary pluralistic world, both to advocates of a secular worldview as well as advocates of other religious faiths. However, Kierkegaard's critique of "Christendom" presents a powerful challenge to the contemporary Christian Church as well, particularly when it attempts to identify itself with a particular culture, and even more when the Church itself becomes part of what Kierkegaard calls "the established order." In this concluding chapter, I shall try to give an account of Kierkegaard's understanding of Christian existence that does justice to both of these challenges.

DESPAIR AND THE QUEST FOR EXISTENTIAL UNITY

One of Kierkegaard's most influential books is *The Sickness Unto Death*. Although the book is pseudonymous, ascribed to "Anti-Climacus," it comes from the later period of Kierkegaard's authorship, when Kierkegaard's works have a strongly Christian character, and differs markedly from the earlier pseudonymous writings that Kierkegaard labels "aesthetic." Kierkegaard wrote *Sickness Unto Death* with the intention of publishing the book under his own name, but struggled over whether he should do so, since he felt that the Christian ideals the book embodies were ones that he personally fell far short of. The solution he hit upon was the invention of "Anti-Climacus," a kind of ideal Christian, who thus is in some way the antipode of Johannes Climacus, who claims not to be a Christian at all. Anti-Climacus is a real pseudonym in the sense that he embodies a standpoint that is not Kierkegaard's own. However, this does not mean that Kierkegaard would disagree with the views found in the book at all, but only that the standpoint expressed in the book is one that he is personally "striving" to achieve.[1]

The Sickness Unto Death is one of the inspirations for what became known in the twentieth century as "existential psychology." In the work, Anti-Climacus gives a profound analysis of despair, understood not merely as a feeling, but as a state of being that is known through the characteristic emotion that we term "despair." Essentially, a person in despair is a person who fails to be fully a self. An awareness of the emptiness of the self results in that feeling we normally call despair, but Anti-Climacus believes that there are many people who are in this state of emptiness or hollowness without being aware of it. The book starts with the famous description of what it means to be a self which I discussed in Chapter 3, in which the self is described as a "relation that relates itself to itself" by "relating itself to another."[2] I shall briefly review some of the points I made earlier before going on to develop the implications of this view of personhood.

I have at several points referred to Kierkegaard's view that the human self is a paradoxical blend of contrasting qualities. In *Sickness Unto Death*, Anti-Climacus continues and develops this theme: "A human being is a synthesis of the infinite and the finite, of the temporal and the eternal, of freedom and necessity, in short, a synthesis" (SUD, 13). However, looking at humans in this manner still does not capture what it means to be a self; selfhood is not merely a relation, it is the activity of relating these disparate elements to each other, and the activity is itself carried on by a being that is self-conscious and thus has a relation to itself. The picture is still more complicated, however, for human selves are not autonomous individuals. When they self-consciously reflect about themselves, they do so in light of an ideal or true self that provides an identity. This ideal that gives an identity is not created by the self but develops through a relation with something outside the self: "The human self is ... that kind of derived, posited relation, a relation that relates itself to itself, and in relating itself to itself relates itself to an Other" (SUD, 13–14).

As creatures of God, humans were made for a relation to God. Metaphysically, humans depend on God for their very being, and are intended for a relationship with God. However, God has endowed

---

[1] See the discussion by the Hongs in the "Historical Introduction" to SUD, especially pp. xx and xxii, where the Hongs discuss passages from the Journals where Kierkegaard talks about himself as "striving" to realize the ideals of Anti-Climacus, and says that he places himself "between" Johannes Climacus, who is not a Christian at all, and Anti-Climacus, who is an extraordinary Christian.

[2] See Chapter 3, pp. 46–50, for a fuller exegesis of this passage.

humans with freedom, and thus has made it possible for them to ground their selves in something other than God: "It is almost as if God, who constituted man as a relation, allows it to slip out of his hand" (SUD, 16). Anti-Climacus tries to show that when humans try to ground their selves in something other than God, the "synthesis" of contrasting elements that compose the self falls apart. This loss of selfhood he calls despair. Despair can be seen more clearly when it is contrasted with the ideal state in which despair is eradicated: "[I]n relating itself to itself and willing to be itself, the self rests transparently in the power that posited it" (SUD, 14).

Because humans are the kind of dependent beings they are, who relate themselves to themselves by relating to something outside the self, there are two forms of despair, according to Anti-Climacus. If humans were completely autonomous, self-determining spirits – if they were the kinds of beings that Jean-Paul Sartre thinks we are, for example – then there would only be one way to forfeit selfhood, "not to will to be oneself" (SUD, 14). In reality, however, there are two ways of failing to be a self: a person can despair by failing to will to be himself or by willing to be himself.

The ideal self is the person God intends for an individual to become, but there are two ways of missing the ideal. The despair of weakness passively fails to actualize the ideal that is recognized; such a self does not will to be itself. However, the despair of defiance actively seeks to create a new self. Self-consciousness allows a person to step back from his actual self and negate that self. A defiantly despairing person in effect refuses to be the ideal self he or she was created to be and seeks to use the self-conscious freedom God has granted to create a new self out of whole cloth.

> But with the help of the infinite form, the negative self, he wants first to take on the task of transforming all this in order to fashion out of it a self such as he wants, produced with the help of the negative self's infinite form – and thus he wants to be himself. That means he wants to begin a little earlier than other people, not at and with the beginning, but "in the beginning"; he does not want to put on his own self, does not want to see his given self as his task – with the help of the infinite form he wants to create his self. (SUD, 68)

Such a person in effect wants to take the place of God, to become his own creator. The resulting picture of the self bears a striking resemblance to Sartrean existentialism, as we saw in Chapter 3.[3]

---

[3] See Chapter 3, pp. 52–55. I shall develop this point in more depth later in this chapter; see pp. 176–180.

Anti-Climacus proceeds to give accounts of despair from two different points of view. First, he gives what one might call a symptomatic description of despair, detailing the various kinds of pathologies that result within the self when a person does not rightly relate to himself. He then presents a phenomenological description of the forms of despair, looking at the degrees of consciousness of despair possible for a human. I shall give a brief account of both of these ways of describing and analyzing despair.

FORMS OF DESPAIR ANALYZED SYMPTOMATICALLY

As already seen, every human being is intended to be a "synthesis" or relation of temporality and eternity, freedom and necessity, infinitude and finitude. Anti-Climacus claims that when a person does not properly relate to himself by relating to God, the result is that the synthesis becomes discordant; the relationship between these contrasting elements becomes a misrelationship. The misrelationship takes the form of a one-sidedness, in which one element of the synthesis atrophies and as a result the other element becomes (relatively) overdeveloped. In each case Anti-Climacus tries to show that a proper relation to God provides the antidote to the pathology.

The descriptions of the various forms of pathology are formulaic, or, as Kierkegaard himself says, "algebraic" in character.[4] Thus, the despair of infinitude is characterized by a lack of finitude, while the despair of finitude lacks infinitude. The despair of possibility lacks necessity, while the despair of necessity is in want of possibility. Interestingly, Anti-Climacus does not sketch forms of despair corresponding to the polarity of temporality–eternity, although this pair is included in the initial account of the elements of the synthesis. Perhaps, having provided four examples, he leaves it to the reader to think through what these two forms of despair might be like. Or, it may well be that the three polarities used to describe the paradoxical structure of the self (eternity–temporality, infinitude–finitude, possibility–necessity) do not really represent different elements, but simply are three ways of describing one fundamental duality. If so, the forms of despair characterized by loss of temporality and eternity may already be present in the other forms. Certainly, there is

---

[4] See *Kierkegaard's Journals and Papers*, Vol. V, entry 6137, where Kierkegaard describes the book as "dialectical algebra."

a sense in which eternity, infinitude, and possibility are linked, while temporality, finitude, and necessity also form a tightly-linked group.

The despair of infinitude is thus described as a despair that lacks finitude. The person who lives in infinitude is a person who lives through the imagination, described as "the medium for infinitizing" (SUD, 30). Imagination itself is essential to human life; it is the "capacity *instar omnium* (for all capacities)" and sets the limit for what a person can achieve in "feeling, knowing, and willing" (SUD, 30–31). The problem for the person in the grip of the despair of infinitude is that the imagination takes the person away from himself into infinitude, but the person lacks the concrete relation to the finite that allows him to return to himself (SUD, 31). With respect to emotion, for example, such an individual becomes lost in sentimental, volatilized feelings that do not engage with his actual life. He may be filled with sorrow for the suffering of the poor, or inspired when he contemplates the courage of humanity in the face of death. However, such feelings do not move him to do anything to alleviate the plight of the poor person he encounters on the way to work or move him to act courageously when threatened by some evil. His emotions are so abstract that they never engage any actual objects in his world.

A similar ailment may affect the will of a person in the grip of the despair of infinitude. He may form grand resolutions and will something grand, but the object of the will never becomes concrete and particular. He may have a wonderful dream or goal, but never thinks the dream through with respect to the concrete steps that he might be able to take. Perhaps he wants to become a physician and find a cure for AIDS, but he does not want to bother to learn chemistry. He may will to wipe out global poverty, but never think about how his own lifestyle might change so he could do something concrete for his neighbor.

The despair of infinitude is possible with respect to knowledge as well. Anti-Climacus says that in a healthy self an increase in knowledge should go hand in hand with increased self-knowledge (SUD, 31). When I seek to gain knowledge, I should have some sense of why this knowledge is valuable and why I should seek it. A person in the grip of the despair of infinitude, however, is enchanted by knowledge itself; he may know all about astronomy or ancient coins or bird plumages. Such knowledge may of course be interesting and enjoyable, and such enjoyment may make such knowledge worthwhile in itself, but a person who simply lives in a world of facts but has no curiosity about himself or his own task as a human being has become a kind of observer of life rather than a true self.

The despair of infinitude seems quite similar to what Anti-Climacus calls the despair of possibility, the kind of despair that lacks necessity. This kind of person becomes lost in an imaginary world of possibilities. We say of such people that they "live in a dream-world" and that their lives are unreal, but Anti-Climacus insists that the loss of actuality is really a loss of necessity. "The mirror of possibility is no ordinary mirror; it must be used with the greatest possible care. In the highest sense, this mirror does not tell the truth. That a self appears to be such and such in the possibility of itself is only a half-truth, for in the possibility of itself the self is still far from or is only half of itself" (SUD, 37). Possibility is like "a child's invitation to some kind of party; the child immediately wants to go," but necessity is like the child's parents, who must give permission if the party is to become actual (SUD, 37).

Though one can become lost in possibility in all kinds of ways, according to Anti-Climacus, two ways are primary (SUD, 37). One is the "desiring" or "craving" kind of possibility. Here one begins by desiring something, but ends by simply desiring the state of desire itself, as when a person is in love with being in love, enjoying not the fulfillment of love by the development of a relationship with an actual person, but the giddy feeling of possibility that overwhelms a person at the beginning of a relationship. The second form is the "melancholy-imaginary" form. This form seems even more unreal, in that a person is now intoxicated not by desire for something really possible, but lives in fear or anxiety or hope with respect to possibilities that may have little relation to the person's actual life.

The opposite forms of despair to infinitude/possibility are described by Anti-Climacus as the despair of finitude that lacks infinitude, and the despair of necessity that lacks possibility. The former is the despair of the bourgeois conformist, who lacks that quality that the Hongs translate as "primitivity" (*Primitivitet*), but that could also be translated as authenticity or originality. The despair of finitude is essentially a fear of being the individual self that one was intended to be:

Every human being is originally [*primitivt*] intended to be a self, destined to become itself, and as such every self certainly is angular, but from this it only follows that it is to be ground into shape, not that it is to be ground down smooth, not that it is from fear of other humans to totally give up itself. (SUD, 33)[5]

---

[5] The Hongs usually translate the Danish terms *Primitivitet* and *primitivt* as "primitivity" and "primitively." It is hard to find a good English equivalent; certainly the Hongs' choices are

In words that seem prophetic of the numbing conformity of contemporary societies, Anti-Climacus goes on to describe the difference between this kind of despair and the despair of infinitude sketched previously:

> But while one kind of despair goes wild in the infinite and loses itself, another kind of despair seems to permit itself to be tricked out of its self by "the others." Surrounded by hordes of people, busy with all sorts of secular matters, more and more shrewd about the ways of the world – such a person forgets himself, forgets his name divinely understood, does not dare to believe in himself, finds it too risky to be himself, far easier and safer to be like the others, to become a copy, a number, part of the crowd. (SUD, 33–34)

If the despair of finitude is the despair of conformism, the despair of necessity could be described as a kind of fatalism. Anti-Climacus uses a brilliant metaphor from language for the way possibility and necessity function in human life. Possibility, he says, is to human existence what vowels are to speech, while "the necessary is like sheer consonants" (SUD, 37). To live in pure possibility is like an infant's utterance of vowel sounds, which fail to express something that is definite and clear. Vowels alone do not make for articulate speech, although without them nothing can be said at all. Similarly, "if a human existence is brought to the point where it lacks possibility, then it is in despair and is in despair every moment it lacks possibility" (SUD, 37). The same thought is expressed in another vivid image, in which human existence is compared to breathing (SUD, 40). One cannot breathe without oxygen, but it is also impossible to breathe pure oxygen. Possibility is a kind of spiritual oxygen that a person cannot live without, but one cannot live on pure possibility either.

Anti-Climacus thinks that a proper relationship to God provides an antidote for both types of despair; whether the individual is lost in possibility/infinitude or mired in necessity/finitude the relation to God offers the possibility of healing. On the one hand, the recognition of one's creaturely status ought to lead a person away from pure possibility/infinitude towards the recognition of finitude/necessity. As God's creature, a human being is assigned a post, so to speak, and to attempt to fly away from one's actual situation is a kind of rebellion. However, God is also the antidote to the despair that is caught in finitude/necessity. God has created us as individuals; spiritually understood, each of us has a unique name. Thus God wants us to have the courage to become the

---

defensible, but "primitivity" has misleading associations. The Danish terms refer to what is part of God's original plan for the self, and thus one could also speak of what is original or authentic to the self.

individuals he has created us to be, and not to lose ourselves through fear of what "the others" will think. Furthermore, God is the one for whom all things are possible, the only ground for hope when all seems lost, humanly speaking (SUD, 38–39).

DESPAIR CLASSIFIED BY DEGREE OF CONSCIOUSNESS

Besides this symptomatic analysis of despair, Anti-Climacus also offers a description of different forms of despair categorized by the degree of consciousness of the despairer. The categorization goes up the scale, so to speak, beginning with the despair that is unaware of its condition, through a form of despair that is conscious of despair but dim and confused about the nature of despair, to forms of despair that are more fully conscious.

One might think that the idea of unconscious despair is impossible. Perhaps it would be if human beings were fully transparent to themselves, Cartesian egos fully defined by consciousness. However, Kierkegaard, like Nietzsche and Freud after him, is a depth psychologist who thinks that full transparency is an ideal for humans but not a reality. If we take despair, as he does, primarily as a state or condition of the self, then it is not surprising that humans may be in this state without noticing it.

Such a view of despair is also implied by the claim Anti-Climacus makes that despair is an essential condition for the one who is in it. One cannot, he says, despair by accident. Once again it might appear that this is not so if we think of the case in which a person (I will imagine him as male) loses a job or a girlfriend and then finds himself in despair. It is natural for the man to think, "If only I still had my job (or girlfriend), I would not be in despair. That loss is the ground of my despair." Anti-Climacus thinks that there is a twofold mistake here. On the one hand, all despair, he says, is over the self, not "something" outside the self (SUD, 19). The real cause of the despair is not the man's loss of the job or the girlfriend, but his unwillingness to be the self who has lost the job or the girlfriend. However, the error is deeper. The loss of a job or a girlfriend is something contingent, but it cannot be a contingent thing that a person is in despair. What the loss of the job or girlfriend really reveals is that the person was in despair all along, that his identity was built on something too fragile to be the basis of selfhood (SUD, 24). When this fragile basis for identity shattered, the self's underlying emptiness was revealed.

Anti-Climacus holds that despair is actually a universal condition, not simply a mental pathology that affects some people and not others

(SUD, 22). The kind of despair that is ignorant of its own condition is far from advantageous; it is in fact the most dangerous kind of despair. "Despair itself is a negativity; ignorance of it, a new negativity. But in order to reach the truth, one must go through every negativity, for the old legend about breaking a certain magic spell is valid: the piece has to be played through backwards; otherwise the spell is not broken" (SUD, 44). Though ignorance of despair may be, from an ethical standpoint, more innocent than conscious despair, the conscious despairer at least has the advantage of recognizing the condition, and this may make a cure possible.

The despair that lacks consciousness of itself is in reality a lack of awareness of what a human being is called to become: spirit. To have no sense of what it means to be a self, or, perhaps even worse, to have a sense of self that is rooted in something other than God, is a kind of spirit-lessness for Anti-Climacus:

Every human existence that is not conscious of itself as spirit or personally conscious of itself before God as spirit, every human existence that is not transparently grounded in God but vaguely rests in and merges in some abstract universal (state, nation, etc.) or, in darkness over his self regards his capacities merely as productive powers without becoming in the deepest sense consciously aware of their source, regards his self, if he tries to understand it at all, as an inexplicable something – every such existence, whatever it achieves, be it most amazing, whatever it explains, be it the whole of existence, however intensively it enjoys life aesthetically – every such existence is nevertheless despair. (SUD, 46)

This is true both of humans in paganism and within Christendom, though Anti-Climacus says that there is one important respect in which paganism is superior. Though paganism lacks spirit, "it still is qualified as directed towards spirit" (SUD, 47). One might say that paganism is moving towards spirit, perhaps even yearns for it. Within Christendom things are different, however: "[P]aganism in Christendom lacks spirit in a direction away from spirit or in a falling away and is therefore spirit-lessness in the strictest sense" (SUD, 47).

Anti-Climacus moves up the ladder of consciousness by looking next at despair that has some degree of consciousness, but he argues that having a consciousness of despair does not necessarily imply that the person who has this consciousness has a true understanding of the nature of the despair. In reality, Anti-Climacus suggests, neither extreme on the ladder of consciousness is actually possible for humans, but we should rather view them as ideal types. The person we have just described as ignorant of despair is an approximation; probably there is no one in despair who is completely ignorant of despair, who does not at some time have some uneasiness and anxiety over the self (SUD, 48). Similarly, it is questionable whether or not "perfect clarity about oneself as being in despair can be combined with being in despair" (SUD, 47). Thus the person who is in despair but is somewhat confused about the nature of the despair is not unusual; all forms of despair involve a kind of interplay between self-awareness and willed self-deception, and humans are actually quite skilled at keeping themselves in the dark "through diversions and in other ways, for example, through work and busyness as means of diversion" (SUD, 48).

In any case, the kind of person we described earlier, who falls into a feeling of despair over some contingent loss, would be a clear example of the person who has some awareness of despair while lacking a true understanding of the condition. Such despair is "despair over the earthly" (SUD, 50). In less acute forms, the despair is over the loss of some particular earthly good. If a person begins to recognize the emptiness of all such earthly goods, he is advancing from despair over "something earthly" to "despair over the earthly" in general. Anti-Climacus says that such a state is "the dialectical initial expression for the next form of despair," the despair of the eternal (SUD, 60).

The difference between the despair of the eternal and despair over the earthly in a person is that the latter is a despair "in weakness" while the former is a despair "over his weakness." "The despairer himself understands that it is weakness to make the earthly so important, that it is weakness to despair. But now, instead of definitely turning away from despair to faith and humbling himself before God over his weakness, he deepens himself in despair and despairs over his weakness" (SUD, 61).

The lower forms of conscious despair, in which people still lack a clear understanding of their own spiritual character, Anti-Climacus characterizes as the "despair of weakness," a kind of despair in which a person is unable to become the self he or she is called to be. This is contrasted with the "despair of defiance," which I will describe below, in which a person actively tries to become a self, but not the self he or she was created to be. Despair of the eternal is still not yet defiance, according to Anti-Climacus, but still a form of weakness: "Like a father who disinherits a son, the self does not want to acknowledge itself after having been so weak" (SUD, 62). However, this form of despair is more conscious and thus more active; it requires a consciousness of the spiritual character of the self in order to despair over having failed to become a self. Anti-Climacus suggests that this form of weakness is actually a kind of prideful self-centeredness. When accused of being prideful, the person denies it, since he sees himself as weak, "just as if it were not pride that places such an enormous weight on the weakness, just as if it were not because he wants to be proud of his self that he cannot bear this consciousness of weakness" (SUD, 65).

At this point it becomes clear that, although despair is "the sickness unto death," it is also in another sense part of the way the self is healed. Even in the Preface, Anti-Climacus had hinted that this is so, telling us that "in the whole book, as the title indeed expresses, despair is interpreted as the sickness, not as the cure. Despair is indeed that dialectical" (SUD, 6). So it is not too surprising that in his discussion of the despair of weakness, he should imply that a proper recognition of weakness is essential to overcoming despair. Anti-Climacus imagines the following advice given to the person who is despairing over his weakness: "[Y]ou must go through the despair of the self to the self. You are quite right about the weakness, but that is not what you are to despair over; the self must be broken in order to become itself, but quit despairing over that" (SUD, 65). It turns out then that there are different ways to despair; there is despair which is part of the process that leads to faith, and there is the despair that pridefully refuses healing.

If the person becomes clear about his failure to become a self, then "there is a shift, then there is defiance" (SUD, 67). Now the person has a full consciousness of being a self; this is no longer despair of the eternal, but "despair through the aid of the eternal." Such a despair is in one sense very close to the truth, because the person has an intense consciousness of his own character as a responsible self, but in another sense is very far removed from the truth: "The despair that is the path to faith also comes about with the help of the eternal; with the help of the eternal the self has the courage to lose itself in order to win itself. Here, however, it is unwilling to begin with losing itself but wills to be itself" (SUD, 67).

In his description of this form of despair, Anti-Climacus struggles to find the right word. Such a despairing self wants to be, as we saw earlier, its own creator; it wants to use its own freedom to create itself. Climacus does not quite know what to call this: "If one wants a generic name for this kind of despair, one could call it stoicism, using the word not to apply only to that sect" (SUD, 68). Surprisingly, for those who think of Kierkegaard only as the "father of existentialism," if he were writing today, I think Kierkegaard would have a better term for what he is trying to describe: existentialism, at least of the type represented by Sartre.

The Sartrean existentialist, as we saw in Chapter 3, sees the human task as the invention of values through a kind of "radical choice."[6] For Sartre, human consciousness is essentially a form of negativity, in which we distance ourselves from whatever we are conscious of and thereby escape any fixed identity. This seems to be just what Anti-Climacus is describing when he says that this kind of self wants to use "the infinite form, the negative self" in order to become its own foundation.

The problem with this kind of self is that the freedom reduces to arbitrariness and the autonomous self it tries to be turns out to have no content. "The negative form of the self exercises a loosening power as well as a binding power; it can quite arbitrarily begin again at any time" (SUD, 69). Thus "it is easy to see that this absolute ruler is a king without a country, he actually rules over nothing; his position, his kingdom, is subordinate to the dialectic that rebellion is legitimate at any moment" (SUD, 69). Ironically, insofar as existentialism is identified with the thought of Sartre, as is largely the case, Kierkegaard, the alleged "father of existentialism" turns out to be a trenchant critic of existentialism.

The epitome of the despair of defiance is described as a figure suffering from "demonic rage." Such figures are rare, says Anti-Climacus, and not directly recognizable, since they typically are caught in what the Hongs translate as "inclosing reserve." There is no good English term for the Danish "*Indesluttetheden*," which describes a person who is "shut-up" within himself, a "form of inwardness with a jammed lock" (SUD, 72). Anti-Climacus poignantly describes such a person as like an author's mistake who has somehow become conscious, and does not want to allow the author to correct the error:

It is, speaking figuratively, as if an error slipped into an author's writing and the error itself became conscious of itself as an error – though perhaps it actually was not a mistake but in a much higher sense an essential component of the whole production – and now this error wants to rebel against the author, out of hatred towards him, forbidding him to correct it and in maniacal defiance saying to him: No, I will not be erased; I want to stand as a witness against you, a witness that you are a mediocre author. (SUD, 74)

Similarly, a defiant sufferer may take a similar attitude. "Once he would gladly have given everything to be rid of this agony, but he was kept waiting." This person would "rather rage against everything and be the wronged victim of the whole world and all of existence" (SUD, 72). It is

---

[6] See Chapter 3, pp. 52–55.

hard not to think that this attitude represented one that Kierkegaard himself, as a person who suffered a great deal, was tempted to hold and had to struggle against constantly, perhaps not always successfully.

MASCULINE AND FEMININE DESPAIR: KIERKEGAARD ON GENDER

At one point Anti-Climacus describes the despair of weakness as "feminine" despair, while defiant despair is described as "masculine" (SUD, 49). A much-discussed footnote is added to this description, in which the two forms of despair are discussed at more length in relation to what would today be termed gender issues.

It is tempting to write Kierkegaard off at this point as simply sharing in the sexual stereotypes of his age.[7] There can be no doubt that at many places in his authorship such stereotypes abound, and some can be found in this footnote: "A woman has neither the egotistical concept of the self nor, in a decisive sense, intellectuality, however much more tender and sensitive she may be than man" (49n). However, I think it is important to recognize the ways in which Kierkegaard resists the usual sexual stereotypes as well, and he does so to a surprising degree.

The first thing to note is that he explicitly says that what he calls masculine and feminine forms of despair are "ideal types," and that neither sex has a monopoly on either form (SUD, 49–50n). Roughly, men are more likely than women to suffer from the despair of defiance, meaning that they are more likely to be self-centered, autonomous individuals who put their own needs and wants ahead of others. Women are more likely to suffer from the despair of weakness, in which they pay too much attention to the needs and expectations of others, failing to act on their own sense of what is right for them. As generalizations, these claims seem right, not only in Kierkegaard's day, but even today in modern western societies.

However, Anti-Climacus is clear that these generalizations are only generalizations. Men can suffer from the feminine despair of weakness and women can suffer from the despair of defiance, even if these are

---

[7] There are some excellent discussions of Kierkegaard's view of men and women and their relationship. See in particular Sylvia Walsh, "On 'Feminine' and 'Masculine' Forms of Despair," in *International Kierkegaard Commentary 19: The Sickness Unto Death*, ed. Robert L. Perkins (Macon, Georgia: Mercer University Press, 1987), pp. 121–134. Several other fine essays can be found in *Feminist Interpretations of Søren Kierkegaard*, ed. Céline Léon and Sylvia Walsh (University Park, Pennsylvania: Pennsylvania State University Press, 1997).

"exceptions" to the social norms (SUD, 49n). As descriptive psychology and sociology, these descriptions of masculine and feminine forms of despair contain a good deal of truth.

Even more interesting is the conclusion of the footnote, in which Anti-Climacus says that the whole distinction between masculine and feminine despair is undercut when we look at human persons in relation to God. "In the relationship to God, where the distinction of man-woman disappears, it is equally true for men as well as women that devotion is the self and that by giving oneself one gains the self" (SUD, 50n). This egalitarian claim is spoiled for some by the concluding sentence: "This holds equally for man and woman, even though in actuality in most cases the woman probably relates to God only through the man." I confess that I wish Kierkegaard had ended the above sentence at the end of the first clause. However, if we read him charitably, we may understand the last clause not as a normative claim, but as a sociological description of a society where women were by and large not given the opportunity for education.

DESPAIR AND SIN

In the last half of *The Sickness Unto Death*, Anti-Climacus proceeds to give a description of despair as sin. Sin is described as intensified or aggravated despair: "Sin is: *before God, or with the conception of God, despairingly not to will to be oneself, or despairingly to will to be oneself*" (SUD, 77; italics original). Since space is limited and this book is an attempt to introduce Kierkegaard as a philosopher and not as a theologian, I shall not treat this section of *Sickness Unto Death* extensively. However, some notice should be taken of the discussion of the famous Socratic claim that sin (or human wrong-doing) is ignorance (SUD, 87–96). On this view, people who do wrong must be ignorant of what they are doing, since we always choose what we perceive as good.

Ultimately, Anti-Climacus rejects such a view, and puts forward what he sees as the Christian alternative. The Socratic view lacks the defining element of sin, which is "the will, defiance. Greek intellectuality was too happy, too naïve, too aesthetic, too ironic, too witty – too sinful for it to come to grasp that anyone could have knowledge and fail to do the good, or knowingly, with knowledge of what is right, do wrong" (SUD, 90). It is a consistent theme in Kierkegaard's writings that human sin is not something humans can understand through their own philosophical resources, and Anti-Climacus affirms this clearly: "there must be a revelation from God to make it clear what sin is" (SUD, 89).

However, what is most interesting in this section is not the contrast drawn between Greek and Christian views, but the claim that there is still something in the Greek perspective which modern Christendom needs to recover:

Socrates, Socrates, Socrates! Yes, one might call your name three times; it would not be too much to call it ten times, if it would be of any help. People think that the world needs a republic, needs a new social order and a new religion – but no one realizes that what the world, confused by its great amount of knowledge, needs is a Socrates. (SUD, 92)

What the modern world needs, according to Anti-Climacus, is a recovery of the Socratic principle that "to understand and to understand are two different things" (SUD, 92). When Socrates sees someone who does not act in accordance with what he says is true, he concludes that he must not genuinely understand what he claims to know: "His understanding is purely imaginary" (SUD, 92). This echoes the Kierkegaardian distinction between understanding that is purely verbal, and the kind of "subjective understanding" that links what is understood to a person's existence. In many ways what the modern world needs is a recovery of this Socratic insight. Only when this is present will that world be ready to hear the addition made possible by Christian revelation: that the lack of existential understanding is willed. Sin "must lodge in that part of a person by which he works to obscure his knowledge" (SUD, 92).

As sin is intensified despair, so the cure for sin is faith, an intensified form of being oneself. "Faith is: that the self in being itself and in willing to be itself is transparently grounded in God" (SUD, 82). All the elements of this definition are important. Though an existing self is a never-finished synthesis of discordant elements, in faith such a self can nevertheless achieve a kind of grounding, achieve a state of "rest," as the Hongs translate the sentence, a state in which the self accepts itself for what it is. Such a self can be transparent, open to itself and to others, with no need to deceive itself or others about itself.

The ultimate contrast then is between faith as a form of being oneself and sin as a refusal of authentic selfhood. It should not be surprising that Anti-Climacus, citing Romans 14:23, draws the corollary that "the opposite of sin is not virtue but faith" (SUD, 82). This statement is often misunderstood as a rejection of virtue theory on the part of Kierkegaard, a reading that puts Kierkegaard in tension with such contemporary thinkers as Alasdair MacIntyre and Martha Nussbaum, who argue that ethical thinking should focus on the virtues rather than simply on duties to act in particular ways. However, it is clear in the context that this Kierke-gaardian claim is not opposed to an ethics of virtue at all. In the Kier-kegaardian quote the term "virtue" refers, in a Kantian way, to the kind of moral goodness that is achievable through the will. The claim being made is that faith as genuine selfhood cannot be achieved simply through autonomous moral striving. Contemporary virtue theory does not use the term "virtue" in this way, but rather to refer to those states of character in a person that are excellent and desirable, however they are achieved. In this sense, it makes sense to think of Kierkegaardian faith itself as a virtue, an excellence that makes a self genuinely human.[8]

LOVING THE NEIGHBOR: *WORKS OF LOVE*

The pre-eminent virtues for Kierkegaard are the ones that have generally been regarded as supreme in the Christian tradition: faith, hope, and love. I have given an extended description of the account of faith in *Sickness Unto Death* that comes into focus by looking at the antipode of faith: despair and sin, which is intensified despair. A treatment of hope could be given by looking at several of Kierkegaard's *Upbuilding Discourses*,[9] but I will forgo that discussion and turn immediately to Kierkegaard's influential account of love in his powerful, non-pseudonymous *Works of Love*. Here, if anywhere in Kierkegaard's authorship, we find a treatment of issues central to ethics in the writer's own voice. Here is a portrait of the life of faith in action.

Works of Love is a long and complex work, and no brief summary can do it justice.[10] Here I will simply describe some of the major themes

---

[8] There are a number of thinkers who have taken the lead in interpreting Kierkegaard as a virtue thinker, including, for example, Robert Roberts and John Davenport. For Robert Roberts, see "Existence, Emotion and Character: Classical Themes in Kierkegaard," in *The Cambridge Companion to Kierkegaard*, ed. Alastair Hannay and Gordon Marino (Cambridge: Cambridge University Press, 1977), pp. 177–206. Roberts reads Kierkegaard as more like Aristotle than like the existentialists, while Davenport advocates an "existentialist" virtue ethics that stresses the executive will in forming virtues, and finds in Kierkegaard's writings an existentialist virtue called "authenticity." For John Davenport, see "Towards an Existential Virtue Ethics: Kierkegaard and MacIntyre," in *Kierkegaard After MacIntyre*, ed. John J. Davenport and Anthony Rudd (Chicago: Open Court, 2001), pp. 265–324.

[9] For an essay that does just this, see Robert Roberts, "The Virtue of Hope in *Eighteen Upbuilding Discourses*," in *International Kierkegaard Commentary: Eighteen Upbuilding Discourses*, ed. Robert B. Perkins (Macon, Georgia: Mercer University Press, 2003), pp. 181–203. This paper treats three of the discourses from *Eighteen Upbuilding Discourses*: "The Expectancy of Faith," "Patience in Expectancy," and "The Expectancy of an Eternal Salvation."

[10] Fortunately, there have been two major treatments of the book recently. The best overall account is found in Jamie Ferreira, *Love's Grateful Striving* (New York: Oxford University Press, 2001). A

treated in the first few chapters and give a sample of the richness of the volume. The book as a whole is an attempt to understand what it means to fulfill the great command, common to Judaism and Christianity, to love one's neighbor as oneself.

Of course both Judaism and Christianity see this command as linked to an even higher command: the duty to love God unconditionally, summarized by Jesus, quoting from the Hebrew Bible he knew, in Luke 10:27: "Love the Lord your God with all your heart and with all your soul and with all your strength and with all your mind."[11] One might think that Kierkegaard's focus on the "second" command to love the neighbor slights the first and greatest command (to love God), but this is not the case. The book begins with a Trinitarian prayer that makes clear the Christian context for the deliberations that follow. Although there is almost no theology proper in the book, the prayer makes it clear that God the Father is the source of all love, God the Son is the one who revealed what genuine love is by being our Savior and Redeemer, and God the Spirit is present whenever the believer is reminded "to love as he is loved and his neighbor as himself" (WL, 3–4). The first chapter follows with an argument that all genuine love has its source in God. Furthermore, the book as a whole tries to show that genuine love for the neighbor must be grounded in love for God, since God is "the middle term" in any true love relationship, a claim I will discuss below.[12] For Kierkegaard there can be no question about competition between love for God and love of neighbor, for one cannot properly love the neighbor without loving God, and one cannot genuinely love God without also loving the neighbor who is made in God's image.

The book begins with the paradox that love is seen as a duty, which Kierkegaard admits is "an apparent contradiction" (WL, 24). We tend to think of genuine love as something that must be spontaneous and free, and we think of duty as something that we are compelled to do, regardless of how we feel, and thus it is difficult to see how there can be a duty to love. If we identify love with an immediate feeling, then it would seem impossible for love to be commanded, for humans do not generally have voluntary control over their immediate feelings. It is probably for this reason that Kant interprets the command to love the neighbor as a

more specialized study that attempts to bring Kierkegaard into conversation with contemporary debates in meta-ethics can be found in my *Kierkegaard's Ethic of Love: Divine Commands and Moral Obligations* (Oxford: Oxford University Press, 2004).
[11] New International Version.   [12] See pp. 187–190.

"practical love," a love that exists in and through action, for he thinks that we do have control over our actions.[13]

Kierkegaard agrees with Kant to some extent, in that he says that "love is known by its fruits," and therefore genuine love must be seen in "works of love." However, Kierkegaard also insists that genuine works of love stem from love, which is something inward. Kierkegaard departs from Kant by recognizing that enduring passions, long-term dispositions to feel towards others in particular ways and act towards those others in particular ways, are partly under our control. It is possible for us to cultivate a passion.[14]

Robert Roberts has developed an account of emotion that allows us to make sense of this.[15] For Roberts, an emotion is a "concern-based construal," a response to something or someone that is grounded in the way we think about and perceive that other. If I construe my neighbor Fred as the grouch who yells at my kids, I am likely to feel anger and irritation, as I perceive him as a grumpy and unloving person. However, if I think sympathetically about his own loneliness, and remember that he is a human being, a person made in God's image, my emotional response to him may be tempered and even transformed. A Kierkegaardian passion is more of a formed emotion, or a disposition to have certain emotions. As an example, think of the love of two people married for many years who have worked hard to preserve and develop their love, rather than the tingly feeling of infatuation two teenagers might feel when they first meet.

If this is right, then we can in general make sense of the idea that love might be a duty, something one must practice and work at if it is to be real and to endure, since we do have some control over the way we characteristically construe persons and situations. However, even if we generally have some control over our enduring passions, the idea of love for the neighbor still offers special problems. Drawing on the parable of

---

[13] See Immanuel Kant, *Groundwork of the Metaphysic of Morals*, trans. H. J. Paton (New York: Harper and Row, 1964), p. 67.

[14] I have made this point a number of times in this book. See Chapter 2, pp. 32–35, and Chapter 3, p. 57.

[15] Originally developed in Robert C. Roberts, "What Is an Emotion: A Sketch," *Philosophical Review*, 97 (1988), pp. 183–209. This account of emotion is developed in detail in Robert C. Roberts, *The Emotions: An Essay in Aid of Moral Psychology* (Cambridge: Cambridge University Press, 2003). Roberts himself restricts the term "emotion" to more immediate, episodic emotions, while I extend his account by terming dispositional states emotions if those dispositional states entail that emotions in Roberts' sense (episodic states) will occur when appropriate. Since we use the term "belief" both to refer to episodic acts of assenting as well as long-term dispositional states, I see no reason why "emotion" should not be used in both ways. It is in the dispositional sense that love is an emotion.

the Good Samaritan, Kierkegaard claims that the neighbor is "all people" (WL, 21). The neighbor is no abstraction, but "the first person you see" (WL, 51), but one cannot use the concept of neighbor in an exclusive or preferential way. I am not allowed to say that those of another race, or another sex, or another faith are not my neighbors, and restrict my love to those who are like me.

Erotic love, friendship, and patriotism are all forms of what we might call "natural" love, where the ground of the love is some connection between the lover and the person loved. I love my wife because she is my wife; my friends because they are my friends. Those who are not my friends are not loved as friends. Thus, all such loves are preferential in nature, and the basis for the preferential exclusiveness is a relation to oneself. For this reason, Kierkegaard argues that all such loves have within them an element of self-love. Kierkegaard notes that Aristotle himself says that the friend is "another self," the "other-I," and argues that neighbor love transcends this love of self: "'the neighbor' is what thinkers would call 'the Other,' that by which the selfishness in self-love is to be tested" (WL, 21).

We can now see why neighbor love requires a different kind of ground than other loves. Any way of relating to the other that selects the other on the basis of some relation to the self will necessarily produce a form of preferential love. Kierkegaard believes that neighbor love, a love that extends to all people and achieves genuine alterity, must be grounded in God's command, for our natural inclinations do not lead us to love in this non-selective way.

Kierkegaard's claim that neighbor love is a universal love "that makes no distinctions" can easily be misunderstood and often has been. Some have thought that he is asking for an inhuman egalitarianism in which people treat strangers in the same way that they treat friends and family members. However, a close reading makes it clear that this is not his meaning at all.[16] Love can "make no distinctions" in terms of who is loved. I am not allowed to draw boundaries and say that some persons are outside the scope of my moral concern. However, this claim is quite compatible with saying that the specific way in which I love the other must reflect the nature of the relationship I have to the other (WL, 141–142). The claim is not that neighbor love must replace married love and

---

[16] For a good account of the critics and a detailed reply, see Jamie Ferreira, *Love's Grateful Striving*, pp. 53–64.

friendship, but that it must become a foundational element in all these special loves, transforming and purifying them (WL, 146).

However, although love for the neighbor does not come easily or spontaneously for us, it is still good for us to love in this way, and the persons we love when we love our neighbors are worthy of this love. God's command is not an arbitrary one. Every person, as a creature made in God's image, possesses what Kierkegaard calls "the inner glory" that humans have just as humans (WL, 87). He compares this inner glory to a "common watermark" that pieces of paper may all have and that can be seen when held up to the light, however different the writing on the paper may be (WL, 89). Similarly, no matter how diverse humans are as individuals, they possess an unconditional worth and dignity as humans, a quality that makes it possible to love them and that makes them worthy of love. It is possible to construe others as persons who possess this "inner glory" and not simply as possessing the differential characteristics that distinguish them as individuals and make them like or unlike ourselves as individuals.

We can therefore see why God can command love of the neighbor, and how it is possible for us to obey the command. For Kierkegaard, God is unconditionally good, and can only command what is good. The goodness of love for the neighbor means that if we humans fully understood ourselves and were unfallen, we should not need to be commanded to love the neighbor. At the conclusion of the book, Kierkegaard poetically imagines the Apostle John striking a "middle tone" in which the duty to love begins to recede from its prominence, and the tension between self-love and love of neighbor begins to break down:

"Good Lord, what is all this that would hinder you from loving, what is all this that you can win by self-love! The commandment is that you *shall* love, but ah, if you understand yourself and life, then it would appear that you do not need to be commanded, because to love people is the only thing worth living for, and without this love you are not really living." (WL, 375)

Kierkegaard's thought here parallels Immanuel Kant, who conceives of a being with a "holy will" as one who lives in accordance with the principles of duty, but does not experience duty as duty.[17] However, just as Kant says that we humans do not possess such a holy will, Kierkegaard thinks that short of eternity, the category of duty is still necessary. Even the

---

[17] See Immanuel Kant, *Groundwork of the Metaphysic of Morals*, trans. H. J. Paton (London: Routledge, 1991), p. 78.

imagined words of the Apostle still possess divine authority, and this diminishing of duty is an ideal that only the saint can really understand. Kierkegaard himself says that he, like most of us, stands in need of duty: "Therefore we do not dare to speak this way. What is truth in the mouth of the veteran and perfected apostle could in the mouth of a beginner very easily be a flirtation by which he would much too quickly run away from the school of the commandment and escape the 'school-yoke'" (WL, 376).

As sinful creatures, we humans do not naturally practice neighbor love. It may be natural for us to love our families and friends, our tribes and our nations, but to love those who are not like us and who may not be able to do anything for us in return does not come easy. We need the category of duty.

Suppose it is true that God commands love of the neighbor? Why should we obey God or seek to please him? What does God's command add to the fact that it would be good for us to love in this way? One might think that the answer would revolve around divine rewards and punishments, with heaven as the reward for the good and hell as the punishment for those who fail to achieve true goodness. However, Kierkegaard consistently refuses to see divine rewards and punishments in this way. Since God is essentially good and essentially loving, God can only will the good of the individual, and any "chastening" that God sends an individual can only be intended for the good of that individual (UDVS, 44–60). God's "chastening" is not then to be feared, but welcomed. No appeal can be made to fear of hell as a motive for obeying God's commands. Nor does Kierkegaard appeal to heaven as an external or extrinsic reward, for a person who would be motivated by such a reward would not be a person who truly loves the good.

The reason I should want to obey God's commands cannot be found simply in the fact that God is omnipotent, but rather in the fact that the omnipotent God is love. I should want to obey God for the same kinds of reasons that motivate a lover to want to please his or her love. The obligations romantic lovers have to each other are grounded in the history of their relationship, including the promises they have made to each other and the loving actions they have performed, actions that call forth love and gratitude from the other, resulting in a desire to please. The ground of our motivation to obey God is similar, only our love-relationship to God is much deeper and stronger than any romantic love-relationship, and the resulting obligations far stronger: "But that eternal love-history has begun much earlier; it began with your beginning, when you came into existence out of nothing, and just as surely as you do not become nothing, it does not end at a grave" (WL, 150).

Kierkegaard stresses very strongly that love of the neighbor requires self-denial; we must not follow our natural inclinations, but must be willing to put the good of the other above our own happiness. It might appear from this that there is a fundamental divergence in Kierkegaard from the Aristotelian tradition that has normally linked the ethical life to the pursuit of happiness. However, the differences are not as sharp as they might appear. The need for self-denial is grounded in the sinfulness of humans. We have just seen that Kierkegaard affirms that genuine love for the neighbor is good for the lover as well as the neighbor, and that for a saint such love would not even need to be commanded. Kierkegaard's view seems to be something like this: the connection between the truly moral life and happiness changes as one's moral character develops. The person who understands happiness in aesthetic terms will see tension between the pursuit of happiness and the demands of duty, such that duty will require self-denial. However, as the person begins to understand the nature of true happiness, this tension begins to diminish and vanishes for the saint, and for all who attain blessedness in eternity.

Even for the person who is not yet a saint, it is possible to come to see that true happiness lies in fulfilling the duty to love the neighbor. Kierkegaard argues that there are goods that we humans seek in our natural, preferential loves that are in fact better realized and safeguarded in the love for the neighbor that is grounded in eternity. In our earthly loves, we seek a love that endures, a love that does not diminish us as persons but a love that enhances our freedom and independence, and a love that gives our lives meaning and protects us from despair (WL, 29–43).[18] Neighbor love, argues Kierkegaard, actually secures these goods in ways that preferential love cannot. Romantic love, for example, though it wants permanence, comes and goes, and the lover who is dependent on such a love is not genuinely autonomous. Furthermore, the lover who is jilted may be tempted by despair. Neighbor love, by contrast, is grounded in God's eternal love and God's eternal command. Such a love can endure, since it is grounded in what is eternal. The person who loves the other as neighbor can go on loving, and his or her love is not dependent on the response of the other. Furthermore, all of us have a divine calling

---

[18] I discuss these points in detail on pp. 146–155 in my *Kierkegaard's Ethic of Love.*

to love our neighbors, and thus every life has meaning and purpose. It is then actually a good thing for us that love for the neighbor is a duty.

One might think that the duty to love the neighbor could be grounded in something other than God's command. Perhaps we ourselves are the source of the duty, either as individuals or as a community. Kant, for example, famously argued that our moral duties are grounded in reason, and that the moral law is one that we legislate for ourselves as rational beings. Kierkegaard, however, simply does not think that a human being can be a "self-legislator" in this sense:

Kant was of the opinion that man is his own law (autonomy) – that is, he binds himself under the law which he himself gives himself. Actually, in a profounder sense, this is how lawlessness or experimentation are established. This is not being rigorously earnest any more than Sancho Panza's self-administered blows to his own bottom were vigorous.[19]

Kierkegaard here seems to anticipate the view of Elizabeth Anscombe, who famously held that "the concept of legislation requires superior power in the legislator" and so Kant's idea of "legislating for oneself" is as absurd as it would be to call every reflective decision of a person a "vote" that always turns out to be a solid majority of 1:0.[20]

However, even if the individual is not superior to the individual, could not human society be the "higher authority" needed to ground the moral law? Perhaps the moral law could be thought of as a kind of rational choice or social agreement that people have made.[21] Once again Kierkegaard firmly rejects such a view, on several grounds. There is no agreement about who establishes the agreement, and little likelihood that an agreement could be reached among actual individuals.

Or should the determination of what is the Law's requirement perhaps be an agreement among, a common decision by, all people, to which the individual has to submit? Splendid – that is, if it is possible to find the place and fix the time for this assembling of all people (all the living, all of them? – but what about the dead?), and if it were possible, something that is equally impossible, for all of them to agree on one thing. (WL, 115)

[19] *Kierkegaard's Journals and Papers*, vol. I, entry 188, p. 76.
[20] Elizabeth Anscombe, "Modern Moral Philosophy," in *Twentieth Century Ethical Theory*, ed. Steven Cahn and Joram G. Haber (Englewood Cliffs, New Jersey: Prentice-Hall, 1995), p. 352. This essay first appeared in *Philosophy*, 33/124 (Jan. 1958).
[21] For a clear example of such a proposal, see David Gauthier, *Morals By Agreement* (Oxford: Oxford University Press, 1986). I provide a detailed exposition of Gauthier's views and an argument for the superiority of Kierkegaard's divine command view of moral obligation in Chapter 11 of *Kierkegaard's Ethic of Love*.

Any agreement reached would be subject to constant renegotiation, leading to moral chaos, or, in Kierkegaard's words, the "doubt and vortex" of the modern world (WL, 115).

Hence, for Kierkegaard, the alternatives to God as a foundation for moral duty do not stand up to critical scrutiny.[22] Our obligation to love the neighbor is best understood as rooted in God and God's commands. We can now understand why he believes that God is the "middle term" in every healthy love relation, and the obligation to love the neighbor goes hand in hand with the command to love God (WL, 58, 107). When we love our neighbors, we love them as creatures made in God's image, and we are motivated to do so by God's command, a command we follow out of love and gratitude.

I have only scratched the surface of *Works of Love* here, focusing mainly on the themes that occur in the early chapters, and are foundational to the book. In reality, most of the book deals with concrete, edifying or "upbuilding" actions. Kierkegaard writes movingly about how love seeks to build up the others, about how love refuses to force the other to conform to our own agendas, and about how love seeks not only to fight for the good, but constantly to be reconciled with the ones we have had to oppose as we struggle for the good.[23] Love "hides a multitude of sins," not only forgiving but in one sense *forgetting* the harms done to one (WL, 280–299). Love expresses itself in mercifulness, a quality that even those with little in the way of material resources can manifest (WL, 315–330).

Above all, love always focuses concretely on the actual person it sees, and not abstractions (WL, 154–174). Kierkegaard's emphasis on "loving the neighbor" means that in one sense when we love, we do so with "closed eyes" (WL, 68). He means by this that when we select the person to love, we do not allow the particularities of class, gender, appearance, and so on to distract us. But this emphasis on loving in this non-selective way is balanced by the claim that when we actually love the person selected, we look at those very particularities, seeking to help people in ways that fit their own unique situations.

---

[22] It is interesting to compare Kierkegaard on this point with the recent work of Nicholas Wolterstorff, *Justice: Rights and Wrongs* (Princeton, New Jersey: Princeton University Press, 2007). In this work Wolterstorff argues for an account of justice that gives primacy to the notion that human persons possess natural rights, and argues that only God provides an adequate foundation for the claim that all human beings have natural rights. Such a claim is logically linked to Kierkegaard's view that all human persons are my neighbors, and that all possess an "inner glory" as those created by God in his image.

[23] See WL, Chapters I, IV, and VIII in Part II.

CHRIST AS THE REDEEMER AND THE MODEL

It would not be appropriate in a book on Kierkegaard as a philosopher to dwell at great length on some of his late writings, since they deal largely with theological themes, particularly with Kierkegaard's increasingly radical frustration with the character of contemporary "Christendom," which he saw as far removed from what he called "the Christianity of the New Testament." However, it is appropriate to give some attention to Kierkegaard's view of Christ and the role Christ should play in the Christian life, because his account of Christ allows Kierkegaard to answer problems that arise in his ethics.

It is obvious that the ethic of neighbor love Kierkegaard presents in *Works of Love* is an extremely demanding one, requiring a degree of self-denial rarely attained, and a willingness to embrace the other, including the enemy, that few people can manage.[24] It is therefore no accident that the book begins with a Trinitarian prayer, in which Christ is described as "Redeemer and Savior." The human situation as Kierkegaard sees it is one in which we found ourselves facing what John Hare has called "the moral gap."[25] It is not surprising then that in *Works of Love* one of the discourses describes Christ as "the fulfillment of the law," the person who perfectly fulfills the law of love (WL, 101).

> While the Law with its demand became the downfall of all people, because they were unable to be what it required and thus only came to know sin: so Christ became the downfall of the Law, because he was what it demanded. Its downfall, its end – for when the requirement is fulfilled, the requirement exists only as fulfillment, and so therefore does not exist as requirement. (WL, 99)

By living a life of love, Christ realizes what the law requires, but in being the realization of this law, he at the same time represents the "abolition" of the law.

Of course no other human being is in Christ's situation: "let us never forget that there is an eternal difference between Christ and every Christian. Even though the Law is abolished, it still stands here with its power and fixes an everlasting chasmic abyss between the God-man and

---

[24] Perhaps one of the rare examples of genuine love of this sort can be found in the Amish response to the killing of Amish schoolchildren at the West Nickel Mines School in Pennsylvania. For a full account of this remarkable response, see Donald Kraybill, Steven M. Nolt, and David L. Weaver-Zercher, *Amish Grace: How Forgiveness Transcended Tragedy* (San Francisco: John Wiley and Sons, 2007).

[25] See John Hare, *The Moral Gap: Kantian Ethics and God's Assistance* (Oxford: Oxford University Press, 1996).

every other person" (WL, 101). This means that for the ordinary Christian, the law is "fulfilled" only when I relate to Christ in faith. "Every Christian believes it [that Christ is the abolition of the law] and appropriates it through his believing" (WL, 101).

Kierkegaard's late writings are dominated by the theme of the "imitation of Christ." For Kierkegaard, Christ is "the Pattern," or "Prototype," as the Hongs translate the Danish *Forbilledet*.[26] Christ is the perfect human; the true Christian must be an imitator of Christ (Danish *Efterfølger*, literally an "after-follower" or one who "follows after"). Kierkegaard's critique of Christendom is essentially that following Christ has been forgotten, and that the true Christian is now identified with the one who is simply an admirer of Christ, rather than a disciple. This is a sharp challenge to the Christian Church, both in Kierkegaard's day, and our own. Kierkegaard believes that living a life as a disciple of Christ will demand radical, costly changes in lifestyle. This recognition leads Kierkegaard to be increasingly suspicious of the "hidden inwardness" that is often extolled in his pseudonymous writings. He now thinks that Christian existence will inevitably lead to a clash with the established order, and that the true Christian must be willing to suffer ridicule and even persecution because of her refusal to go along with the egoistic materialism that dominates modern societies. Genuine Christianity is, one might say, necessarily a counter-cultural and subversive movement, and one can hardly expect any established order to welcome it.

Nevertheless, though his emphasis is on the imitation of Christ, he retains a clear understanding that Christ is not only the Pattern, but also the Redeemer, who atones for the sin of the world. The balance between these two ways of conceiving Christ is particularly clear in a "Prayer" from the posthumously published *Judge for Yourself!*

Help us all, each one of us, you who both will and can, you who are both the Pattern and the Redeemer, and in turn both the Redeemer and the Pattern, so that when the striving one almost droops under the Pattern, crushed, almost despairing, the Redeemer raises him up again; but at the same moment you are again the Pattern so that he may be kept in the striving. (JY, 147)

The Christian life then has a kind of natural rhythm, in which the person who accepts Christ as the Pattern is humbled and must have recourse to

---

[26] I think that "prototype" as a translation is somewhat misleading, since a "prototype" is sometimes an early, test version of something, to be improved upon by later versions. *Forbilledet* means "pattern" in the sense of "ideal" or "perfect model." It is more like a concretized Platonic form than a prototype.

Christ as atoning Redeemer, and the person who receives mercy and forgiveness through Christ's atonement is re-energized to strive to imitate Christ.

One may wonder if in his late writings Kierkegaard has rejected his earlier emphasis on "indirect communication," since he is now critical of "hidden inwardness" and demands a form of direct witness from the Christian. There is a sense in which this is so, but it is not really a break with his previous views, since he had always held that Christian communication, as contrasted with ethico-religious communication, required direct as well as indirect communication. In any case, the maieutic or "midwife" ideal that indirect communication is intended to serve is still honored. It is true that the Christian must bear direct witness to faith. Nevertheless, faith is still something the individual must appropriate for herself as a gift from God. The testimony of the witness may be direct in form, but the freedom and autonomy of the hearer is still respected.

CONCLUSION: KIERKEGAARD'S CHALLENGE TO A SECULAR WORLD

In this chapter I have shown how Kierkegaard's philosophical thought culminates in a Christian vision. He argues that authentic selfhood and freedom from despair require Christian faith, and that the basic moral obligation to love all human beings as neighbors is best understood as rooted in God's command to love all those who are created in God's image. The guilt that we encounter when we strive to realize this ideal again drives us to faith in Christ, understood as the "God-man," the Absolute Paradox who is the object of faith, as discussed in Chapter 7.

One might wonder what relevance these claims have for a western world that is supposed to be secular and "post-Christian." To be sure, much of the contemporary world is hardly secular. Hinduism remains vibrant in India and Buddhism continues to flourish in much of the rest of Asia. The resurgence of Islam in much of the world, and the incredible growth of Christianity in Africa and parts of Asia also show that secularization is hardly inevitable. What Kierkegaard might have to say to a religiously pluralistic world is an open and fascinating question. There is no doubt that his own primary audience was Christendom, not adherents of other faiths. However, Kierkegaard's veneration of the non-Christian Socrates, his claim that "truth is subjectivity," and his analysis of "Religiousness A" provide some basis for discussion with non-Christian believers.

Although the world as a whole remains vigorously religious, there is little doubt that the intelligentsia in the west, particularly in Europe, is far more secular than was the case even in Kierkegaard's day. What might Kierkegaard have to say to these secular intellectuals, to whom Kierkegaard's Christian faith may appear outmoded or even quaint? The first thing he might wish to say is that questions of faith or lack of faith should not be made on the basis of alleged "eras" or "epochs." Kierkegaard argues in many places that one cannot conclude that Christianity is true merely because it is popular or has endured for many centuries. Christendom provides no support for genuine Christianity. However, for the same reasons, one cannot safely conclude that Christian faith is false merely because its popularity has declined among intellectuals. One cannot safely decide not to be a Christian because we live in a "post-Christian" world, any more than one can safely decide to be a Christian because one lives in an allegedly Christian world.

Rather, in a genuinely philosophical spirit, Kierkegaard wants us to see that decisions for and against religious faith are grounded in our perception of our existential situation as human beings. Fundamentally, this situation does not change with the times. Regardless of the age in which we are born, we have the task of becoming whole persons, confronting the meaning and purpose of life and the problems of guilt and death. Kierkegaard would ask the secular critic who is dismissive of religion to take a fresh look at things. At the very least he would ask that the critic take into account Kierkegaard's arguments about the role religious faith plays in the development of authentic selfhood and in the ethical life. And he would ask the critic to ponder whether the decline of faith is really grounded in new intellectual developments, or rather, as Kierkegaard himself thinks, in the loss of imaginative and emotional power.

In asking for a religious voice to be heard, Kierkegaard is by no means asking for any special favors for religion. As we have seen, he is an intense critic of Christendom, and thinks that genuine Christianity can never be identified with any human culture, whether that culture be Danish, American, or whatever. "Established Christianity" is virtually an oxymoron for him. Constantinian Christianity is for him part of the problem rather than a vanished ideal.

If one thinks that a liberal, democratic society is one in which religious convictions must be set aside in public life, then Kierkegaard's claims about the connection between faith and authentic selfhood and ethics might seem dubious. Certainly, some have argued for such a separation of religion and public life, on the grounds that religion is a divisive force in society, and that allowing religious convictions to operate in the public sphere leads to intolerance and violence. The issues raised here are too complex to be settled at the end of a book whose primary purpose is to provide an introduction to the thought of one philosopher.[27]

Here I can only signal the fact that a strong case can be made that a society that demands that religious faith be privatized is in fact less liberal and free than one that allows religious individuals to participate in public life in an integral manner, without relegating their deepest convictions to a "private" world with no connection to where they spend the greatest part of their lives. The supposed neutrality of a religion-free public world is a myth; excluding convictions about God from public life is no more liberal than requiring individuals to have such convictions.

In any case, Kierkegaard can teach us that when it comes to bringing religious convictions into public life, it makes a difference what those convictions are like. As a Christian, Kierkegaard is critical of religions, including forms of Christianity, that attempt to use power to prop up faith. He is a follower of one who won a victory over evil by being willing to suffer death on a cross. Kierkegaard believes that the followers of Christ must be willing to suffer in the same way: they must be witnesses to love and witnesses to peace, even at the cost of martyrdom. Those of us Christians who are not capable of such costly discipleship must at least humbly confess that we are not Christians of the first rank.

---

[27] For a good discussion of these issues, and a defence of the kind of view I sketch below that would allow voices such as Kierkegaard's to be heard, see Nicholas Wolterstorff, "Why We Should Reject What Liberalism Tells Us About Speaking and Acting for Religious Reasons," in *Religion and Contemporary Liberalism*, ed. Paul J. Weithman (Notre Dame, Indiana: University of Notre Dame Press, 1997), pp. 162–81.

For further reading:
Some personal suggestions

One of the readers for this book for Cambridge University Press suggested that it should contain a relatively short, annotated bibliography, a "suggestions for further reading," rather than the more traditional "Works Cited" bibliography. Both the editor and I liked this suggestion, and the result is below. The books that appear do so for various reasons. Some are selected because they are my own, for the benefit of those who want expanded accounts of some of the themes in the book. Others are included because they are simply books that I love and that have influenced me strongly. Others are on the list because in my judgment they are unusually high in quality, and still others are included because they are widely read and have been influential. Obviously, this list could be expanded indefinitely, and both the selections and the comments about them reflect the personal views of the author.

KIERKEGAARD'S OWN WRITINGS

In Danish, three editions of Kierkegaard's collected works (*Samlede Værker*) have been published by Gyldendals. The pagination of the first edition is included in the margins of the Princeton University Press edition (see below) of *Kierkegaard's Writings*. All of the published works as well as the surviving journals and papers are being published in a new edition (*Søren Kierkegaard's Skrifter*) in fifty-five volumes by Gad Publishers in Copenhagen.

Most of the early translations of Kierkegaard into English were done by David Swenson and/or Walter Lowrie, and were published by Princeton University Press and Oxford University Press. These translations are much loved for their literary quality.

The standard, scholarly English edition is currently *Kierkegaard's Writings* from Princeton University Press. The general editor for the series was Howard V. Hong and most of the translations were personally done by Howard Hong and his wife, Edna Hong. The Hong translations are distinguished by accuracy and informative reference notes, as well as appendices that include many relevant portions from Kierkegaard's Journals. The Hongs also translated an edition of *Kierkegaard's Journals and Papers* for Indiana University Press, though Princeton University Press is at work on a new translation that will be based on the new Danish edition.

A number of readable translations of various works of Kierkegaard have been done by Alastair Hannay for Penguin. A superior translation of *Fear and Trembling*, highly accurate and readable but with fine scholarly notes, has been done for Cambridge University Press by Sylvia Walsh, with an extensive introduction by the author of the present work.

OTHER BOOKS ON KIERKEGAARD BY THE AUTHOR

Kierkegaard on Faith and the Self: Collected Essays. Waco, Texas: Baylor University Press, 2006. A collection of "greatest hits," articles written over a 25-year period with two new essays, focusing particularly on issues of faith and reason, psychology, and ethics.

Kierkegaard's Ethic of Love: Divine Commands and Moral Obligations. Oxford: Oxford University Press, 2004. This book discusses Kierkegaard as an ethicist, with brief looks at such works as *Either/Or, Fear and Trembling, Concluding Unscientific Postscript,* and *Upbuilding Discourses in Various Spirits.* However, the bulk of the book is devoted to an account of the ethic presented in *Works of Love,* which is read as a "divine command" view of moral obligations. Arguments are given that this kind of ethic is superior to its secular, contemporary rivals.

Faith Beyond Reason. Edinburgh: Edinburgh University Press. Grand Rapids, Michigan: Wm. B. Eerdmans, 1998. This book discusses in what ways Kierkegaard is and is not a "fideist," by arguing that he offers a critique of reason that is itself reasonable.

Passionate Reason: Making Sense of Kierkegaard's Philosophical Fragments. Bloomington, Indiana: Indiana University Press, 1992. A chapter by chapter commentary, focusing particularly on the issues raised by Kierkegaard's understanding of the incarnation and his view of the relation of faith to history.

Kierkegaard's Fragments *and* Postscript: *The Religious Philosophy of Johannes Climacus.* Atlantic Highlands, New Jersey: Humanities Press, 1983. Reprinted Amherst, New York: Humanity Books, 1999. This work gives an overview of the crucial "Johannes Climacus" pseudonymous books by analyzing the key concepts found in the works.

BIOGRAPHIES

Garff, Joakim. *Søren Kierkegaard: A Biography.* Princeton, New Jersey: Princeton University Press, 2005. This highly acclaimed biography, translated by Bruce Kirmmse, is readable and informative, but somewhat marred by the author's cynical and debunking view of Kierkegaard's own self-understanding.

Kirmmse, Bruce, ed. *Encounters with Kierkegaard: A Life as Seen by His Contemporaries.* Princeton, New Jersey: Princeton University Press, 1996. Not strictly a biography, but a compilation of everything written about

Kierkegaard by his contemporaries. All the material for a do-it-yourself biography.

Lowrie, Walter. *A Short Life of Kierkegaard*. Princeton, New Jersey: Princeton University Press, 1942. Lowrie, who provided the majority of the early translations of Kierkegaard into English, introduced several generations of readers to Kierkegaard. Though not wholly uncritical, Lowrie was a great lover of the Dane.

SOME UNUSUAL AND USEFUL ANTHOLOGIES FROM KIERKEGAARD'S WRITINGS

Lefevre, Perry D. *The Prayers of Kierkegaard*. Chicago: The University of Chicago Press, 1956. Some of these prayers have been set to music by Samuel Barber.

Oden, Thomas, ed. *The Humor of Kierkegaard*. Princeton, New Jersey: Princeton University Press, 2004.

　　ed. *The Parables of Kierkegaard*. Princeton, New Jersey: Princeton University Press, 1978.

OTHER BOOKS ABOUT KIERKEGAARD

Some of the best scholarship about Kierkegaard in the English language can be found in the volumes of the *International Kierkegaard Commentary*, edited by Robert L. Perkins and published by Mercer University Press.

Bukdahl, Jørgen. *Kierkegaard and the Common Man*. Grand Rapids, Michigan: Wm. B. Eerdmans, 2001. A fascinating study of Kierkegaard's political and social attitudes, by a Danish scholar with a translation by Bruce Kirmmse.

Davenport, John J. and Rudd, Anthony, eds. *Kierkegaard After MacIntyre*. Chicago: Open Court, 2001. A challenge to the influential reading of Kierkegaard by Alasdair MacIntyre as a proponent of "radical choice." Many essays read Kierkegaard as a virtue ethicist.

Denzil, G. M. Patrick. *Pascal and Kierkegaard: A Study in the Strategy of Evangelism*. London: Lutterworth Press, 1943. Hard to find but interesting comparative study by a Scotsman who was a returned missionary and takes seriously Kierkegaard's own claim to be a missionary to "Christendom."

Eller, Vernard. *Kierkegaard and Radical Discipleship*. Princeton, New Jersey: Princeton University Press, 1968. Reads Kierkegaard, quite convincingly, as an Anabaptist-style Christian who was a radical critic of established western society.

Elrod, John W. *Kierkegaard and Christendom*. Princeton, New Jersey: Princeton University Press, 1981. Good study of Kierkegaard as a social and political thinker.

Ferreira, M. Jamie. *Love's Grateful Striving: A Commentary on Kierkegaard's Works of Love*. New York: Oxford University Press, 2001. Splendid commentary on Kierkegaard's most important work in ethics; demolishes many widely-held misunderstandings and criticisms.

Transforming Vision: Imagination and Will in Kierkegaardian Faith. Oxford: Oxford University Press, 1991. Sees the "leap of faith" more as an imaginative reorientation than an arbitrary act of will.

Gouwens, David J. *Kierkegaard as Religious Thinker*. Cambridge: Cambridge University Press, 1996. One of the best books on Kierkegaard as a theologian.

Kirmmse, Bruce. *Kierkegaard in Golden Age Denmark*. Bloomington, Indiana: Indiana University Press, 1990. Groundbreaking work by an historian that sets Kierkegaard's thought in the context of nineteenth-century Denmark; gives attention to the importance of industrialization and social change in this period.

Lippitt, John. *Humor and Irony in Kierkegaard's Thought*. Basingstoke: Palgrave Macmillan, 2000. Clearly written and informative study of an important dimension of Kierkegaard's thought.

Mackey, Louis. *Kierkegaard: A Kind of Poet*. Philadelphia: University of Pennsylvania Press, 1971. Takes a literary approach to Kierkegaard that undermines traditional philosophical approaches.

Points of View. Tallahassee, Florida: University Press of Florida (Florida State University Press), 1986. Extends the literary approach of his first book by arguing that there is no single "point of view" for understanding Kierkegaard's authorship; even the non-pseudonymous books are by a "persona."

Malik, Habib C. *Receiving Søren Kierkegaard: The Early Impact and Transmission of His Thought*. Washington, D.C.: Catholic University of America Press, 1997. Delivers just what the title promises.

Mullen, John Douglas. *Kierkegaard's Philosophy: Cowardice and Self-Deceit in the Present Age*. New York: New American Library, 1981. Very well-written and personally challenging introduction to Kierkegaard, though marred by an overly "existentialist" reading at the end.

Poole, Roger. *Kierkegaard: The Indirect Communication*. Charlottesville, Virgina: University of Virginia Press, 1993. Good example of a "deconstructionist" or "postmodern" reading of Kierkegaard.

Rae, Murray. *Kierkegaard's Vision of the Incarnation: By Faith Transformed*. Oxford: Oxford University Press, 1997. Good study of the key Kierkegaardian view of the incarnation as "the Absolute Paradox."

Roberts, Robert. *Faith, Reason, and History: Rethinking Kierkegaard's Philosophical Fragments*. Macon, Georgia: Mercer University Press, 1986. A clear treatment, from the perspective of analytic philosophy.

Swenson, David. *Something About Kierkegaard*. Minneapolis, Minnesota: Augsburg Publishing House, 1941. A classic set of essays by one of the pioneer translators of Kierkegaard in America.

Taylor, Mark C. *Kierkegaard's Pseudonymous Authorship: A Study of Time and the Self*. Princeton, New Jersey: Princeton University Press, 1975. Good study of the spheres of existence in their relation to time, except for a misunderstanding of "Religiousness A."

Walsh, Sylvia. *Kierkegaard: Thinking Christianly in an Existential Mode*. Oxford: Oxford University Press, 2008. Thoughtful introduction to Kierkegaard's theology.

  Living Christianly: Kierkegaard's Dialectic of Christian Existence. University Park, Pennsylvania: Pennsylvania State University Press, 2005. Focuses on the "inverse dialectic" in which for Kierkegaard the positive (blessedness, eternal life) is conditioned by the negative (suffering, dying to self).

  Living Poetically: Kierkegaard's Existential Aesthetics. University Park, Pennsylvania: Pennsylvania State University Press, 1994. This book deals with more than "the aesthetic" in Kierkegaard by seeing all three of the stages as differing views of what it means to live artistically.

Westphal, Merold. *Becoming a Self: A Reading of Kierkegaard's* Concluding Unscientific Postscript. West Lafayette, Indiana: Purdue University Press, 1996. Penetrating study of one of Kierkegaard's most important works. Westphal, who is an established Hegel scholar, relates Kierkegaard to Continental philosophers both of Kierkegaard's time and our own.

  Kierkegaard's Critique of Reason and Society. Macon, Georgia: Mercer University Press, 1987. Fine collection of essays that gives illuminating treatments of Kierkegaard's view of faith and reason and also his political and social thinking.

Index

Lightning Source UK Ltd.
Milton Keynes UK
UKHW020039151119
353577UK00022B/463/P